TRANSFORMATIONAL LEADERSHIP:

THE INFLUENCE OF EXERCISE HABITS ON LEADERSHIP STYLES AND LEADER EFFECTIVENESS

Publications by

Carol. R. Himelhoch

Dey, E.L., Ross, P., White, C.B., & Himelhoch, C.R. (2007). A different kind of diversity outcome: Medical school experiences associated with physician choices to serve the underserved. Presented at the American Educational Research Association conference (AERA) Annual Meeting, Chicago, IL.

Dey, E. L., Antonaros, M., & Himelhoch, C. R. (2007). Strangers in a strange land: Faculty leadership in context. Presented at the American Educational Research Association conference (AERA) Annual Meeting, Chicago, IL.

Antonaros, M.E., Himelhoch, C.R., & Ball, S.R. (2011, April). Unpacking leader effectiveness: Exploring gender, institutional type, and other common predictors. Presented at the American Educational Research Association conference (AERA), New Orleans, LA.

Himelhoch, C.R. (2012, September). Synergistic learning community: Bringing out the best in others in an on-line course. Invited Speaker at the Lilly Conference on College and University Teaching, Traverse City, MI.

Himelhoch, C. R. (2014). *Transformational leadership and high-intensity interval training*. Spring Lake, Michigan: MindBodyMed Press.

MindBodyMed Press Mini-Monograph Series

TRANSFORMATIONAL LEADERSHIP:

THE INFLUENCE OF EXERCISE HABITS ON LEADERSHIP STYLES AND LEADER EFFECTIVENESS

Carol R. Himelhoch, PhD

University of Michigan Educated Professor of Management
Siena Heights University

Mary Antonaros Raymond, PhD

University of Michigan Educated Associate Professor of
Professional Communication
Siena Heights University

Spring Lake | Michigan | United States

Edited by Michele Spilberg Hart, MA

Publisher: MindBodyMed Press, LLC, PO Box 221, Spring Lake, Michigan, United States, www.MindBodyMedPress.com

Ordering Information: Quantity sales. Special discounts are available on quantity purchases by corporations, associations, book clubs and others. For details, contact the publisher at the address above.

Cover Image: Ratushnyi, S. (n.d.). Just keep running [Vector illustration]. Retrieved from https://www.123rf.com/profile_skillsup?mediapopup=40327907

Publisher's Cataloging-in-Publication data

Names: Himelhoch, Carol Rose, author. | Raymond, Mary Antonaros, author.

Title: Transformational leadership: the influence of exercise habits on leadership styles and leader effectiveness / Carol R. Himelhoch, PhD; Mary Antonaros Raymond, PhD

Description: Includes bibliographical references. | Spring Lake, MI: MindBodyMed Press, LLC, 2018.

Identifiers: ISBN 9780990329749 | LCCN 2018949859

Subjects: LCSH Leadership--Case studies. | Sports--Psychological aspects. | Exercise--Psychological aspects--Case studies. | Physical fitness--Psychological aspects. | Work environment--Psychological aspects. | Executive ability. | BISAC BUSINESS & ECONOMICS / Leadership | SOCIAL SCIENCE / Research | PSYCHOLOGY / Industrial & Organizational Psychology

Classification: LCC HD57.7 .H558 2018 | DDC 658.4 1--dc23

MEDICAL DISCLAIMER

Healthcare is an ever-changing field. MindBodyMed Press, its editors, and authors of the mini-monographs, monographs, and creative nonfiction books have made every effort to provide information that is accurate and complete as of the date of publication and consistent with standards of good practice in the healthcare setting. As research and practice advance, however, standards may change. For this reason, it is recommended that readers evaluate the applicability of any recommendations in light of particular situations and evolving standards.

MindBodyMed Press mini-monographs, monographs, and creative nonfiction books are designed for educational purposes only and MindBodyMed Press, its editors, and authors are not engaged in rendering medical advice or professional services. The information provided in this book should not be used for diagnosing or treating a health problem or a disease. It is not a substitute for professional care. Members of the public using this book are advised to consult with a physician regarding personal medical care. If you have or suspect you may have a health problem, consult your healthcare provider.

Although the author and publisher have made every effort to ensure that the information in this book was correct at press time, the author and publisher do not assume and hereby disclaim any liability to any party for any loss, damage, or disruption caused by errors or omissions, whether such errors or omissions result from negligence, accident, or any other cause.

Always consult your primary healthcare provider before beginning any exercise program.

TABLE OF CONTENTS

Carol R. Himelhoch and Mary Antonaros Raymond

LIST OF FIGURES

LIST OF TABLES

Carol R. Himelhoch and Mary Antonaros Raymond

ACKNOWLEDGEMENTS

Special thanks to Dr. Allan Afuah, Professor of Corporate Strategy and International Business Administration at The University of Michigan's Stephen M. Ross School of Business, for taking the time to read and endorse our work. Allan has been a great friend and mentor to both of us through the years. We also wish to thank Dr. Beth Smith, Assistant Professor in Biokinesiology and Physical Therapy at University of Southern California, for her help in establishing a common unit of measure to apply to the coding of all leisure exercise forms encountered in our research. We are grateful to Beth also for reviewing and recommending our monograph.

We would also like to thank Dr. Alan Moore and Dr. David Lucas, both of Siena Heights University. They encouraged us to explore curvilinear relationships among the Big Five personality taxonomy and leadership styles when we were conceptualizing our study. Dr. Stephen Ball, also of Siena Heights University and husband of co-author Carol Himelhoch, was a great help because he "cracked the code" in determining how to compute and input variables for polynomial regression analyses in SPSS as a means of sidestepping limitations in the SPSS software. Page limits in many journals force many researchers to report fractionalized results. Many thanks to Dr. Werner Absenger, of MindBodyMed Press, for providing a publication outlet for sharing our research in its entirety. Thanks also to Michele Spilberg Hart, MA, for editing our manuscript.

FOREWORD BY

DR. ALLAN AFUAH

In what ways do personality characteristics, demographic characteristics, and leisure exercise habits influence leadership styles and leader effectiveness? When are "dark side" traits most likely to occur? What are "dark side" traits, anyway? These questions ran through my head as I was reading the original manuscript of this book, and I found the answers to these questions much more exciting than I had originally expected.

As Professor of Corporate Strategy and International Business in the Ross School of Business at the University of Michigan, I have read my fair share of manuscripts, articles, books, and other scholarly works. Few have been as innovative and, frankly, provocative as the text you are reading at this moment. Many of us, myself included, look beyond diet and nutrition to put our best feet forward, and this book fills an important gap in leadership research.

I have personal experience with physical fitness. As Professor of Corporate Strategy and International Business in the Ross School of Business, I am well versed in stress management techniques. Maintaining an exercise regimen and a healthy diet both enhance my productivity. I have experienced a personal health challenge when I realized I had some food allergies and was deficient in D and B vitamins. Making simple dietary changes literally turned my life around. In fact, when I see students who seem stressed or depressed, I encourage them to take care of themselves. I have even been known to give my students bottles of Vitamin D as gifts. I value self-care because it helps us function at full capacity.

I also have personal experience working with Himelhoch and Raymond. I began serving as a member of Himelhoch's dissertation committee at the University of Michigan in 2000, and I began serving on Raymond's dissertation committee in 2009. I became friends and mentors to both authors when I began serving on their respective dissertation committees, and I am proud of their scholarly progress as they have advanced into faculty positions. Knowing both of the authors as well as I do puts me in a position to unequivocally recommend their work.

SCOPE OF THE BOOK

Transformational leadership is known to be the best fit for organizations competing in rapidly changing environments, while transactional leadership is best suited in stable environments. Both leadership styles have their place. Of all leadership theories, transformational leadership has received the most attention by researchers. The focus has been on many aspects of leadership styles and traits, including antecedents. However, the greatest gap in antecedent research is the role of leisure exercise habits. When exploring trait theories, the Big Five model has the most predictive potential in connection with leadership styles. However, correlations have been weak. Lord, DeVader, and Alliger (1986) were the first to suggest that curvilinear relationships may uncover relationships that are masked in linear models, and much still needs to be explored to understand what was masked in linear models.

Himelhoch and Raymond's book fills gaps in antecedent research because it examines the influence of exercise habits and personality on leadership behaviors, using a curvilinear lens. The authors do an excellent job of exploring how much and at what intensity exercise is useful for leaders. They emphasize the value of diversity, and advise against using fitness in hiring decisions. In fact, they learned through their research that many of the best leaders do not exercise at all. However, they do explore patterns for what levels of exercise habits are optimal and what levels are detrimental in their influence on leader behaviors.

WHY SHOULD I READ THIS BOOK?

It is easy to assume that, because exercise is beneficial to one's health, more is better. Similarly, one may believe that the more intense one's positive personality traits are, the more effective a leader he or she will be. Himelhoch and Raymond's book is valuable because they unpack those assumptions, and explore nuanced relationships. This study is unique because it explores "at what intensity of exercise and at what concentrations are personality traits significant antecedents of leader behavior, while also factoring in demographic" (p. 77) characteristics. Their work advances the exploration of why certain leaders engage in transformational, transactional, or passive-avoidant leadership.

As mentioned in the book, Lord, DeVader, and Alliger (1986) uncovered flaws in methodology that led prior researchers to dismiss the relationship between personality and leadership styles (p. 90). Himelhoch and Raymond's research begins to fill those methodological gaps through examining curvilinear relationships. Specific findings provide guidelines for managers interested in improving their leadership. In particular:

- The optimal perceived rate of exercise exertion to promote inspirational motivation is "just below the maximum perceived intensity" (p. 96).
- Exercise six days per week to optimize idealized attributes and idealized behaviors.
- Exercise seven days per week to maximize Contingent Reward.
- No exercise at all is associated with the following effectiveness variables: Idealized Attributes, Idealized Behaviors, Inspirational Motivation, Individual Consideration, and Contingent Reward.
- "The Big Five factors, in relation to their influence on leadership styles and leader effectiveness, are paradoxical. Those normally considered strengths may be weaknesses; those considered liabilities may be assets under certain conditions" (p. 97). However, relationships one would expect were found with certain Big Five dimensions and effectiveness measures. For example, openness, agreeableness, extraversion, conscientiousness, and emotional stability contribute to desired leadership behaviors and effectiveness.
- Certain demographic characteristics were also salient.

Himelhoch and Raymond offer the following caveat in interpreting their study:

Caution is warranted whenever physical characteristics are discussed in connection with leadership, as prior research has demonstrated followers' preferences for physically formidable leaders, either in association with height, weight, body mass index, gender, and physical strength (Murray, 2014). Given these caveats, the authors make a case for looking for alignment between the business' situation and the leader's traits when hiring new managers, or teaching existing managers how to develop those traits. For example, in a business in which contingent reward is desired, such as a company with many technical operational details, hiring a leader who possesses strong "thoroughness" and "extraverted" personality dimensions. When a business' circumstances dictate competence in innovation and creativity, one may seek or train a leader in dimensions associated with a transformational leadership style.

It is important to note that Himelhoch and Raymond do not recommend hiring or training leaders based on physical fitness or their leisure conditioning routines. Their data show that many effective leaders do not exercise at all. What they do propose is that organizations make formal efforts to promote and encourage exercise, because they found correlations between exercise at specific levels (i.e., six days or seven days per week depending on the desired leadership style and effectiveness measure) and desired leadership styles and effectiveness outcomes.

Now that I have reviewed some important themes of the book, I invite you to read the details. Himelhoch and Raymond present a thorough exploratory study, in which they apply quantitative methods to examine complex and nuanced relationships. Their use of visual graphs help the curvilinear relationships come to life. Through their conscientious and thorough approach, full disclosure of limitations, suggestions for future research, this tome will no doubt be read with interest and then frequently revisited as a part of your personal library.

Allan Afuah, PhD
Professor of Corporate Strategy and International
Business The Stephen M. Ross School of Business
The University of Michigan

MindBodyMed Press Mini-Monograph Series

TRANSFORMATIONAL LEADERSHIP:

THE INFLUENCE OF EXERCISE HABITS ON LEADERSHIP STYLES AND LEADER EFFECTIVENESS

Carol R. Himelhoch, PhD

University of Michigan Educated Professor of Management
Siena Heights University

Mary Antonaros Raymond, PhD

University of Michigan Educated Associate Professor of
Professional Communication
Siena Heights University

MindBodyMed
Press
Your mind. Your body. Unite them.

Spring Lake I Michigan I United States

Edited by Michele Spilberg Hart, MA

ABSTRACT

In this paper, we addressed the question, "In what ways do personality characteristics, demographic characteristics, and leisure exercise habits influence leadership styles and leader effectiveness?" Participants included 189 leaders across a broad range of industries, with their perceptions corroborated through surveying a sample of their employees. Constructs from the Big Five model and the Multifactor Leadership Questionnaire (MLQ) were combined with leisure exercise habits and exercise frequencies in polynomial regression equations. We found that the "Goldilocks Paradox" applies both to exercise habits and personality dimensions, as curvilinear relationships among personality dimensions and exercise habits suggested optimal levels for desired leadership styles and leader effectiveness. Gender, managerial level, and race were significant in certain dimensions of leadership style and leader effectiveness. Transformational leadership is most heavily associated with effectiveness, although dimensions of transactional leadership are effective under certain conditions.

Keywords: Transformational leadership, transactional leadership, passive-avoidant leadership, gender, age, race, Big Five factors, exercise intensity, exercise frequency, leader effectiveness

SYNOPSIS

For those interested in a succinct synopsis of this book, we condense the main points into the following six pages. Reading the entire manuscript is essential, however, to fully grasp the methods, findings, and implications.

RESEARCH QUESTION

The general question of why certain leaders engage in transformational, transactional, and passive-avoidant leadership behaviors stipulates a focus on antecedents. For this study we asked, *In what ways do personality characteristics, demographic characteristics, and leisure exercise habits influence leadership styles and leader effectiveness?* Sub-questions are covered in the results section below.

RESEARCH METHODS

Leaders and employees completed surveys to gauge leadership styles, Big Five personality dimensions, and exercise habits. We integrated the MLQ and Big Five questionnaires into our instrument. A total of 189 leaders completed the survey. The same survey questions were posed to 95 employees, all of whom who report to the 27 out of 189 leaders who granted us access to their employees. The MLQ variables were compressed through factor analysis. We used one-way ANOVA to examine significant differences in both Exercise Frequency and Perceived Rate of Exertion (PRE) for all of the leader behavior and outcome variables in the MLQ as well as for all of the Big Five factors. We also performed curve-fitting analyses on all relationships, to determine if further testing of curvilinear relationships was warranted. Similarly, we performed curve-fitting analyses on all leadership-style variables and all Big Five personality variables in connection with the outcome variables Satisfaction, Extra Effort, and Effectiveness. We performed multiple regression analyses and polynomial regression analyses to integrate both linear and curvilinear relationships that were significant in the curve-fitting analyses.

RESULTS FOR EACH RESEARCH QUESTION

1. In what ways do a leader's perceived rate of exertion and his or her leisure exercise frequency influence leadership style and leader effectiveness?

Our data suggest that the optimal PRE to promote Inspirational Motivation is strenuous exercise at just below the maximum perceived intensity. The most advantageous number of days per week to exercise to advance Idealized Attributes and Idealized Behaviors is six. However, seven days per week is the most favorable regularity associated with Contingent Reward. Relationships between exercise and other facets of transformational, transactional, or passive-avoidant leadership styles are not salient. Moreover, leaders who do not exercise at all are competent across leadership dimensions associated with effectiveness, including Idealized Attributes, Idealized Behaviors, Inspirational Motivation, Individual Consideration, and Contingent Reward. Other factors contribute to effective leadership, although exercise does play a role.

2. How do the Big Five personality dimensions influence leadership style and leader effectiveness?

The Big Five Factors go beyond explaining the perceptions held by leaders. They also influence how leadership is executed. The Big Five factors, in relation to their influence on leadership styles and leader effectiveness, are paradoxical. Those normally considered strengths may be weaknesses, while those considered liabilities may be assets under certain conditions. Certainly, there is modest correlation between many of the individual factors and leadership styles. However, when taken together, the bivariate dimensions of openness (Active Imagination), agreeableness (Trust), extraversion (Outgoingness), conscientiousness (Lazy), and emotional stability (Relaxed) contribute to a multivariate effect on the leadership styles and effectiveness variables that is noteworthy. These dimensions do influence the use of Idealized Attributes, Idealized Behaviors, Intellectual Stimulation, Inspirational Motivation, Extra Effort, Satisfaction, and Contingent Reward.

3. In what ways do demographic factors like supervisory level (firstline, middle, senior manager), age, gender, race, and income influence leadership style and leader effectiveness?

Income does not influence leadership style or leader effectiveness. Managerial level does have a linear association. The other demographic variables have modest correlations. Women, more than men, are likely to behave consistently with the Idealized Behaviors and Individual Consideration dimensions. Women also perform better than men on Effectiveness and Satisfaction factors. Minorities use Individual Consideration more than whites, but whites affect Satisfaction more than minorities do. Younger leaders use more Inspirational Motivation, inspiring enthusiasm for accomplishing future goals and realizing the organizational vision.

4. In what ways do the perceptions of leader effectiveness and leadership style differ between leaders and their employees?

Employee and leader perceptions concerning leadership styles and leader effectiveness are congruent when examined across most of the 45 MLQ dimensions. This was expected because we assumed that effective leaders tend to have accurate self-assessments. The congruence aligns with the association between self-awareness and performance, established by researchers Atwater and Yammarino (1992).

VISUAL DEPICTION OF RESULTS

In the following three figures, the thickest arrows reflect strong relationships, medium-width arrows depict moderate relationships, and the arrows comprising dotted lines represent the weakest relationships.

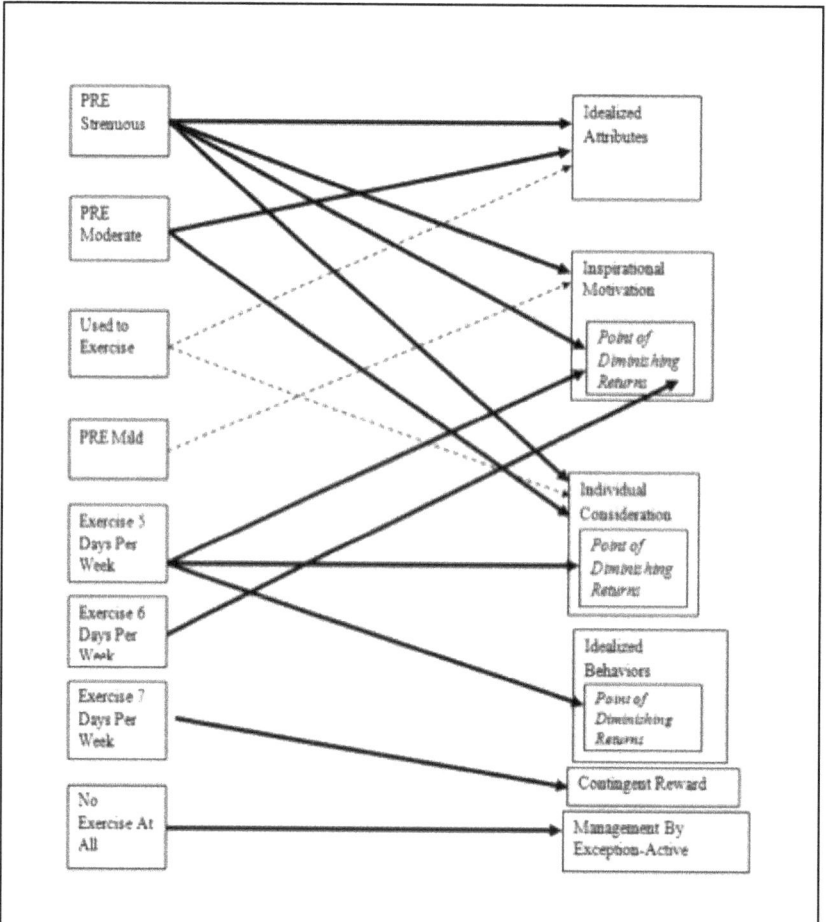

Figure 44. Conceptual representation of the relationship between PRE as well as exercise frequency and leadership.

Carol R. Himelhoch and Mary Antonaros Raymond

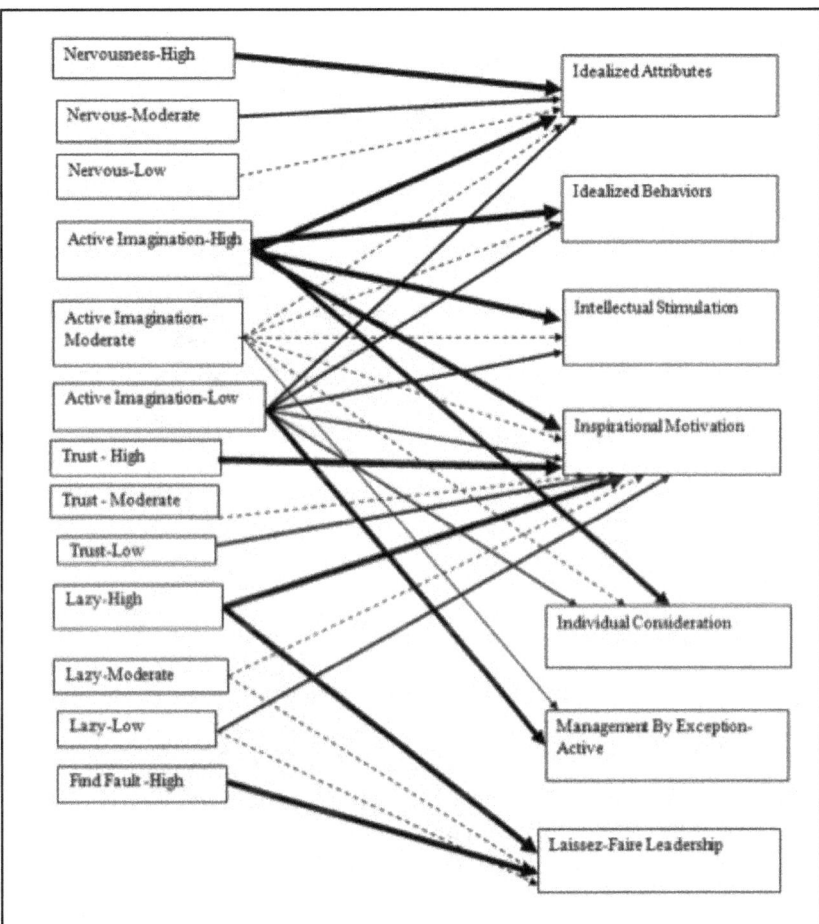

Figure 45. Conceptual connections between the significant big five dimensions and leadership styles.

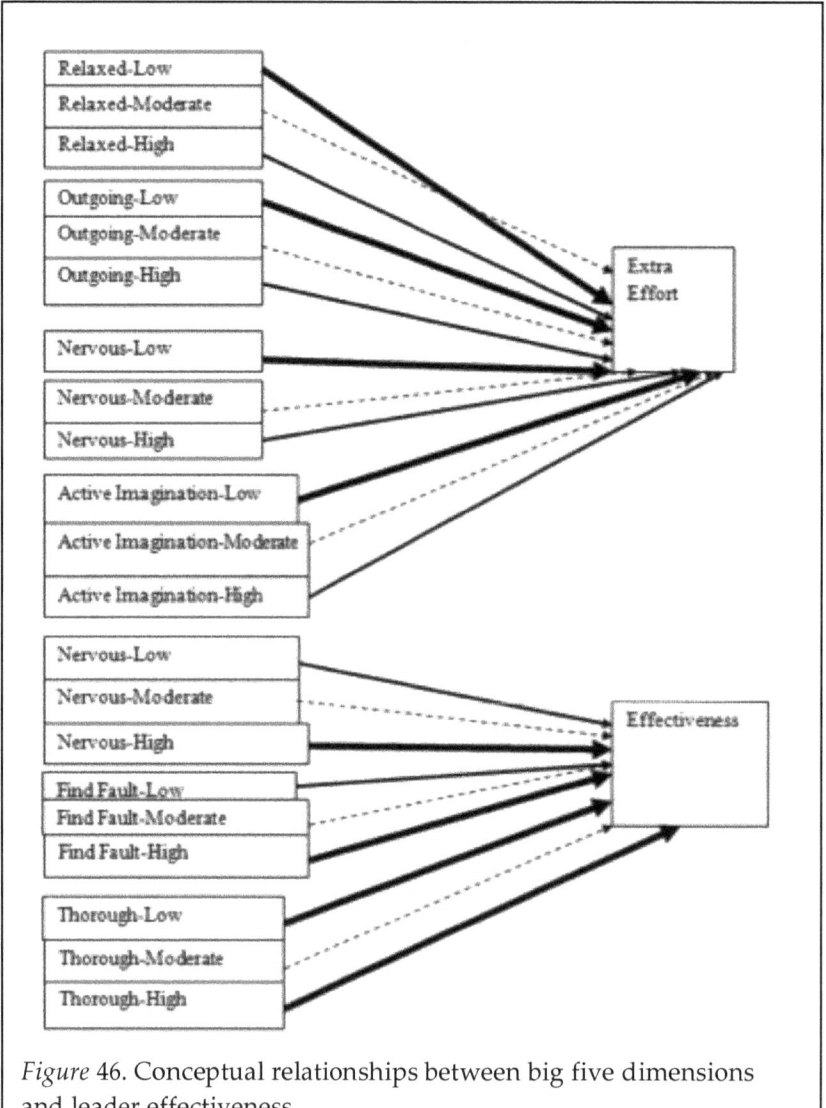

Figure 46. Conceptual relationships between big five dimensions and leader effectiveness.

MindBodyMed Press Mini-Monograph Series

TRANSFORMATIONAL LEADERSHIP:

THE INFLUENCE OF EXERCISE HABITS ON LEADERSHIP STYLES AND LEADER EFFECTIVENESS

Carol R. Himelhoch, PhD

University of Michigan Educated Professor of Management
Siena Heights University

Mary Antonaros Raymond, PhD

University of Michigan Educated Associate Professor of
Professional Communication
Siena Heights University

MindBodyMed
Press
Your mind. Your body. Unite them.

Spring Lake | Michigan | United States

Edited by Michele Spilberg Hart, MA

[1]

PROBLEM DEFINITION

BACKGROUND

Finding top talent is an essential source of competitive advantage for organizations in a rapidly changing business environment (Lawler, 2008). Hiring those with an optimal mix of interpersonal skills and technical competence is an important concern for organizations that are interested in advancing their positions in the marketplace and preserving their viability. In addition to their investments in recruitment and selection, substantial resources are allocated toward developing leaders and their team members, especially within the professions and among firms participating in the knowledge economy (Clark & Waldron, 2016).

Skilled leadership is an important dimension of high value human capital. Most leadership research has focused on the consequences of leadership style, such as linkages to levels of organizational performance, the intensity of organizational commitment, the degree of satisfaction with management, and the extent to which employees put forth extra effort as well as the span of their organizational citizenship behaviors and turnover intentions (Bommer, Rubin, & Baldwin, 2004). Clark and Waldron (2016) cited the research of Bommer et al. (2004), who recommended focusing on leadership antecedents to predict who will and who will not make the most effective leaders. Leadership antecedents, or precursors, may help explain why leaders behave as they do.

Antecedent research is not entirely new. Most antecedent research concerns transformational leadership behavior (TLB), a leadership style in which the leader creates an inspirational vision of change, then motivates employees to execute plans with great commitment (Bass, 1985, 1990). Only one study located by the authors, conducted by De Hoogh, Hartog, and Koopman (2005), also looked at antecedents of transactional leadership behavior, a style associated with the use of rewards and punishment to promote compliance. De Hoogh and colleagues (2005) examined personality characteristics in particular, and found that these antecedents are moderated by perceptions of how dynamic (undergoing change) the work environment is. Perhaps because transformational leadership is associated with "transforming employees into high performers" (Jin, Seo, & Shapiro, 2016, p. 64), there is a dearth of antecedent research on leadership styles other than TLB.

Much research on TLB antecedents has already investigated organizational context dimensions, such as organizational life cycle, structure, and culture (Hunt & Conger, 1999); goals, tasks, and technology (Shamir & Howell, 1999); or even societal structures (Conger & Kanugo, 1987). Some early TLB antecedent research focused on the leader's traits. Leaders who were more agreeable, open to change, extraverted, and had a more positive self-image tended to exhibit TLB (Walter & Bruch, 2009). Judge, Bono, Ilies, and Gerhardt (2002) found that the personality characteristics of extraversion, conscientiousness, and openness to experience connect to leadership emergence (acceptance of the leader by his or her peers in self-directed teams), and that openness to experience is associated with leader effectiveness. Judge et al. (2002) incorporated the Big Five personality taxonomy (John & Srivastava, 1999), which has become standard among the majority of scholars studying personality dimensions in leadership. The Big Five dimensions include degrees of extraversion, agreeableness, conscientiousness, neuroticism, and openness to experience.

In addition to Big Five personality dimensions, trait research has covered gender, intelligence, risk-taking propensity, sensitivity, and self-confidence (Walter & Bruch, 2009). In one meta-analysis of 45 studies, which compared the leadership styles of women and men, Eagley Johannesen-Schmidt and van Engen (2003) found small gender differences. Women use TLB and contingent reward (conveying expectations and providing recognition upon goal attainment) more than men, and men are more apt to use transactional (contractual) and passive-avoidant (reactive) leadership styles. One study of 400 managers, by Oshagbemi (2004), found that older leaders and younger leaders both use delegative leadership styles, although older leaders consult employees more when making decisions. Other scholars found that younger workers use more TLB (Barbuto, Fritz, Matkin, &

Carol R. Himelhoch and Mary Antonaros Raymond

Marx, 2007). Kim and Yoon (2015) found that leaders in the most senior-management positions are apt to use TLB in governmental agencies. Studies of fraternal twins found that when one sibling is a transformational leader, the other sibling usually is also. However, other studies found that the leader's experiences and environment explain a larger percent of the variance in TLB (Jin et al., 2016, p. 64). According to Jin et al. (2016), Bono and Judge's meta-analysis (2004) found that "a large proportion (88 to 95%) of between-person variability in transformational leadership remains unexplained by leader traits (e.g., personality)" (Jin et al., 2016, p. 65).

More antecedent research is needed. According to Bommer et al. (2004), "If we are to understand how to influence, improve, or modify the frequency and/or display of TLB downstream, it is necessary to shift our focus upstream towards the study of TLB as a dependent variable" (p. 196). The same necessity to study antecedents to TLB applies to all leadership styles. While there is clear benefit in knowing antecedents to desirable TLB, understanding what may lead to counterproductive leader behaviors is also worthwhile. Despite the research conducted between the 2004 Bommer study and the Jin et al., research (2016), the question remains: Why do leaders engage in behaviors associated with different leadership styles?

Bernard and Ruth Bass were the first to discuss the behavioral antecedent exercise as a method of coping with leaders' "occupational demands" (Bass & Bass, 2008, p. ii). In their successive editions of The Bass Handbook of Leadership, initially copyrighted in 1974 and updated most recently in 2008, they stated: "Two-thirds of executives exercise at least three times per week, and 90% of these do aerobic exercises. Endurance, strength, and flexibility need to be developed and maintained" (p. ii). Atwater and Yammarino (1993) later found physical fitness is an antecedent that explained 28% of the variance in leader behavior, although the variable was not explored comprehensively.

Exercise and fitness as independent variables predicting leadership styles remains largely unexplored. In one British study, researchers surveyed 400 women leaders with a background in team sports (Female Executives, 10 October, 2014). Seventy-four percent of these female senior managers viewed a background in sports as a career enhancement. Sixty-one percent perceived that sports added to their career accomplishments, with motivational skills, team-building proficiency, and the aptitude to carry projects through to completion as the top three abilities promoted by participation in sports. One exploratory study examined how the lived experiences of athletes participating in high-intensity interval training (HIIT) intersected with their leadership styles (Himelhoch, 2014), and found a connection between their exercise intensity and their perceived TLB. However, Himelhoch's qualitative study cannot be generalized to a larger population because the sample was too small, and the participants were interviewed after they started HIIT. Although they reported connections, one can never know if the participants were transformational leaders before they were avid athletes.

Research Objective

Although leadership scholars favor TLB in dynamic environments (Nanjundeswaras & Swamy, 2014), other leadership styles, such as transactional leadership, are effective under certain circumstances (Atwater, Camobreco, Dionne, Avolio, & Lau, 1997). Transactional leadership entails setting clear expectations and establishing quasi-contractual terms with employees for achieving or failing to achieve goals. In contrast, a style considered ineffective under any circumstances is passive-avoidant leadership. As its title suggests, passive-avoidant leadership involves minimal leader engagement, unless in reaction to problems (Avolio & Bass, 2004). Our quantitative study extended Himelhoch's (2014) initial research on HIIT athletes and TLB, and explored antecedents to a range of leadership styles. The antecedents in our study included personal characteristics such as managerial level, age, race, gender, and personality, plus a full assortment of leisure exercise habits, including no exercise at all. Leadership styles incorporated transactional, transformational, and passive-avoidant leadership. Additionally, we verified the leaders' perceptions by checking how their employees perceive their leadership styles.

Rarely is the mind-body relationship applied to managerial research. Perhaps that is because disciplinary lenses narrow researchers' foci to tackle problems using tools exclusive to their fields. However, most complex problems are multidimensional and need to access knowledge from diverse perspectives.

As boundaries between disciplines are crossed, and as research engages more with stakeholders in complex systems, traditional academic definitions and criteria of research quality are no longer sufficient—there is a need for a parallel evolution of principles and criteria to define and evaluate research quality in a transdisciplinary research (TDR) context (Belcher, Rasmussen, Kemshaw, & Zornes, 2016, p. 1).

The assumption of a mind-body connection guided the Himelhoch (2014) study and also directed our research, thereby leveraging both business and medical models.

Obesity is a relevant concern in organizations. According to Smith and Smith (2016), more than 2.1 billion people are obese across the globe. In the United States, 33% of children and 35% of adults are obese or overweight. Obesity is a top cause of death, ranked fifth among causes, which accounts for roughly 34% of deaths per year. Although healthcare costs caused by obesity are difficult to measure precisely, Smith and Smith estimated hundreds of billions of dollars annually in the United States. The increase in employee-benefit expenses is derived from these high healthcare costs, many of which could be eliminated if obesity were not so endemic (Harolds, 2016). However, the concern goes beyond the domain of cost containment. Obesity is associated with an unfavorable quality of life and sense of well-being (Giuli, Papa, Marcellini, Boscaro, Faloia, Lattanzio, Tirabassi, & Bevilacqua, 2016). "Obesity has become a pressing health problem worldwide, resulting in significant morbidity in both the physical health and psychological status of those affected" (Pinto-Bastos, Ramalho, & Conceicado, 2016, p. 309). Leaders are not immune to the psychological effects of obesity on the well-being of themselves and their employees. Kerman, Racicot, and Fisher (2016) surveyed 448 managers and found that the psychological climate created by unhealthy leaders is a mediating variable affecting job satisfaction and employee commitment.

Some research on leadership has examined the absence of anxiety and distress on leader behavior (Barling, Bergenwall, Byren, Dioniski, Dupre, Robertson, & Wylie, 2012). The aim of this study was to explore the positive potential that healthy habits offer, habits over which a leader has some control, and which could combat poor health caused by factors like obesity. Diet and exercise are two obvious behaviors that are within the purview of most individuals. This study considered exercise, in particular. We assumed that if actionable habits, like exercise, were antecedents to desired leader behaviors, the prospect to improve organizational performance is feasible. The supposition of positive potential was based on previous studies, such as those mentioned above, which found linkages to positive organizational outcomes and TLB, like improved organizational performance, employee commitment, extra effort, organizational citizenship, and satisfaction with management.

Certainly, some individuals are unable to exercise. Many well-known leaders are/were not athletes, including Franklin Delano

Roosevelt, Stephen Hawking, Congresswoman Barbara Jordan, and newspaper magnate Dean Singleton, to name a few. Multiple paths lead to effective leadership. However, if research were to demonstrate that exercise is one actionable antecedent to effective leadership styles, and if physically able leaders were to participate in athletics, they, their employees, and their organizations may benefit.

RESEARCH QUESTION

The general question of why certain leaders engage in transformational, transactional, and passive-avoidant leadership behaviors stipulates a focus on antecedents. We narrowed the question further to isolate the dimension of leisure exercise habits, personality characteristics, and demographic factors in order to explore their influence on leader behaviors and leader effectiveness. Additionally, we surmised that applying the assumption of a linear relationship might miss important and nuanced connections.

A study of personality characteristics and leader effectiveness by Ames and Flynn (2007) found that employees perceive that leaders who are very low or very high in assertiveness are less effective, yet leaders with a moderate degree of assertiveness are considered more effective by their employees. According to Hereford (2011), "dark side" traits occur when "positive traits and behaviors [are] used in extremes" (p. vi). As such, her study uncovered a curvilinear relationship between forceful behavior and leader effectiveness. The implication is that forceful behavior, used in moderation, was found more effective than in low or extremely high doses.

We extended Hereford's (2011) assumption to exercise frequency and intensity. Perhaps there is a "dark side" dimension of exercise. Eijsvogels, Molossi, Lee, Emery, and Thompson (2016) studied relationships between exercise and mortality, and found that mortality declines at mild and moderate exercise levels, but increases very slightly when exercise intensity is taken to an extreme. Gay, Buchner, and Schmidt (2016, in press) sought to identify the optimal dose of exercise intensity for patients with high risk of Type 2 diabetes. They established a curvilinear relationship, concluding that fractionalized (defined as short bouts of activity throughout the day) moderate-level exercise was best for controlling glucose levels long-term. Brown and Bray's (2015) study of the effects of isometric exercises on cognition concluded that "exercise until exhaustion is associated with reduced cognitive performance and that higher intensity isometric exercise leads to greater performance impairments in a linear dose-response manner" (p. 487). Although unexplored, we wondered whether or not a curvilinear relationship exists between exercise frequency and intensity and leadership behaviors.

For this study we asked: In what ways do personality characteristics, demographic characteristics, and leisure exercise habits influence leadership styles and leader effectiveness?

Sub-Questions

1. In what ways do a leader's perceived rate of exertion (PRE) and his or her leisure exercise frequency influence leadership style and leader effectiveness?
2. How do the Big Five personality dimensions influence leadership style and leader effectiveness?
3. In what ways do demographic factors like supervisory level (firstline, middle, senior manager), age, gender, race, and income influence leadership style and leader effectiveness?
4. In what ways do the perceptions of leader effectiveness and leadership style differ between leaders and their employees?

We posited the last question as a validity check. When asking leaders their perceptions of how they behave, there was a chance their employees held differing assessments.

HYPOTHESES

Rest days for recovery are recommended for optimal physical performance gains (Buschman, 2016; Foster, 1998). Applying a similar logic, we surmised deleterious effects on leadership styles and leader effectiveness among those who embrace the mindset of overtraining. We hypothesized curvilinear relationships between the following variables:

1. Perceived rate of exertion (PRE) and leadership style.
2. Exercise frequency and leadership style.
3. The Big Five personality factors and leadership style.
4. PRE and leader effectiveness.
5. Exercise frequency and leader effectiveness.
6. The Big Five personality dimensions and leader effectiveness.

In addition to the curvilinear relationships, we surmised that:

7. Women, minority, and younger leaders use TLB more than men, non-minority, and older leaders.

8. Senior-level leaders use TLB more than less-experienced leaders.

9. Women and minorities perform better along the dimensions of *Effectiveness* as defined in the MLQ because *Effectiveness* is associated with TLB.

10. Leaders' perceptions of their leadership style and effectiveness is moderately aligned with that of their employees.

11. Those with the lowest rate of PRE and exercise frequency are more apt to use transactional or passive-avoidant leadership styles.

We would like to make special note of Hypothesis 10. According to Atwater and Yammarino (1992), the leader's self-awareness is a predictor of his or her performance. Therefore, a complete mismatch in perceptions was unlikely among successful business leaders who participated in our study.

CONSTRUCTS

The constructs used herein can be grouped into three categories. The leadership constructs and outcome variables came from the MLQ, a validated instrument developed by Avolio and Bass (2004). It contains measures of transformational, transactional, and passive-avoidant leadership. It also addresses the outcome variables associated with leader effectiveness. The Big Five personality inventory, developed by Cattell (1943) and refined by Goldberg (1993), is the basis of much of the trait research in the leadership domain. The second grouping of constructs in our study was based on the Big Five model. Finally, we included dimensions associated with exercise frequency and perceived levels of exertion in our study.

Leadership Constructs

The constructs linked with transformational, transactional, and passive-avoidant leadership styles come from the MLQ, developed by Avolio and Bass (2004), which we used with permission. They conceptualized transactional leadership as a quid-pro-quo exchange process. Transformational leadership, also viewed as a more sophisticated negotiation, presents long-term implications for developing employees' capabilities, their performance, and organizational outcomes. Figure 1 depicts their conceptualization of transactional and transformational leadership exchanges.

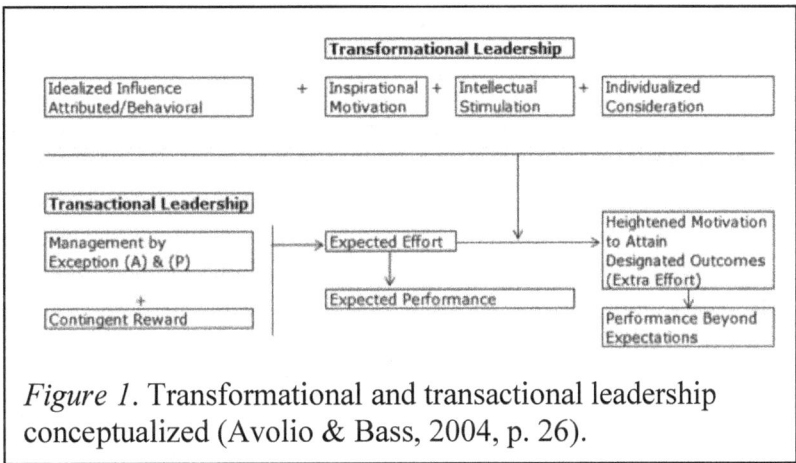

Figure 1. Transformational and transactional leadership conceptualized (Avolio & Bass, 2004, p. 26).

Transformational Leadership

Transformational leaders diverge from those with a more transactional style through the identification of team members' needs as they strive to nurture and develop employees' interests. Ultimately, the aim is to build team members into leaders. We used the variables associated with transformational leadership in the MLQ which were defined by Avolio and Bass (2004) as follows:

Idealized Influence –These leaders are admired, respected, and trusted. Followers identify with and want to emulate their leaders. Among the things the leader does to earn credit with followers is to consider followers' needs over his or her own needs. The leader shares risks with followers and is consistent in conduct with underlying ethics, principles, and values.

Idealized Attributes (IA)

- Instill pride in others for being associated with me.
- Go beyond self-interest for the good of the group.
- Act in ways that build others' respect for me.
- Display a sense of power and confidence.

Idealized Behaviors (IB)

- Talk about my most important values and beliefs.
- Specify the importance of having a strong sense of purpose.
- Consider the moral and ethical consequences of decisions.
- Emphasize the importance of having a collective sense of mission (p. 107).

Inspirational Motivation (IM) – These leaders behave in ways that motivate those around them by providing meaning and challenge to their followers' work. Individual and team spirit is aroused. Enthusiasm and optimism are displayed. The leader encourages followers to envision attractive future states, which they can ultimately envision for themselves.

- Talk optimistically about the future.
- Talk enthusiastically about what needs to be accomplished.
- Articulate a compelling vision of the future.
- Express confidence that goals will be achieved (p. 107).

Intellectual Stimulation (IS) – These leaders stimulate their followers' effort to be innovative and creative by questioning assumptions, reframing problems, and approaching old situations in new ways. There is no ridicule or public criticism of individual members' mistakes. New ideas and creative solutions to problems are solicited from followers, who are included in the process of addressing problems and finding solutions.

- Re-examine critical assumptions to question whether they are appropriate.
- Seek differing perspectives when solving problems.
- Get others to look at problems from many different angles.
- Suggest new ways of looking at how to complete assignments (p. 108).

Individual Consideration (IC – These leaders pay attention to each individual's need for achievement and growth by acting as a coach or mentor. Followers are developed to successively higher levels of potential. New learning opportunities are created along with a supportive climate in which to grow. Individual differences in terms of needs and desires are recognized.

- Spend time teaching and coaching.
- Treat others as individuals rather than just as a member of the group.
- Consider each individual as having different needs, abilities and aspirations from others.
- Help others to develop their strengths (p. 108).

Transactional Leadership

The quid pro quo negotiation process that we mentioned earlier in the chapter defines transactional leadership. More specifically in the MLQ (Avolio & Bass, 2004), transactional leadership contains two dimensions: *Contingent Reward* and *Management by Exception-Active*. Both styles are considered constructive and involve corrective transactions.

Contingent Reward (CR) – Transactional contingent reward leadership clarifies expectations and offers recognition when goals are achieved. The clarification of goals and objectives and providing of recognition once goals are achieved should result in individuals and groups achieving expected levels of performance (Avolio & Bass, 2004, p. 108).

- Provide others with assistance in exchange for their efforts.
- Discuss in specific terms who is responsible for achieving performance targets.
- Make clear what one can expect to receive when performance goals are achieved.
- Express satisfaction when others meet expectations (Avolio & Bass, 2004, p. 108).

Management by Exception Active (MBEA) – The leader specifies the standards for compliance, as well as what constitutes ineffective performance, and may punish followers for being out of compliance with those standards. This style of leadership implies closely monitoring for deviances, mistakes, and errors and then taking corrective action as quickly as possible when they occur (Avolio & Bass, 2004, p. 109).

- Focus attention on irregularities, mistakes, exceptions, and deviations from standards.
- Concentrate my full attention on dealing with mistakes, complaints and failures.
- Keep track of all mistakes.
- Direct my attention toward failures to meet standards (Avolio & Bass, 2004, p. 109).

Passive-Avoidant Leadership

Passive-avoidant leadership is a form of management-by-exception, but it is more reactive, hence the term "passive." Unlike the more active form, passive leaders do not create quid pro quo agreements, spell out what they expect, or share goals and standards for which employees should strive. Passive-avoidant leadership influences outcomes opposite to those desired by the manager. In this respect, it resembles "laissez-faire styles - or no leadership" (Avolio & Bass, 2004, p. 109). Both styles have unfavorable effects on employees.

Management-by-Exception: Passive (MBEP)

- Fail to interfere until problems become serious.
- Wait for things to go wrong before taking action.
- Show a firm belief in "if it ain't broke, don't fix it."
- Demonstrate that problems must become chronic before I take action (p. 109).

Laissez-Faire (LF)

- Avoid getting involved when important issues arise.
- Am absent when needed.
- Avoid making decisions.
- Delay responding to urgent questions (p. 109).

Effectiveness Outcomes of Leadership

The MLQ also contains variables associated with leader effectiveness. "Success is measured with the MLQ by how often the raters perceive their leader to be motivating, how effective raters perceive their leader to be at interacting at different levels of the organization, and how satisfied raters are with their leader's methods of working with others" (Avolio & Bass, 2004, p. 109).

Extra Effort is defined as influencing others to accomplish more than they expected, increasing their wish to thrive, and increasing the eagerness of others to "try harder" (Avolio & Bass, 2004, p. 109). *Effectiveness* is defined as meeting the job-related needs of others, representing the team well to those in higher authority, meeting the requirements of the organization, and leading a team that is effective (Avolio & Bass, 2004, p. 110). *Satisfaction* with leadership has two dimensions: (1) Using leadership methods perceived to be pleasing; and (2) working well with others (Avolio & Bass, 2004).

We assumed that by augmenting transactional leadership with transformational behaviors, the results would be "a greater amount of *Extra Effort*, *Effectiveness*, and *Satisfaction*" from employees (p. 27). It is unrealistic to presuppose a leader will be purely transformational, solely transactional, or exclusively passive. Rather, leaders employ a combination of behaviors from all three domains. When the majority of behaviors align with one particular style, the leader is considered mostly one over the others.

The Big Five Constructs

The Big Five dimensions came from the Big Five Inventory, which was charted in the following table developed by John and Srivastava (1999). The Big Five taxonomy does not measure personality. Rather, it arranges and organizes personality scales, thereby enabling a structure for spotting similarities and differences in the scales (Kaiser & Hogan, 2011). The dimensions in Table 1 fall into independent categories, and can be conceptualized as "Extraversion (sociable, assertive, active); Agreeableness (trusting, accommodating, caring); Conscientiousness (reliable, dependable, hardworking); Emotional Stability (adjusted, composed, resilient); and Intellect-Openness to Experience (educated, imaginative, unconventional)" (Kaiser & Hogan, 2011, p. 221). We used questions from the Big Five Inventory-10 (BFI-10), a shortened version of the original 44-item instrument, which was validated by Rammstedt and John (2007).

TABLE 1

The Big Five Factors (John & Srivastava, 1999, p. 110)

Big Five Dimensions	Facet (and correlated trait adjective)
Extraversion vs. introversion	Gregariousness (sociable)
	Assertiveness (forceful)
	Activity (energetic)
	Excitement-seeking (adventurous)
	Positive emotions (enthusiastic)
	Warmth (outgoing)
Agreeableness vs. antagonism	Trust (forgiving)
	Straightforwardness (not demanding)
	Altruism (warm)
	Compliance (not stubborn)
	Modesty (not show-off)
	Tender-mindedness (sympathetic)
Conscientiousness vs. lack of direction	Competence (efficient)
	Order (organized)
	Dutifulness (not careless)
	Achievement striving (thorough)
	Self-discipline (not lazy)
	Deliberation (not impulsive)
Neuroticism vs. emotional stability	Anxiety (tense)
	Angry hostility (irritable)
	Depression (not contented)
	Self-consciousness (shy)
	Impulsiveness (moody)
	Vulnerability (not self-confident)
Openness vs. closedness to experience	Ideas (curious)
	Fantasy (imaginative)
	Aesthetics (artistic)
	Actions (wide interests)
	Feelings (excitable)
	Values (unconventional)

Exercise Intensity

We used the three constructs to measure leisure exercise behaviors: *Frequency of Exercise* was defined using the number of times per week the leaders engage in leisure exercise, which ranged from none at all to seven or more days per week (with "more" defined as exercising more than once per day). *Type of Exercise* we framed by asking open-ended questions in the survey. Participants were asked to identify the types of leisure-exercise activities in which they engage. *Perceived Rate of Exertion (PRE)* was a construct comprising three levels. We defined *Strenuous exercise* as activities in which one's heart beats rapidly and produces a sweat. *Moderate exercise* we described as exercising to a level that raises the heart rate to a point where one sweats and feels he or she is working, yet is able to carry on a conversation. We explained mild exercise as activity that does not induce sweating, unless it is a hot, humid day, and there is no noticeable change in breathing patterns. We found it difficult to define "extreme" exercise. We anticipated our data analysis would help us understand the parameters of extreme exercise and their effects on leadership dimensions.

SCOPE/DELIMITATIONS AND LIMITATIONS

We confined our research to perceptions, including how leaders regard themselves and those of their team members. In the employee survey, we invited only those for whom we received their leader's permission. Some leaders did not grant access because they recently asked them for feedback and shared their concerns over survey fatigue. Others did not explain why they declined our request for access. Therefore, one limitation of both scope and data generalizability is the potential for bias toward more favorable perceptions when corroborating the self-reports of leaders.

Another limitation of the study was the sample size. It was difficult to persuade leaders to participate in our web-based survey, a concern that is not isolated to our research (Sauermann & Roach, 2013). Therefore, we missed the opportunity to identify patterns that could have emerged had more leaders participated. In addition, our confirmatory factor analysis (Chapter Three) produced a lower reliability level on the composite variable *Satisfaction*, which would have probably been higher had the sample size been larger. As a result, our confidence in our findings for that particular outcome variable is weaker than in all other dimensions. Regardless, the sample was ample for inferential analyses.

We relied on leaders' self-reports, which were corroborated through surveying a sample of their employees. Both points of data collection depended on the perceptions of both groups. This methodological limitation could have been minimized through observational research that examined leaders in action. However, time, cost, and access barriers precluded our use of this triangulation technique.

We also depended on self-reported leisure exercise habits. We did not measure physical exertion through blood tests, VO2max, heart rate during and after exertion, or through other medical tests. We framed our research using a social science lens, relying only on self-assessments and perceptions held by leaders and their employees. Additionally, we applied a decision rule, described in Chapter Three, which selected one PRE per individual. Although pragmatic, we risked overlooking fine distinctions in PRE for leaders who participate in multiple forms of exercise.

Finally, our data collection plan did not determine business conditions in the industries employing the leaders we surveyed. Much research suggests that personality tendencies are situational in that certain traits emerge to fit the constraints posed by current circumstances; such traits may not reflect the norm for the leader under average conditions (De Hoogh et al., 2005). Other studies have confirmed leader effectiveness dimensions are situational, also. For example, TLB is not ideal in routine situations, and transactional leadership is a poor fit when innovation and visionary competencies are needed (Kaiser & Hogan, 2011). We did not measure these situations in this study. Rather, we coupled our findings with what has already been shown concerning situational leadership through these prior studies.

SUMMARY

Research focusing on antecedents to leadership style and leader effectiveness is in its infancy. The purpose of this study was to develop a deeper sense of why leaders behave as they do. We surmised nuanced relationships between employee characteristics, leisure exercise habits, leadership styles, and leader effectiveness. Our study examined these connections across a range of leadership styles, and relied on validated models of personality (the Big Five) and leadership (the MLQ).

Chapter Two offers a review of relevant literature. In it we canvass studies across both management and psychology domains to better understand theoretical models and prior research that informed our inquiry. We explored also the potential of "dark side" traits and behaviors, which may not be assets uniformly in all circumstances. We turn now to share what we learned from our secondary research.

[2]

LITERATURE REVIEW

Since we examined the ways in which personality characteristics, demographic characteristics, and leisure exercise habits influence leadership styles and leader effectiveness, we first needed to narrow the leadership behaviors and personality characteristics to be explored. In addition to framing the problem and research questions in Chapter One, we introduced the leadership constructs associated with transformational, transactional, and passive-avoidant leadership that come from the Multifactor Leadership Questionnaire (MLQ), developed by Avolio and Bass (2004), and the Big Five personality taxonomy. We will now provide more detailed information. Below is an overview of transformational, transactional, and passive-avoidant leadership styles, a review of the Big Five personality constructs, and a presentation of extant literature that is relevant to each of our research sub-questions.

TRANSFORMATIONAL, TRANSACTIONAL, AND PASSIVE-AVOIDANT LEADERSHIP STYLES

While several leadership theories exist, the focus of this literature review is on the full-range leadership model of transformational, transactional, and passive-avoidant leadership to elucidate whether personality characteristics, demographic characteristics, and leisure exercise habits influence leadership styles and leader effectiveness. Because the MLQ has been used in leadership research so extensively, its constructs provided a solid framework upon which we relied.

Transformational Leadership

Transformational leadership behaviors, or TLBs, (Avolio, 2011; Bass, 1997; Basu & Green, 1997; Howell & Avolio, 1993) go beyond meeting the basic needs of employees and engages them in such a way as to raise them to new levels of morality. A transformational leader establishes high standards and goals; gives meaning, purpose, and direction to followers and their work; leads followers with enthusiasm, inspiration, charisma, motivations, and emotions (Bass, 1990; Harms & Credé, 2010, as cited in Furtner, Baldegger, & Rauthmann, 2013), and creates an atmosphere of intrinsic motivation whereby extrinsically motivated needs are reduced (Shamir, House, & Arthur, 1993, as cited in Furtner et al., 2013). TLB expresses the importance and values associated with desired outcomes in ways that are easily understood by employees, while communicating higher levels of expectations for them (Avolio & Bass, 1988; Conger & Kanungo, 1987; as cited in Jung & Avolio, 2000). As aforementioned, leaders who utilize transformational leadership behaviors (TLBs) "transform employees into high performers" (Jin Seo, & Shapiro, 2016, p. 64).

Transformational leadership is likely to emerge in times of rapid change and distress, and it is also likely to surface in organizations that have unclear goals and structures, well-educated members, and a high level of trust (Basu & Green, 1997). In contrast to the transactional leader who practices contingent reinforcement of followers, transformational leaders inspire, intellectually stimulate, and are individually considerate of them. Transformational leadership may be directive or participative, but it requires higher moral development (Basu & Green, 1997).

Transactional Leadership

Transactional leadership (Avolio, 2011; Avolio, Bass, & Jung, 1999; Burns, 1978; Lowe, Kroeck, & Sivasubramaniam, 1996) is based on an exchange of valued intangible items that could be economic, personal, political, emotional, or psychological. In contrast to transformational leadership, it has been characterized as a contractual or exchange process between leaders and followers (Jung & Avolio, 2000). Jung and Avolio (2000) describe the fundamental aspects of transactional leadership:

The transactional leader identifies specific followers' expectations and provides rewards in exchange for followers' performance. Bass labeled this form of exchange stating that, 'transactional leadership is contingent reinforcement (1985, p. 121).' Ideally, the leader and his or her followers agree on what followers need to do to get rewards or to avoid punishment. There is no concerted effort to change followers' personal values, nor necessarily a need to develop a deep sense of trust and commitment to the leader. Instead, the transactional leader works with followers' current needs and tries to satisfy those needs with desired outcomes once agreed upon performance levels are achieved. (Jung & Avolio, 2000, p. 951)

Clearly, not all forms of transactional leadership are ineffective. Atwater, Camobreco, Dionne, Avolio, and Lau (1997) found that leaders who engage in contingent reward behaviors are more effective than those who do not.

Further, in its more constructive form, transactional leadership is augmented by working with individuals and/or groups, setting up and defining agreements to achieve specific objectives, discovering individuals' capabilities, and specifying the compensation and rewards that can be expected upon successful completion of tasks (Avolio & Bass, 2004, as cited in Furtner et al., 2013). In its corrective form, it focuses on actively setting standards. In its passive form, it involves waiting for mistakes to occur before taking action. In its active form, there is close monitoring for the occurrence of mistakes. In either its passive or active form, it focuses on identifying mistakes (Avolio & Bass, 2004, as cited in Furtner et al., 2013).

Passive-Avoidant Leadership

The most noteworthy form of passive-avoidant leadership is laissez-faire behavior. Laissez-faire leadership tends to be the least effective leadership behavior, displaying negative correlations with leader effectiveness (Lowe, Kroeck, & Sivasubramaniam, 1996, as cited in Cable & Judge, 2003). It is thus is considered a particularly passive and ineffective leadership style, as the leading of employees is avoided or practically nonexistent (e.g., Avolio, 2011; Bass & Avolio, 1995; Judge & Piccolo, 2004; as cited in Furtner et al., 2013). Many scholars and practitioners have found it useful to label Contingent Reward (CR) and Management-by-Exception: Active (MBEA) as Transactional Leadership and Management-by-Exception: Passive (MBEP) and Laissez-faire as Passive-Avoidant Leadership (Avolio & Bass, 2004).

Big Five Personality Constructs

According to John and Srivastva (1999), there was a renewed surge of interest in research on the personality traits of effective leaders. Personality has been studied from innumerable theoretical perspectives, with varying levels of breadth or depth. Several personality scholars sought to create the theoretical structure that would transform the human race into speaking a common language, but such an integration could not be achieved by any one theoretical perspective. What personality psychology needed was a descriptive model, or taxonomy, of its subject matter (John & Srivastava, 1999). One of the main goals of scientific taxonomies is the definition of overarching domains within which large numbers of specific interests can be understood in a simplified way. Thus, in a personality psychology, a taxonomy would permit researchers to study specified domains of personality characteristics, rather than separately examining the myriad specific attributes that make human beings individual and unique. A taxonomy would also facilitate the accumulation and communication of empirical findings by offering a standard vocabulary (John & Srivastava, 1999).

John and Srivastava (1999) explored personality from many theoretical perspectives, and concluded the universal appeal of the Big Five framework emanates from its grounding language that emerges naturally in conversations concerning personality. They stated:

> *After decades of research, the field is finally approaching consensus on a general taxonomy of personality traits, the 'Big Five' personality dimensions. These dimensions do not represent a particular theoretical perspective but were derived from analyses of the natural language terms people use to describe themselves and others...the Big Five taxonomy serves an integrative function because it can represent diverse systems of personality description in a common framework.* (John & Srivastava, 1999, p. 103)

According to John and Srivastva (1999), the Big Five personality dimensions are the result of the lexical approach and discovery that led Chaplin, John, and Goldberg (1988) and other esteemed scholars to argue for a prototype conception in which each category is defined in terms of its clear cases rather than its boundaries. Later, a 44-item inventory that measures an individual on the Big Five Factors (dimensions) of personality (Goldberg, 1993) was created, and each of the factors is then further divided into personality facets (as cited in John & Srivastava, 1999). As aforementioned in Chapter One, an even more condensed instrument, which was found valid in measuring the Big Five dimensions, is the BFI-10, developed by Rammstedt and John in 2007.

The Big Five factors, per Table 1 in Chapter One, are extraversion, agreeableness, conscientiousness, emotional stability, and intellect. Several researchers have studied transformational and/or charismatic[1] and transactional leadership in connection with the Big Five factors, but they are complex and layered constructs because they tend to be activated by relevant situational conditions. De Hoogh et al. (2005) address these complexities in a clear and direct manner.

Recent work demonstrates that stable individual differences in leadership do exist (e.g., Judge, Bono, Ilies, & Gerhardt, 2002). However, unambiguous links between the five factors and leader behavior have been difficult to establish (e.g., Bono & Judge, 2004; Crant & Bateman, 2000; Judge & Bono, 2000; Ployhart, Lim, & Chan, 2001). To date there has been little attention in the leadership literature for the principle of trait activation, which holds that personality traits require trait-relevant situations for their expression. In other words, an individual will behave in trait-like ways only in those situations that are relevant to the given trait (Tett & Burnett, 2003). Drawing on trait activation theory, the relationship between personality and charismatic and transactional leadership may differ depending on the context and such relationships may only be present in situations in which these leadership styles encompass viable, trait-relevant responses (De Hoogh et al., 2005, p. 839-840).

---

[1]According to Levine, Muenchen, and Brooks (2010), "charismatic leadership is similar to transformational leadership, as it examines the relationship between the leader and the followers and focuses on issues relating to vision, risk taking, enthusiasm and confidence (Hoyt & Ciulla, 2004). Some theorists have suggested that charismatic leadership is a sub-dimension of transformational leadership; others state that the two theories overlap, as each identifies unique and important aspects of the leadership process (Yukl, 1999)" (p. 577). We agree with these scholars, and therefore use the two terms interchangeably when appropriate.

Connecting the Literature to the Research Questions

Now that we have shared the literature pertaining to the leadership and Big Five constructs, we will focus on the literature relevant to the central research question and sub-questions. We share extant research that concerns personality characteristics and leadership style, demographic characteristics and leadership style, and leisure exercise habits and leadership style. We follow that general discussion with an assessment of the literature relating to each of the sub-question in our study.

Research Question

As a refresher, the central research question is: In what ways do personality characteristics, demographic characteristics, and leisure exercise habits influence leadership styles and leader effectiveness? The purpose and perspective of this question is unique in many ways. There has been virtually no empirical research examining how personality and demographic characteristics combined with leisure exercise habits influence leadership styles. The literature does not yet directly answer this question, although there is research that explores portions of the question.

Personality Characteristics and Leadership Style

Leadership style is a vital component that influences leader effectiveness, outcomes, and productivity. One of the influencing factors on one's leadership style is his or her personality characteristics. However, few researchers have examined leaders' personality characteristics and leadership styles. In this subsection, we address some of the most relevant findings that currently exist in the literature.

Cable and Judge (2003) tested theoretical linkages between the Five Factor model and managers' upward influence tactic strategies, and found that managers scoring high on extraversion were more likely to use inspirational appeal and ingratiation, while those scoring high on openness were less likely to use coalitions. These authors also found that those scoring high on emotional stability were more likely to use rational persuasion and less likely to use inspirational appeal. Further, those scoring high on agreeableness were less likely to use legitimization or pressure, and those scoring high on conscientiousness were more likely to use rational appeal (Cable & Judge, 2003). Additionally, results confirmed that managers' upward influence tactic strategies depended on the leadership style of their supervisor. Managers were more likely to use consultation and inspirational appeal tactics when their supervisor was a transformational leader, but were more likely to use exchange, coalition, legitimization, and pressure tactics when their supervisor displayed a laissez-faire leadership style (Cable & Judge, 2003).

Judge, Bono, Ilies, and Gerhardt (2002) found that *Extraversion* emerged as the most consistent correlate of leadership, as it was not only the strongest associate of leadership in their combined analysis, but it also displayed a nonzero effect in all analyses, when controlling for the other Big Five traits, and when broken down in the moderator analysis by criteria and sample type. These results suggest that Extraversion is the most important trait of leaders and effective leadership. Results also confirmed that Extraversion is more strongly related to leader emergence (acceptance of the new leader by his or her peers in self-managed teams) than to leader effectiveness. The authors posit that if attempted leadership is more likely to result in leader emergence than it is in leader effectiveness, the results for Extraversion make sense, as both sociable and dominant people are more likely to assert themselves in group situations (Judge et al., 2002). After Extraversion, Conscientiousness and Openness to Experience were the strongest and most consistent correlates of leadership, with Conscientiousness more strongly related to leader emergence than to leader effectiveness. Further, in business settings, Openness to Experience (along with Extraversion) was the strongest dispositional correlate of leadership, although it failed to emerge as a significant predictor of leadership in the multivariate analysis (Judge et al., 2002).

Demographic Characteristics and Leadership Style

Myriad studies have investigated demographic characteristics and leadership style, with the bulk of the literature focusing on gender differences in leadership style. Many studies on gender differences in leadership yield conflicting results. A number of studies from a variety of scholarly arenas (sociology, psychology, business, education) contended that women and men exhibit dissimilar leadership styles and react differently when placed in similar situations (Astin & Leland, 1991; Benismon & Neumann, 1993; Billing

& Alvesson, 1994; Cantor & Bernay, 1992; Eagly, Karau & Johnson, 1992; Eagly, Makhijani & Klonsky, 1992; Helgeson, 1995; Kezar, 2000; Rosener, 1990; Statham, 1987; Shakeshaft, 1987, 1999). For example, participative and transformational leadership styles were found to be used slightly more by women than men, with the main difference attributed to women relying more on individual consideration (being supportive and emphasizing the development of employees' skill and confidence levels). Moreover, men were found to follow exception-management styles more than women while women relied more on contingent-reward behaviors (Eagly, Johannesen-Schmidt, & van Engen, 2003, as cited in Antonaros, 2010).

Age is a demographic characteristic that has not been examined nearly as much as gender when considering the connection to leadership style. Some research indicates that younger leaders have a higher tendency for transformational preference (Barbuto, Fritz, Matkin, & Marx, 2007). Other studies have found that older managers consulted more widely and favored more participation in comparison with younger managers, although both younger and older managers practiced directive and delegative leadership styles at about the same degree (Oshagbemi, 2004).

Race and ethnicity are other demographic characteristics that greatly need to be researched. While many researchers will report the results of their instrument measures with demographic characteristic data, we could not locate any research that explicitly explores race and/or ethnicity and leadership style.

In short, competing results render the answer to questions of demographic characteristics and leadership style inconclusive, most likely caused by the serious limitations in the majority of the research.

Leisure Exercise Habits and Leadership Style

There is some, but not much, research on the connections between leisure exercise habits and leadership style. Most of these studies focus on physical fitness, but not specifically leisure exercise. Physical fitness has been related to ratings of leadership (Bass, 1990). A positive correlation has been found between physical aptitude and others perceiving the leader to possess more leadership ability (Rice, Yoder, Adams, Priest, & Prince; 1984). Also, physical fitness in the form of varsity athletic participation was found to be the best predictor of follower ratings of transformational leadership among midshipman (Atwater & Yammarino, 1993).

Researchers have found that engaging in regular exercise is positively correlated with leadership behaviors and styles. For example, McDowell-Larsen, Kearney, Leigh, and Campbell (2002) examined how regular exercise affected leadership scores on two multi-rater leadership assessment instruments – the Executive Success Profile (ESP) and the Campbell Leadership Index (CLI). Results from their study showed that observers rate exercisers significantly higher than non-exercisers on many of the ESP and CLI scales. Further, the weighted averages of all the scales for both instruments were significantly higher than the averages of non-exercisers (McDowell-Larsen et al., 2002).

Additionally, attributes of leaders that influenced their use of contingent and noncontingent punishment, and subsequently the results of using punishment on leader effectiveness have been examined (Atwater, Dionee, Camobreco, Avolio, & Lau, 1998). Results directed that leaders with higher levels of physical fitness and moral reasoning were more likely to use contingent punishment, while those with lower self-esteem were more likely to use noncontingent punishment (following random operant conditioning with punishment). Noncontingent punishment negatively affected leader effectiveness, while contingent punishment positively influenced leader effectiveness (Atwater et al., 1998).

While the literature clearly indicates that physical fitness has a positive effect on leadership style, little research exists that shows the ways in which leisure exercise habits influence leadership style. Additional exploration of this topic is needed.

Research Sub-Question One:

In what ways do a leader's perceived rate of exertion and his or her leisure exercise frequency influence leadership style and leader effectiveness?

As aforementioned, a few studies have found connections between physical fitness and leadership style (Atwater & Yammarino, 1993; Atwater et al., 1998; McDowell-Larsen et al., 2002; Rice et al., 1984). Himelhoch (2014) examined the connections between transformational and HIIT, and found positive connections between the two. However, the ways in which a leader's PRE and his or her leisure exercise frequency influence leadership style and leader effectiveness has not yet been examined. We hope that this monograph will contribute to a growing body of research on this topic.

Research Sub-Question Two:

How do the Big Five personality dimensions influence leadership style and leader effectiveness?

Knowing how each of the personality characteristics applies to leader behaviors helps to further elucidate antecedents to TLB, other leadership styles, and leader effectiveness. There is a dearth of research in this area, as unambiguous links between the five personality dimensions and leader behavior have been difficult to establish (De Hoogh et al., 2005). However, a few studies have focused on the connections between the Big Five personality dimensions and leadership. Curvilinear relationships do exist among personality, behavior, and leadership (Hereford, 2011). A small positive correlation has also been found between bold traits and forceful behavior, although a curvilinear relationship was not found between bold traits and leadership effectiveness. Findings from Hereford's (2011) study indicate that relatively low and high amounts of forcefulness yielded the lowest scores of perceived leadership effectiveness and relatively moderate amounts of forcefulness yielded significantly higher ratings of leadership effectiveness criteria. These results indicate that forceful behavior in moderate amounts is a predictor of success in leadership positions (Hereford, 2011).

Also, De Hoogh et al. (2005) found that four of the Big Five dimensions are differently relevant to charismatic and transactional leadership depending in the degree to which the work environment is perceived as dynamic. Contrary to De Hoogh et al.'s expectations, no direct relationship was found between openness to experience and charismatic leadership. They found a positive relationship between openness to experience and charismatic leadership only in a work environment perceived as dynamic. Additionally, leaders scoring high on openness to experience were rated more charismatic by employees in work situations that were perceived as dynamic. Conversely, they were rated less charismatic in work situations that were viewed as more stable. Employees in work situations that were perceived as dynamic rated leaders scoring high on openness to experience more charismatic (De Hoogh et al., 2005). According to De Hoogh et al. (2005), these findings align with those by Ployhart, Lim, and Chan (2001), and suggest that openness to experience is more relevant to charismatic leadership in a dynamic rather than a stable environment.

A study that examined the Five Factor model of personality, transformational leadership, and team performance under conditions similar to typical and maximum performance contexts (defined as challenges that exceed the norm) found that neuroticism and agreeableness were negatively related to transformational leadership ratings (Beng-Chong & Plyhart; 2004). Additionally, transformational leadership related more strongly to team performance in the maximum rather than the typical context. Transformational leadership also fully mediated the relationship between leader personality and team performance in the maximum context but only partially mediated the relationship between leader personality and team performance in the typical context (Beng-Chong & Ployhart, 2004).

Research Sub-Question Three:

In what ways do demographic factors like supervisory level (firstline, middle, senior manager), age, gender, race, and income influence leadership style and leader effectiveness?

Researchers have indicated that there is a relationship between certain demographic factors and leadership style. As previously discussed, there is a good deal of research that examined gender, leadership style, and leader effectiveness (Antonaros, 2010; Astin & Leland, 1991; Benismon & Neumann, 1993; Billing & Alvesson, 1994; Cantor & Bernay, 1992; Eagly, Karau & Johnson, 1992; Eagly, Makhijani & Klonsky, 1992; Helgeson, 1995; Kezar, 2000; Rosener, 1990; Statham, 1987; Shakeshaft, 1987, 1999), as well as age and leadership style (Barbuto et al., 2007; Oshagbemi, 2004), although the latter does not address leader effectiveness. There is also very limited research on race, leadership style, and leader effectiveness. Some studies have found that leadership skills command a higher wage premium within managerial occupations than elsewhere (Kuhn & Weinberger, 2005), but little can be found on the influence of income on leadership style and leader effectiveness.

There has been surprisingly little research on the relationship between supervisory level and leadership style, and even less that also examines these factors along with leader effectiveness. Of the research that does exist, the majority focuses on CEOs, presidents, vice presidents, and other supervisors at the very top of the organizational hierarchy. There have been empirical observations regarding the relationship between transformational leadership and the leader's hierarchical position (Bass, Waldman, Avolio, & Bebb, 1989). Colbert,

Kristof-Brown, Bradley, and Barrick (2008) found that higher vice president perceptions of goal importance are associated with both CEO transformational leadership and vice president attitudes. Also, at the organizational level, CEO transformational leadership was positively related to within-team goal importance congruence, which was positively related to organizational performance (Colbert et al., 2008).

Fewer studies have addressed the leadership styles of middle- and lower-level managers, although some research does exist. Sparks and Schenk (2001) examined the key leadership relationships between individual member distributors and the 'sponsor' members who recruited them into the organization. While sponsors were expected to provide leadership to the members they recruited, they did not possess any direct supervisory roles. Still, the researchers found that transformational leadership did indeed transform followers by encouraging them to see the higher purposes in their work.

Waldman and Yammarino (1999) note that cohesive intragroup and intergroup relationships are likely to be spawned by CEO charismatic styles, and cascading leadership often results from role modeling processes, which in turn encourages the cooperative pursuit of goals of all levels. This means that intergroup cohesion makes it possible to achieve simultaneously the potentially divergent goals of organizational performance units such that the ultimate performance of the organization has the potential to be maximized (Waldman & Yammarino, 1999). Ultimately, transformational leadership needs to be enacted at all organizational levels to create a positive intergroup and intragroup work environment, which in turn will help to maximize productivity, enhance employee satisfaction, and achieve organizational goals.

While limited research exists to answer even portions of this research sub-question, clear patterns have emerged that indicate that transformational leadership on all supervisory levels can improve follower productivity, satisfaction, and morale.

Research Sub-Question Four:

In what ways do the perceptions of leader effectiveness and leadership style differ between leaders and their employees?

It is common for leaders to have differing perceptions of their leadership style and leader effectiveness than their followers. Perceptions are factors that individuals take into account when making judgments about others. While perceptions typically are not directly assessed in the formal measurement process, they do influence those perceptions that are assessed. Examples of formally assessed perceptions include some of the more intangible measures of effectiveness such as employee satisfaction, congruence between followers' expectations and their perceptions of their leader, and group cohesion (Antonaros, 2010).

A plethora of factors affect the perceptions of leadership style and leader effectiveness, including the perceiver's demographic factors such as gender, age, racial and ethnic background, and educational background. Although superiors' and employees' assessments are perceptual and may well be subject to bias, learning the perceptions of those whom work with and for leaders is a vital component of the leader effectiveness construct (Birnbaum, 1989; Bowen & Shapiro, 1998; Martin & Samels, 1997; Rosser, 2003).

Research has found that transformational leadership, which is often connected with communal leadership behaviors, is highly correlated with leader effectiveness. These findings are consistent with the literature in that transformational leaders who exert communal and relational leadership behaviors are usually viewed as more effective leaders than their transactional counterparts who enact agentic behaviors (Antonaros, 2010; Omar & Davidson, 2001).

The implications in the literature that address the influence of transformational and transactional leadership styles on leader effectiveness are uncertain in light of arguments that the effectiveness of these styles is likely contingent on features of the group or organizational environment (Vroom & Yetton, 1973, as cited in Antonaros, 2010). Meta-analyses reviewing the effects of transformational versus transactional leadership on effectiveness have also confirmed the importance of moderating conditions (Foels, Driskell, Mullen & Salas, 2000; Gastil, 1994, as cited in Antonaros, 2010).

LIMITATIONS OF THE LITERATURE

As is typical of any exploratory study, we found noteworthy gaps in prior research that has been conducted on topics relevant to our research question and sub-questions. First, there is scarce research that connects research domains of leadership styles, leadership effectiveness, demographic characteristics, and leisure exercise habits. Second, we found methodological challenges among the research that has been conducted to date. Finally, we note problems with the validity in employee ratings of their leaders. We address these limitations in the final section of this chapter.

Dearth in Literature

We found several areas in which research is lacking within each of our research questions. The limited research in each of these areas is a limitation that has prevented us from accessing data; however, we expected this shortage because our study, although quantitative, is exploratory.

Methodological Challenges

Several methodological challenges exist when attempting to examine gender differences in leadership style and its influence on leader effectiveness. The first of these challenges involves single-source variance (Dansereau, Yammarino & Makham, 1995). Many models reviewed in this examination were validated on limited sources of information due to the lack of literature on the topic. A small number of researchers examining a particular topic may artificially inflate the relationships under investigation (Yukl, 2006). The early studies of Big Five dimensions were limited because they examined linear relationships. When small correlations were found, the momentum in trait research was lost. Recently, the research trajectory has been revitalized with the use of curvilinear analyses to explore more nuanced relationships between the Big Five factors and leadership styles and effectiveness (Judge, Piccolo, & Kosalka, 2009; Lord, DeVader, & Alliger, 1986).

The second challenge involves biased perceptions of participants in these studies. Biases may involve deeply rooted stereotypes, such as those concerning gender, age, or race, as well as more personal and individualized judgments that employees and colleagues may hold for a leader. One solution to this challenge may be to ask one employee to describe the leader's behavior and another to provide the effectiveness measure (Avolio, Bass & Jung, 1999). Although a step in the right direction, still both the leader and the employees have a vested interest in the relationship and thus may provide a biased perception in assessments.

Carol R. Himelhoch and Mary Antonaros Raymond

Validity and Reliability of Measures

Another challenge is that the existing research on leader performance assessment has been the development of valid and reliable measures of leader effectiveness (Heck & Marcoulides, 1996; Marcoulides & Heck, 1993; Pike, 1994; Pitner, 1988, as cited in Antonaros, 2010).

> *Leader effectiveness has been measured by various indexes and by many sources such as self-report, superiors, and subordinates. Some models have been more effective in predicting leaders' emergence than effectiveness. Others have been more successful in predicting the well-being and cohesion of the group, such as subordinate satisfaction, employee turnover, and subordinates' levels of morale. Several studies have predicted group performance measures by subordinates' or superiors' assessments, while others have used performance criteria such as financial indexes, sales, or organizational goals met. The parameter of models and the measures used to assess leadership are important to consider, as some models may be better in predicting one criterion* (Antonaros, 2010, p. 55)

However, reliability issues surface because such assessments often fail to reflect the true effect of a leader on his or her employees. Sometimes superiors do not take the time to provide accurate and comprehensive performance reviews; at other times, superiors may be largely unaware of or unfamiliar with an individual's performance. Some superiors also have difficulties dealing with conflict and would rather give average ratings than have to deal with the emotions and distress associated with unflattering ratings. Moreover, an employee may rate a leader as effective simply because the leader did not make him or her work hard, or the leader may be rated ineffective if he or she makes employees work too hard (Hughes, Ginnett, & Curphy, 1999; Reeves, 2004, as cited in Antonaros, 2010).

Given the flaws in various assessment processes, Hughes et al., (1999) stated that no one perfect or ideal method of assessing leader effectiveness had been identified (Antonaros, 2010). These authors suggest that a better way to judge leader effectiveness may be to ask employees to rate their level of satisfaction or the effectiveness of their leaders. Other than conducting a real-time assessment through a direct observational method, surveying employees' opinions on leader effectiveness is the most capable way of telling the direct impact of leadership on employee levels of job satisfaction. This leads back to Yukl's (2006) recommendation of including a variety of criteria when exploring leader effectiveness. While virtually impossible to wholly capture and measure the nuances and myriad of fine details of leader effectiveness, multiple criteria are essential when attempting to measure leader effectiveness (Antonaros, 2010). We use the effectiveness measures in the MLQ because the instrument has been validated in numerous studies since 2004, despite the sub-optimal methodical limitations cited above.

The disconnect of findings, lack of empirical evidence, and competing results in the interdisciplinary literature render the answers to our research questions inconclusive. There are serious limitations in the majority of the research that have been addressed in this section. It is clear that the influence personality characteristics, demographic characteristics, and leisure exercise habits on leadership styles and leader effectiveness needs to be empirically examined. Now that the relevant literature on our research questions has been analyzed, the next chapter presents the methods that we used for the study.

[3]

METHODS

INTRODUCTION

The purpose of this quantitative study was to explore antecedents to a range of leadership styles and the degree of leader effectiveness associated with those behaviors. The antecedents included personal characteristics, such as managerial level, age, race, gender, and personality plus a full assortment of leisure exercise habits, including no exercise at all. Leadership styles included transactional, transformational, and passive-avoidant leadership.

This chapter shares the methods employed to test our hypotheses. We provide a description of our survey instrument, which integrated leisure exercise habits, dimensions from Avolio and Bass' (2004) MLQ as well as from the Big Five instrument (John & Srivastava, 1999), and leaders' demographic characteristics. We incorporate also our sampling methods and analysis techniques. We present the characteristics of our sample, and our plan for data analysis. We include the results of the confirmatory factor analysis, which we used for data compression.

RESEARCH METHOD

Although our research was exploratory, we extended Himelhoch's (2014) qualitative research on HIIT as an antecedent to TLB. To investigate a range of leisure exercise habits across a set of leadership styles, the quantitative method was most appropriate. Quantitative methods provide an opportunity to test hypotheses using inferential statistical methods like the ANOVA and polynomial regressions that we performed. Our quantitative research was guided in part by theories established by research on transformational, transactional, and passive-avoidant leadership. As mentioned in Chapter One, studies suggesting curvilinear connections between the Big Five dimensions and leadership behaviors also provided the theoretical foundation for our research (Ames & Flynn, 2007; Hereford, 2011). We did not find conjectural connections between exercise and leadership beyond the Atwater and Yammarino (1993) and Himelhoch (2014) studies. However, research concerning the "dark side" dimension of exercise (Brown & Bray, 2015; Eijsvogels et al., 2016; Gay et al., 2016) supports a theoretical extrapolation to exercise and leadership that we examined. The quantitative method was the most suited because we had defined our variables (Creswell, 2009; Newman, 2006).

THE SURVEY INSTRUMENT

The survey instrument opened with a description of the purpose of our research. The instrument was designed to measure leaders' leisure exercise habits and their leadership styles as they perceive them. The instrument contained four sections. The first grouping asked for frequency of exercise and provided open-ended questions concerning strenuous, moderate, and mild activities. The second set of questions was taken directly from Avolio and Bass' MLQ (2004), and was used with permission. Section Three contained Likert-scaled questions on the Big Five dimensions outlined in Chapter One, which we took from the BFI-10 (Rammstedt & John, 2007). The final section contained demographic questions, which included age, gender, race, employer's industry and location, position (firstline, middle, or senior manager), and whether or not the leaders would grant us permission to survey their employees. The instrument administered to employees contained the same questions in Section Two of the leader survey.

POPULATION AND SAMPLING

The population included all leaders of all organizations in the United States. To narrow our focus, we purchased a mailing list containing email addresses of 10,000 managers across all industries. Electronic mailing lists are difficult to keep current. The list contained approximately 6,500 addresses that were not out of date. The response rate was three percent, which is emblematic of low response rates typical of web-based surveys (Sauermann & Roach,

2013). Tables 2-12, referenced in the appendix, provide supporting data on the sample.

Characteristics of the Sample

A total of 189 leaders completed the survey. The subset of respondents who answered questions concerning position and gender totaled 174. Table 2 depicts the number of men and women occupying first-line, middle- and senior-level management positions. Seventy-one percent were male; as were 62% of the first-line supervisors, 74% of the middle managers, and 75% of the senior managers. Twenty-nine percent of those in sample were female; 38% of the women occupied first-line supervisory positions; 26% held middle-management positions; 25% of the women were senior managers.

The breakdown of participants' age by position held is depicted in Table 3. Eighty-six percent of the respondents were between 25 and 64 years of age. The variation in race was minimal, as depicted in Table 4. Ninety-six percent of the participants were white; three percent were Black or African American; one percent were from multiple races. No participant self-identified as American Indian or Alaskan Native, Asian, or Native Hawaiian or Other Pacific Islander. To manage this low variation, we re-categorized participants into a dummy variable, placing respondents either into minority and non-minority categories (0 = minority; 1 = non-minority) for later use in the inferential analyses.

Respondents were from a variety of industries and their organizations spanned multiple locations. Table 5 shows the location of the leaders' organizations. Table 6 depicts the industries, based on Standard Industry Classification (SIC) codes, which employed participants in the study. Health services employed the largest number of leaders (12.6%), followed by engineering, accounting, research, management and related services (6.3%), business services, marketing, and advertising (5.1%), justice, public order, and safety (4.6%), social services and nonprofits (3.4%), educational services (3.4%), hotels, rooming houses, camps, and other lodging places (3.4%), amusement and recreation services (2.9%), chemicals and allied products (2.9%), electronic, electrical equipment, computers and computer equipment (2.9%), food and kindred products (2.9%), and miscellaneous manufacturing industries (2.9%), among the others listed below.

Frequency of exercise was defined using the number of times per week the respondents engage in leisure exercise, and ranged from none at all to seven or more days per week (with "more" defined as exercising more than once per day). The majority of the participants exercise between two and five days per week. Those who exercise the most belonged to the 55 to 64 age bracket. Table 7 describes the frequency with which participants exercise, sorted into age categories.

The survey contained open-ended questions, which asked participants to identify the types of leisure exercise activities in which they engage. Table 8 reports the exercises identified, along with the number of respondents who reported that they perform each type of activity.

The respondents described their leisure exercise habits in categories, which were based on the PRE that they reported. Strenuous exercise was defined on the questionnaire as "activities in which your heart beats rapidly and you work up a sweat." We designated moderate exercise in the instrument as "exercising to a level that raises your heart rate to a point where you sweat and you feel you are working, yet you are able to carry on a conversation." The definition for mild exercise in the questionnaire was exercise that "does not induce sweating, unless it is a hot, humid day, and there is no noticeable change in breathing patterns." The code of 4 was assigned to strenuous exercise, 3 to moderate exercise, 2 to mild exercise, 1 to those who indicated that they used to exercise, and 0 to those who reported that they not exercise at all. Table 9 depicts frequencies for respondents' PRE for the exercises performed. We used a decision rule in designating the PRE in cases that respondents engage in multiple exercises that span the strenuous, moderate, and mild categories. The most strenuous form of exercise that was reported by a respondent was assigned if the individual reported multiple forms of exercise across PRE categories. For example, if a participant reported that he or she runs at the strenuous level five days per week, walks briskly at the moderate level one day per week, and practices yoga at the mild level one day per week, we classified his or her exercise habits as strenuous.

We sought a common unit of measure to apply to the vast range of exercises in which respondents engage. Metabolic equivalents (METS) were used because, according to Jette, Sidney, and Blümchen (1990), they are "a simple, practical, and easily understood procedure to quantify the energy cost of activities. METS are also routinely used to describe the functional capacity or aerobic power of an individual and to provide a repertoire of activities in which he or she can safely participate" (p. 555). The article, by Jette et al., contains a list of METS that were calculated for a 70-kg person for most of the activities listed in Table 10. We searched the Internet to find any missing values. The one form of exercise for which we were unable to locate METS values was CrossFit®. However, we used Jared White's (2014) website http://creationbasedhealth.com/crossfit-calories-burned/, which contained estimated calories burned for a range of body weights in CrossFit®. We plugged in values for a 150-pound man into the formula used to calculate METS (the closest to 154 pounds, which is the 70kg equivalent). White's calculation was based on known METS values for intense calisthenic training with weights. It is difficult to apply a common unit of measure to CrossFit® because its programming entails a constantly varying mix of exercise modalities. Although an optimal common unit of measure does not exist, METS data are essentially satisficing [accepting an option that is available as satisfactory] because all exercise forms can be assessed with this measure to some extent, albeit imperfect. To validate our decision rule, we asked an expert in kinesiology, Beth Smith, a CrossFit® athlete with a doctor of physical therapy degree and a PhD in kinesiology, to review the METS values used in the study. In the absence of being able to measure METS directly, she concurred that the values we used were a reasonable approximation. The METS values used for each form of exercise are contained in Table 10.

We computed total exercise intensity by summing three computed variables. First, total strenuous exercise per week was computed by multiplying the METS value of each strenuous exercise by the number of times per week it was performed, multiplied again by the average minutes per week the strenuous activity was performed. We used the same formula used to calculate total moderate and total mild exercise, but inserting the respective METS, times per week on average, and minutes per week on average into each equation. The range of values for total exercise intensity was 0-43, 816.50, with a mean and standard deviation of 2,241.73 and 3,671.37 respectively.

We ran Crosstabs to describe the total exercise intensity of leaders, sorted by position. Although the sample size for each METS value was too low to identify patterns, Table 11 suggests that 40.8% of senior managers, 33.3% of middle managers, and 25.9% of first-line supervisors exercise regularly at a range of METS intensities. A one-way ANOVA test demonstrated that the difference in exercise intensity, based on METS values, among first-line, middle- and senior-managers is not statistically significant.

Although differences in exercise intensity as measured by METS values were not statistically significant, such was not the case when examining participants' PRE. There was a statistically-significant difference among groups as determined by one-way ANOVA $F(2, 171) = 4.984$, $p = .008$ in respondents' PRE. A post-hoc Duncan test revealed that the mean *PRE* for first-line supervisors was 2.64. This differed from the mean of middle managers of 2.93, and of senior managers of 3.14. The differences among the three groups were statistically significant.

DATA COMPRESSION

The MLQ contains 45 items. To determine whether or not these items could be summarized into a smaller number of derived constructs, we ran a confirmatory factor analysis, using the scaled variables already validated through over a decade of research that incorporated the MLQ. We decided to use these factors in all subsequent analyses because the constructs remained unchanged from those validated through the Avolio and Bass (2004) research. We present the composite variables in the order of loadings in the MLQ in Tables 12 and 13, both of which are located in the Appendix.

DATA ANALYSIS METHODS

The leader survey relied on self-reported perceptions. To corroborate those perceptions, we surveyed the employees to whom leaders granted us access. The same questions asked of leaders were given to employees, except the questions were phrased to ask for employee perceptions of their leaders on the identical dimensions. We used one-way ANOVAs to look for significant differences between leader and employee perceptions. We computed dummy variables in which employees were coded as zero and leaders were coded as one, and input them into the equation.

We also used one-way ANOVA to examine significant differences in both Exercise *Frequency* and *PRE* for all of the leader behavior and outcome variables in the MLQ as well as for all of the Big Five factors. We performed curve-fitting analysis on all relationships also, to determine if further testing of curvilinear relationships was warranted. Similarly, we performed curve-fitting analyses on all leadership-style variables and all Big Five personality variables in connection with the outcome variables *Satisfaction, Extra Effort, and Effectiveness*.

Finally, we performed multiple regression analysis and polynomial regression analyses to integrate both linear and curvilinear relationships that were significant in the curve-fitting analyses.

Carol R. Himelhoch and Mary Antonaros Raymond

Because regression tests for linear relationships, the testing of non-linear relationships necessitated transforming the variables before running the regression equations. We transformed variables into squared or cubed variables, to match the significant relationships uncovered through curve-fitting analyses. The inclusion of the power terms X_i^2 and X_i^3 in a regression equation adds one or two curves respectively to the regression line. Polynomial regression equations are represented by the formula $Y_i = a + b_1X_i + b_2X_i^2 + b_3X_i^3 + ... + b_kX_i^k + e_i$, where a = constant; b_k = the coefficient for the independent variable to the kth power; e_i = random error. The regression coefficient indicates the degree of the quadratic or cubic aspect of X's relation to Y, controlling for the linear effect.

We implemented the regression models hierarchically, starting with the linear model, then moving progressively to higher-order terms on the successive steps. The first step reflected the linear relationship in the multiple regression equations, represented as $Z = aX + bY + c$. In step two we squared the terms to reflect quadratic relationships; we cubed the terms in step three to reflect cubic relationships. The hierarchical multiple regression equations provisioned the testing of a linear model first, followed by the quadratic component of the predictor variables, which were followed finally by adding the cubic component of the predictor variables.

Summary

In this chapter, we justified the quantitative methods employed in our exploratory study. We include a description of the questionnaire, the characteristics of our sample, results of the data compression techniques that we employed, and the subsequent analysis methods used on the data.

In the next chapter we share the results of these analyses. Presented first is the analysis of differences between leader and employee perceptions. The one-way ANOVA and curve-fitting results pertaining to leader perceptions are included next. Finally, we include the regression analysis results.

[4]

PRESENTATION AND ANALYSIS OF THE DATA

INTRODUCTION

The purpose of our study was to explore the nuanced relationships between leadership style antecedents, such as personality characteristics, demographic characteristics, leisure exercise habits, and leadership behaviors (TLB, transactional, passive-avoidant) and leader effectiveness. We hypothesized curvilinear relationships between each of the PRE, exercise frequency, and the Big Five factors to both TLB and leader effectiveness, which are the dependent variables. We surmised certain linear relationships between the gender, age, position, and minority demographic variables and TLB. We also hypothesized a moderate corroboration of leader self-perceptions when checked against those of held by their employees. We administered surveys to 189 organizational leaders across a range of industries. The same survey questions were posed to 95 employees who report to the 27 out of 189 leaders who granted us access to their employees.

In this chapter we share the results of our research. In the first section we present similarities and differences between leader and employee perceptions of leadership styles and leader effectiveness. Next, we provide the results of the ANOVA and curvilinear regressions, in which we input all variables including the composite variables from the factor analyses.

LEADER AND EMPLOYEE DIFFERENCES

We administered the survey to leaders, and the data collected from it were based on how leaders perceived their own behaviors and effectiveness. To reduce the inherent bias in self-reported data, we solicited permission to survey employees for corroboration. Fourteen percent (27 out of 188) of the leaders surveyed granted permission. Some declined because 360 evaluations were underway or for no reason given; however, we suspect there may be indeterminate differences among leaders who granted access to their employees and leaders who did not.

Ninety-five employees and 27 leaders completed the 45 questions in the MLQ. Using a one-way ANOVA to test for significant differences, we created a dummy variable as the factor to load in the equation, in which employees were coded as zero and leaders were coded as one. Of the 45 questions, there were only five dimensions for which leader and employee perceptions reflected statistically significant differences. **Therefore, our hypothesis, in which we expected moderate differences, was supported.** All ANOVA results are presented in Table 14, located in the Appendix.

There is a statistically-significant difference between groups as determined by one-way ANOVA $F(1, 118) = 5.234$, $p = .024$ in the question "Provides me assistance in exchange for my efforts." Employees perceive their leaders as stronger than their leaders perceive themselves in helping them in response to their endeavors. The mean employee value is 3.22, whereas the employee mean is 2.73.

The second statistically significant difference is in the question "Concentrates his/her full attention on dealing with mistakes, complaints, and failures," with the one-way ANOVA $F(1, 117) = 14.062$, $p = .000$. Employees perceive their leaders as focusing more on these exceptions than their leaders do, as the mean employee response is 2.26 and the mean leader response is 1.23.

The dimension "Displays a sense of power and confidence" comprised the third statistically significant difference, which is reflected in the one-way ANOVA $F(1, 118) = 9.039$, $p = .003$. Employees view their leaders as more self-confident than their leaders view themselves (means = 3.14 and 2.54 respectively).

"Considers me as having different needs, abilities, and aspirations from others," is a dimension leaders perceive as a greater strength than do their employees. The one-way ANOVA $F(1, 118) = 11.519$, $p = .010$ showed a mean perception of honoring individual differences of 3.23 for leaders and 2.48 for employees.

The final statistically significant difference as determined by a one-way ANOVA $F(1, 118) = 3.982$, $p = .048$ concerns the dimension "Leads a group that is effective." Leaders see the group they lead as more effective than do their employees, with mean values of 3.5 and 3.10, respectively. Appendix Table 14 depicts the descriptive statistics and one-way ANOVA results explained in this section.

LEADER PERCEPTIONS

The remaining sections in Chapter Four contain the results of the analysis of variance (ANOVA) performed on all composite variables, looking first for significant differences when isolating PRE, followed by the same analysis, but substituting exercise frequency for PRE. Curvilinear relationships were also tested between the Big Five factors and all the composite MLQ dimensions, and are shared in the section that follows the ANOVA results. Finally, we present the outcome of the curvilinear multiple regressions run on all the independent and outcome variables.

SIGNIFICANT DIFFERENCES IN PERCEIVED RATE OF EXERTION

We checked all the composite variables for statistically significant differences in the PRE. Statistically significant differences were determined by one-way ANOVA for *Idealized Attributes, Inspirational Motivation,* and *Individual Consideration,* which we share below. Tables 15-16 depict the details, and are presented in the Appendix.

The difference in *Idealized Attributes,* per the one-way ANOVA $F(4, 173) = 2.593$, $p = .038$, was illuminated through the post-hoc Duncan test reported in Table 15. Those who engage in strenuous and moderate exercise (means = 3.20 and 2.99 respectively) differ from those who used to exercise (mean = 2.45) for the *Idealized Attributes* dimension; however, there are no other statistically significant differences for the other levels of perceived exertion rates. Those who exercise strenuously and moderately use *Idealized Attributes* more than those who used to exercise. Therefore, *Idealized Attributes,* a dimension of TLB, is greatest for those with the most strenuous PRE. **Therefore, our hypothesis of a "dark side" of the most strenuous PRE as an antecedent to *Idealized Attributes* was not supported by the data.**

The difference in *Inspirational Motivation* was determined by one-way ANOVA $F(4, 178) = 4.645$, $p = .001$. Per Table 16, a post-hoc

Duncan test revealed that those who participate in strenuous exercise (mean = 3.29) differ from those who used to exercise (mean = 2.75) and those who participate in mild exercise (mean = 2.76) on the *Inspirational Motivation* dimension. However, no statistically significant differences were found for the other levels of PRE. Those who engage in strenuous exercise employ *Inspirational Motivation* more than those who partake in mild exercise or those who used to exercise.

Through a curve-fitting analysis we discovered that the relationship between *Inspirational Motivation* and PRE is cubic, as depicted in Figure 2 in the Appendix. The level of *Inspirational Motivation* decreases between no exercise and mild exercise, then increases as one moves toward strenuous exercise. At the highest levels of perceived strenuous exercise, there appears to be a point of diminishing returns. **The curvilinear relationship supports our hypothesis that there is a "dark side" of the influence of PRE on *Inspirational Motivation* for the most extreme levels of PRE. Those who report zero PRE use more *Inspirational Motivation* than those who perceive mild exertion, but employ lower levels of *Inspirational Motivation* than those who exercise at the moderate to high intensity levels. It is only at the greatest extremes that the curve turns in a downward direction again.** We examine this relationship further in the regression-analyses section because, through multiple regression, we introduce other independent variables that influence the curvilinear association.

Individual Consideration was another scaled variable for which there is a statistically significant difference in PRE. Per a one-way ANOVA $F(4, 179) = 4.246$, $p = .003$, depicted in Table 17 in the Appendix, there is a statistically-significant difference among those who used to exercise (mean = 2.71) and those who exercise at the moderate and strenuous levels (means = 3.25 and 3.50 respectively). Strenuous exercisers rely more heavily on *Individual Consideration* than moderate exercisers; moderate exercisers use *Individual Consideration* more those who used to exercise. Table 17 displays these differences. **Our dark-side hypothesis was not supported. Those who perceive the greatest level of exertion lead with higher levels of *Individual Consideration*, a core dimension of TLB. The relationship is linear, but not curvilinear.**

SIGNIFICANT DIFFERENCES IN EXERCISE FREQUENCY

We examined all the scaled variables for statistically significant differences in the *Exercise Frequency* using one-way ANOVA. This section shares the statistically significant differences in *Exercise Frequency* that we found for *Idealized Behaviors, Inspirational Motivation, Individual Consideration,* and *Management by Exception Active.*

In the one-way ANOVA $F(8, 175) = 3.265$, $p = .002$ for *Idealized Behaviors*, those who exercise one day per week (mean = 2.63) differ from those who exercise four days a week (mean = 3.20) and five days a week (mean = 3.38), as depicted in Appendix Table 18. Therefore, those exercising the most (five days per week) employ the TLB *Idealized Behaviors* more than those exercising less frequently. Exploring curvilinear relationships provides even more detail.

The lower mean in *Idealized Behaviors* for those who exercise seven or more days a week than all frequencies but one day per week can be explained by the cubic curvilinear relationship between the variables. Figure 3 in the Appendix displays the drop, then rise in *Idealized Behaviors* as exercise frequency increases to five days per week, after which there is a decline. **The curvilinear relationship supports our hypothesis that there is a "dark side" of the influence of** *Exercise Frequency* **on** *Idealized Behaviors* **for the most extreme levels of** *Exercise Frequency.* **In this case, extreme exercise is at a frequency of six days per week. Results indicate that those who do not exercise use more** *Idealized Behaviors* **than those who used to exercise.** *Idealized Behaviors* **increase as leaders exercise one or more days per week. This TLB peaks at a frequency of exercising five days per week, at which point** *Idealized Behaviors* **begin to decline again.**

Per the one-way ANOVA $F(8, 175) = 4.118$, $p = .000$ on *Inspirational Motivation*, there are statistically-significant differences among those who exercise one day a week (mean = 2.57), those who exercise seven or more days a week (mean = 3.24), and those who exercise five days a week (mean = 3.46), as shown in the Appendix in Table 19. Therefore, when considering statistically significant relationships, exercising five days a week is better than seven days per week, although exercising at both five and seven days per week is better than exercising one day a week.

The greater level of *Inspirational Motivation* for those who exercise five days a week over those who exercise seven or more days a week could be explained by the cubic curvilinear relationship between the two variables, as depicted in the Appendix in Figure 4. **The curvilinear relationship supports our hypothesis that there is a "dark side" of the influence of** *Exercise Frequency* **on** *Inspirational Motivation* **for the most extreme levels of** *Exercise Frequency.* **In this case, results demonstrate that extreme exercise is that exceeding a frequency of six days per week. Those who do not exercise use** more *Inspirational Motivation* than those who used to exercise and who exercise one day per week. *Inspirational Motivation* increases as leaders exercise one or more days per week. This TLB peaks at a frequency of exercising five days per week, at which point *Inspirational Motivation* begins to decline again.

Significant differences in *Individual Consideration* as determined by a one-way ANOVA $F(8, 176) = 2.748$, $p = .007$, were found among those who exercise two days a week and who used to exercise (means = 2.95 and 2.97 respectively) and those who do not exercise at all (mean = 3.50). Table 20, in the Appendix, displays the post-doc Duncan test results.

The higher *Individual Consideration* among those who do not exercise can be explained by the cubic curvilinear relationship between the variables, as shown in as Figure 5 in the Appendix. **The curvilinear relationship supports our hypothesis that there is a "dark side" of the influence of *Exercise Frequency* on *Individual Consideration* for the most extreme levels of *Exercise Frequency*. In this case, extreme exercise is that exceeding a frequency of six days per week. Those who do not exercise use more *Individual Consideration* than those who used to exercise and who exercise one, two, and three days per week. *Individual Consideration* increases as leaders exercise four days per week. This TLB peaks at a frequency of exercising five days per week, at which point *Individual Consideration* begins to decline again.**

Significant differences in *Management by Exception Active* were determined through a one-way ANOVA $F(8, 174) = 2.240$, $p = .027$ between no exercise at all (mean = 2.66) and all other exercise frequencies, per Table 21 in the Appendix. Those who do not exercise at all are more inclined to use an active management-by-exception leadership style. **This result supports the hypothesis that those with the lowest levels of exercise frequency are more apt to use a transactional leadership style.**

CURVILINEAR RELATIONSHIPS BETWEEN THE FIVE-FACTOR MODEL OF PERSONALITY AND THE TLB

Prior to running regression analyses, we checked to see if nonlinear relationships were present among the Big Five personality dimensions and the scaled outcome variables. Research by Hereford (2011) suggests that the previously assumed linear relationships do not explain the associations fully. We share the significant relationships through Figures 6 and 7 in the Appendix. We provide more detail in the regression analyses sections.

Quadratic relationships were found between *Idealized Attributes* and *I Get Nervous Easily* and *I Have An Active Imagination*. Figure 6 shows a decline in the use of the *Idealized Attributes* leadership style as the level of nervousness increases, with a slight increase at the highest levels of unease.

Idealized Attributes are highest when the level of *Active Imagination* is low, then decreases until there is a turn in the curve at the highest levels of *Active Imagination*. This quadratic relationship is depicted in Figure 7. **Our hypothesis of a curvilinear relationship in between these particular Big Five factors and TLB is supported.**

There is a quadratic relationship also between *Idealized Behaviors* and *Active Imagination*, which follows a similar pattern to that described in the Appendix in Figure 8 for the relationship between *Idealized Attributes* and *Active Imagination*. *Idealized Behaviors* are highest at the lowest levels of *Active Imagination*, decline, and then increase toward the highest levels of *Active Imagination*. **Again, our hypothesis concerning the Big Five dimensions and TLBs is supported.**

There is a quadratic relationship between *Inspirational Motivation* and *Trusting* as well as with *Lazy*, and a cubic relationship between *Inspirational Motivation* and *Active Imagination*. All relevant figures are presented in the Appendix. Figure 9 displays a decline, and then rise in *Inspirational Motivation* as the leader's level of trust increases. Figure 10 illustrates a decline, then rise in *Inspirational Motivation* as the level of laziness increases. Figure 11 demonstrates the cubic relationship between *Inspirational Motivation* and *Active Imagination*. **The three relationships depicted in Figures 9-11 suggest a confirmation of our hypothesized curvilinear relationships between these three Big Five variables and *Inspirational Motivation*.**

We found a cubic relationship between *Inspirational Motivation* and the leader's level of *Active Imagination*. *Inspirational Motivation* declines from its highest point at the lowest level of *Active Imagination*, but turns and increases around the moderate and higher levels. At the top level of *Active Imagination*, *Inspirational Motivation* begins to decline again.

There is a quadratic relationship between *Intellectual Stimulation* and *Active Imagination*, per Figure 12. *Intellectual Stimulation* declines, and then begins to rise again as the level of the leader's active imagination increases.

Figures 13 and 14 in the Appendix also show how the data confirm our hypothesis of a curvilinear relationship between the

Big Five dimensions, both of *Find Fault in Others* **and** *Agreeableness* **with the TLB** *Individual Consideration.* There is a quadratic relationship between *Individual Consideration* and *Find Fault* and *Individual Consideration* and *Active Imagination. Individual Consideration* declines and then rises as the leader's tendency to find fault in others increases (Figure 13), and drops then rises as the leader's level of *Active Imagination* increases (Figure 14).

Curvilinear Relationships Between the Five-Factor Model of Personality and the Transactional and Passive-Avoidant Leadership Styles

We also examined relationships between Big Five dimensions and transactional and passive-avoidant leadership behaviors. **The data analyses suggest curvilinear associations between the Big Five dimensions and transactional and passive-avoidant leadership styles, as depicted in Figures 15-19, all located in the Appendix.** There is a quadratic relationship between *Contingent Reward* and *Lazy* and *Relaxed*. The leader's use of the transactional style, *Contingent Reward*, declines and then rises with the leader's level of laziness (Figure 15) and the degree to which the leader is relaxed (Figure 16).

There is a quadratic relationship between *Management by Exception-Active* and *Active Imagination*. The highest levels of *Management by Exception-Active* are used by leaders with the lowest levels of *Active Imagination*. As *Active Imagination* increases, active *Management By Exception-Active* decreases, but rises again at stronger levels of *Active Imagination* for the leader, as depicted in Figure 17.

There is a quadratic relationship between *Laissez-faire* and *Lazy* as well as *Find Fault*. With both, *Laissez-faire* leadership style increases as the independent variables increase, then turn and decline toward the highest levels. Figures 18 and 19 illustrate these relationships.

Curvilinear Relationships Between the Five-Factor Model of Personality and the Leader Effectiveness Variables

We found a cubic relationship between *Extra Effort* and *Lazy, Relaxed,* and *Outgoing,* and a quadratic relationship between *Extra Effort* and *I Get Nervous Easily* and *I Have an Active Imagination*. We present these relationships in Figures 21-29 in the Appendix. Promoting *Extra Effort* from employees declines, then rises, then declines again as the leader's level of laziness increases, per Figure 20. **These findings support our hypothesized curvilinear relationships between the Big Five dimensions and measures of leader effectiveness.**

The extra effort put forth by employees declines, rises, then declines as the leader's level of a relaxed state increases, per Figure 21.. Employees' *Extra Effort* declines, rises, then declines again with an increase in the leader's level of outgoingness. The cubic relationship is depicted in Figure 22. The *Extra Effort* put forth by employees declines, then rises again as the leader's tendency to get nervous increases, which is depicted in Figure 23. As the leader's level of *Active Imagination* increases, his or her employees' *Extra Effort* declines, and then rises again, per Figure 24.

There is a cubic relationship between *Effectiveness* and *Relaxed* and *I Get Nervous Easily*, and a quadratic relationship between *Effectiveness* and *Find Fault* and *Thorough*. As displayed in Figure 25, *Effectiveness* declines, rises, then declines again as the leader's state of relaxation increases. *Effectiveness* rises, drops, then rises again with the leader's level of nervousness, per the Appendix in Figure 26. As leaders' tendency to find fault in others increases, their level of effectiveness declines, and then rises again, as seen in Figure 27. *Effectiveness* declines, then rises, as the leader's level of thoroughness increases. This quadratic relationship is illustrated in Figure 28. There is a quadratic relationship between *Satisfaction* and *Relaxed*. As the leader's state of relaxation increases, employee satisfaction declines, and then rises again, per Figure 29.

POLYNOMIAL REGRESSIONS

To test the relationship between all of the leadership styles as well as leadership outcome variables with leader characteristics and exercise habits, we conducted polynomial regression analyses to include both linear and curvilinear relationships. We performed curve-fitting analyses first, to determine which variables were linear, quadratic, or cubic. We share the results of each regression equation in the following sections. We used the same process for all independent variables. Each section contains a discussion of the relationships that were statistically significant.

Idealized Attributes

We performed the first polynomial regression on the dependent variable Idealized Attributes and the independent variables *Age,*

Gender, Race, Position, Lazy, Relaxed, Outgoing, Find Fault, Thorough, Nervous, Active Imagination, PRE, and *Exercise Frequency.* The linear model yielded an r-square result of .22, which suggests that 22% of the variance in *Idealized Attributes* is explained by the regression equation. In the quadratic step, we added the variables *Nervous Squared, Exercise Frequency Squared, PRE Squared,* and *Active Imagination Squared.* The r-square result improved by .07, with 29% of the variance in *Idealized Attributes* explained by the equation. In the third step, we added the variables *Exercise Frequency Cubed* and *PRE Cubed.* The r-square increased by 9%, with the cubic regression equation explaining 38% of the variance in *Idealized Attributes.* The results are presented in the Appendix in Table 22.

Three independent variables were significant predictors of *Idealized Attributes* in step one. PRE is associated with the outcome variable positively, with a beta value of .25. Higher levels of the leader's PRE are associated with higher levels of idealized attributes. Similarly, more outgoing and relaxed leaders are associated with higher levels of *Idealized Attributes,* with betas for *Outgoing* and *Relaxed* at .19 and .17 respectively.

In the second step, *Active Imagination Squared* (beta = 1.17) and *Outgoing* (beta = .19) are positively associated with *Idealized Attributes.* *Nervousness* (beta = -.72) is negatively associated with *Idealized Attributes,* which implies that the more nervous the leader is, the less his or her behavior will reflect the *Idealized Attributes* dimension of transformational leadership.

We found seven significant relationships in the third step. The frequency with which the leader exercises yielded a significant cubic relationship, with the curve bending from its initial negative position (beta for *Exercise Frequency* = -3.4), to positive (beta for *Exercise Frequency Squared* = 7.24), then back to negative (beta for *Exercise Frequency Cubed* = -4.22). Suggested in this cubic relationship is that at the lowest levels of exercise frequency, leaders exhibit higher levels of *Idealized Attributes.* The curve turns upward as exercise frequency increases, with higher exercise frequency associated with the highest levels of *Idealized Attributes.* At the highest levels of exercise frequency, leaders levels of *Idealized Attributes* decrease. *Idealized Attributes* are highest among those leaders who exercise five days per week (reflected as 6 in the Figure 30, in the Appendix).

The results reflect also a quadratic relationship between *Idealized attributes* and *Active Imagination. Active Imagination* (beta = -1.05) is negatively associated with *Idealized Attributes,* but *Active Imagination Squared* (beta = .95) is positively associated with *Idealized Attributes.*

Therefore, at low levels of *Active Imagination*, the leader is more likely to possess an *Idealized Attributes* style. At higher levels of *Active Imagination*, the leader is less likely to adopt the transformational leadership dimension *Idealized Attributes*. A higher level of *Nervousness* in the leader is associated with lower *Idealized Attribute* behaviors (beta = -.73). *Relaxed* and *Outgoing* leaders are associated with higher levels of *Idealized Attributes* (betas = .18 and .19 respectively). **Therefore, our hypotheses of curvilinear relationship between *Exercise Frequency* and the *Idealized Attributes* dimension of TLB are supported. There is also a curvilinear relationship between the Big Five dimension *Active Imagination* and *Idealized Attributes*, which also supports our hypotheses.**

Idealized Behaviors

In the second equation, we regressed Idealized Behaviors on the independent variables *Age, Gender, Race, Position, Lazy, Thorough, Nervous, Active Imagination, Exercise Frequency, PRE* and *Strenuous Exercise Intensity*. The linear model yielded an r-square result of .20, which suggests that 20% of the variance in *Idealized Behaviors* is explained by the regression equation. In the quadratic step, we added the variables *Active Imagination Squared, Exercise Frequency Squared, PRE Squared,* and *Strenuous Exercise Intensity Squared*. The r-square result improved by .08, with 28% of the variance in *Idealized Attributes* explained by the equation. In the third step, we added the variables *Exercise Frequency Cubed, PRE Cubed,* and *Strenuous Exercise Intensity Cubed*. The r-square increased by six percent, with the cubic regression equation explaining 34% of the variance in *Idealized Behaviors*. The results are presented in Table 23 in the Appendix. **Therefore, our hypotheses of curvilinear relationship between Exercise Frequency and the Idealized Behaviors dimension of TLB is supported. The data also support our hypothesis of a curvilinear relationship between the Big Five dimension Active Imagination and Idealized Behaviors. Our hypotheses concerning Gender and this TLB is supported as well.**

The two significant predictors of *Idealized Behaviors* were *Gender* (beta = .22) and *Position* (beta = .18) in step one. In the data set, we used the coding men = 1 and women = 2. Therefore, the small positive relationship suggests that women are slightly more likely than men to exhibit *Idealized Behaviors*. A similar interpretation applies to *Position*. The higher the level of managerial position the leader occupies, the more likely he or she is to adopt *Idealized Behaviors*; the lower the level of managerial position, the less likely he or she will adopt this transformational dimension.

In step two, *Gender* maintain ns a significant positive association with *Idealized Behaviors* (beta = .24); however, *Position* is not statistically significant. *Active Imagination* is negatively associated with *Idealized Behaviors* (beta = -1.53). Higher levels of the leader's *Active Imagination* are associated with lower levels of this transformational dimension. However, *Active Imagination Squared* is positively associated with *Idealized Behaviors* (beta = 1.62). Therefore, the relationship between *Active Imagination* and *Idealized Behaviors* is best represented by a quadratic function.

The quadratic relationship found between *Active Imagination* and *Idealized Behaviors* in step two was maintained in step three, with a negative relationship for *Active Imagination* (beta = -1.38), and a positive relationship for *Active Imagination Squared* (beta = 1.44). A positive relationship was maintained also for *Gender* (beta = .24). *Nervous* was negatively associated with *Idealized Behaviors* (beta = -.18), which suggests that the higher the leader's position on this neurotic dimension, the less likely he or she will employ *Idealized Behaviors*. Much like the cubic relationship depicted in Figure 30 above, the frequency with which the leader exercises yielded a significant cubic relationship, with the curve bending from its initial negative position (beta for *Exercise Frequency* = -2.09), to positive (beta for *Exercise Frequency Squared* = 4.99), then back to negative (beta for *Exercise Frequency Cubed* = -3.01). The implication is that at the lowest levels of *Exercise Frequency*, leaders exhibit higher levels of *Idealized Behaviors* than for those who used to exercise. The curve turns upward as *Exercise Frequency* increases, with higher *Exercise Frequency* associated with higher levels of *Idealized Behaviors*. At the highest levels of exercise frequency, leaders levels of *Idealized Attributes* behaviors decline. Idealized behaviors are highest among those leaders who exercise five days per week (reflected as 6 in the Figure 31, in the Appendix).

Inspirational Motivation

For the third curvilinear relationship, we regressed hierarchically *Inspirational Motivation on Age, Gender, Race, Position, Reserved, Trusting, Lazy, Outgoing, Find Fault, Thorough, Nervous, Active Imagination, Exercise Frequency, PRE, Strenuous Exercise Intensity*, and *Total Exercise Intensity* in step one. In step two, we added the independent variables *Trusting Squared, Lazy Squared, Active*

Imagination Squared, Exercise Frequency Squared, PRE Squared, Strenuous Exercise Intensity Squared, and *Total Exercise Intensity Squared.* We added *Active Imagination Cubed, Exercise Frequency Cubed, Exercise Frequency Cubed, PRE Cubed, Strenuous Exercise Intensity Cubed,* and *Total Exercise Intensity Cubed* in step three.

The linear model yielded an r-square result of .29, which suggests that 29% of the variance in *Inspirational Motivation* is explained by the regression equation. The r-square result in step two improved the results by .04, with 33% of the variance in *Inspirational Motivation* explained by the equation. In the third step, the r-square increased by nine percent, with the cubic regression equation explaining 42% of the variance in *Inspirational Motivation.* The results are presented in Table 24 in the Appendix.

Position, Outgoing, and *Nervous* were the statistically significant independent variables in the linear equation in step one. The more upward the leader's managerial level in the organization (beta for *Position* = .18), the more likely he or she will be to use *Inspirational Motivation.* Similarly, the more *Outgoing* the leader, the more he or she will adopt this transformational dimension (beta for *Outgoing* = .18). The Big Five dimension of *Neuroticism* is negatively associated with *Inspirational Motivation* (beta = -.18 for *Nervous*), which suggest that the more nervous the leader the less likely he or she will use inspirational-motivation-type behaviors in interactions with employees.

In step two, statistically significant associations resulted among the independent variables *Trusting* (negative relationship), *Find Fault* (negative relationship), and *Strenuous Exercise Intensity* (positive relationship) and the outcome variable *Inspirational Motivation.* However, the beta values were too small to deem these statistically significant relationships noteworthy.

In step three, *Age* (beta = -.15) was negatively associated with *Inspirational Motivation.* Younger leaders are more likely than older leaders to use leadership strategies consistent with the *Inspirational Motivation* dimension. *Nervous* was also negatively associated with *Inspirational Motivation,* with a beta value of -.16.

Much like the cubic relationships depicted in Figures 30 and 31 above, the leader's PRE while exercising yielded a significant cubic relationship, with the curve bending from its initial negative position (beta for PRE = -1.71), to positive (beta for PRE = 4.91), then back to negative (beta for PRE = -3.21). The implication is that leaders who do not exercise exhibit higher levels of *Inspirational Motivation* than those who used to exercise. The curve turns upward from its low point of "used to exercise," with *Inspirational Motivation* levels increasing with movement along the curve toward a higher point for the strenuous exercise. At the highest levels of PRE, leaders levels of inspirational-motivation-related behaviors decline. *Inspirational Motivation* levels are highest among those leaders who perceive that they participate in strenuous exercise (PRE was coded with 0 = do not exercise; 1 = used to exercise; 2 = exercise at the mild level, 3 = exercise at the moderate level; 4 = exercise at the strenuous level). Figure 32, in the Appendix, displays the relationship between *Inspirational Motivation* and PRE. Table 24 depicts the regression results for all three steps. **Therefore, our hypothesis of curvilinear relationship between PRE and the *Inspirational Motivation* dimension of TLB is supported. Our hypothesis that younger leaders are more likely to use TLB than older workers is supported along the *Inspirational Motivation* dimension.**

Intellectual Stimulation

We performed the fourth curvilinear regression on the dependent variable Intellectual Stimulation and the independent variables *Age, Gender, Race, Position, Exercise Frequency, Moderate Exercise Intensity, Trusting,* and *Active Imagination*. The linear model yielded an r-square result of .10, which suggests that 10% of the variance in Intellectual Stimulation is explained by the regression equation. In the quadratic step, we added the variables *Active Imagination Squared, Moderate Exercise Intensity Squared,* and *Active Imagination Squared*. The r-square result improved by .04, with 14% of the variance in *Intellectual Stimulation* explained by the equation. In the third step, we added the variable *Moderate Exercise Intensity Cubed*. The r-square increased by one percent, with the cubic regression equation explaining 15% of the variance in *Intellectual Stimulation*. The results are presented in Appendix Table 25.

As depicted in Table 25, *Position* and *Exercise Frequency* are positively associated with *Intellectual Stimulation* in step one. The higher one's managerial position in the organization and higher levels of the leader's exercise frequency are associated with greater *Intellectual Stimulation* from the leader. The beta values are .15 and .23 respectively.

In step two, *Exercise Frequency* correlated positively with *Intellectual Stimulation* (beta = .20), while *Moderate Exercise Intensity* was correlated negatively (beta = -.41), and *Active Imagination Squared* had a positive association (beta = 1.05).

Significant predictor variables in step three include *Exercise Frequency* (beta = .19), *Moderate Exercise Intensity* (beta = .87), *Active Imagination* (beta = -.95), *Moderate Exercise Intensity Squared* (beta = -.194), and *Active Imagination Squared* (beta = 1.09). From these data, one can conclude that quadratic relationships exist among *Intellectual Stimulation* and *Moderate Exercise Intensity* as well as the leader's active-imagination level. This relationship is displayed in Figure 33 in the Appendix. The data also show that higher levels of *Exercise Frequency* are associated with higher levels of intellectually stimulating leader behavior.

Therefore, our hypotheses of curvilinear relationship between PRE and the *Intellectual Stimulation* dimension of TLB are supported. There is also a curvilinear relationship between the Big Five dimension *Active Imagination* and *Intellectual Stimulation*, which also supports our hypothesis.

Individual Consideration

We ran a curvilinear regression of Individual *Consideration on Age, Gender, Race, Position, PRE, Lazy, Relaxed, Thorough, Find Fault, Active Imagination, PRE Squared, Find Fault Squared, Active Imagination Squared,* and *PRE Cubed.* The r-square in step one was .22, and improved by .04 in step two to .26. By step three, the r-square jumped .04 to .30, which suggests that 30% of the variance in *Individual Consideration* is explained by this polynomial equation.

In step one, significant positive associations are found among *Gender* (beta = .21), *Thorough* (beta = .21), *Active Imagination* (beta = .15) and *Individual Consideration.* Women are slightly more likely than men do adopt this transformational leadership style. The more *Thorough* and the greater the leader's *Active Imagination*, the more likely the leader will use behaviors consistent with the *Individual Consideration* dimension.

Gender (beta = .23) and *Thorough* (beta = .21) persist in their positive relationships to *Individual Consideration* in step two. The leader's PRE also appears as significant in step two, but as part of a curvilinear relationship that is apparent when moving to step three.

As reflected in step thee in Table 26 in the Appendix, *Individual Consideration* levels are higher among those who do not exercise (beta for PRE = -2.24) than those who perceive that they exercise at the mild level. As the leader perceives he or she is exercising at the mild-to-moderate level through the *Strenuous* level, he or she employs greater levels of *Individual Consideration* (beta = 5.80 for PRE *Squared).* At the highest levels of PRE, *Individual Consideration* turns downward again (the beta for *Individual Consideration Cubed* = -3.55). Figure 34, also in the Appendix, depicts this curvilinear relationship. *Gender* (beta = .24) maintains its positive association with *Individual Consideration* in step three. *Race* emerges with a negative correlation to *Individual Consideration* in step three (beta = - .16). The dummy variable for race is coded such that minorities = 0 and white = 1. Therefore, minorities are more likely than Caucasians to exhibit behaviors consistent with *Individual Consideration*.

Therefore, our hypothesized relationship between PRE and *Individual Consideration* was supported. Our hypotheses that women are more transformational leaders than men, and that minorities are more likely to be transformational than non-minorities are supported for the *Individual Consideration* dimension.

Contingent Reward

The transactional leadership style dimension *Contingent Reward* was regressed on leader characteristics and exercise habits in a curvilinear regression. The independent variables used in the linear equation included *Age, Gender, Race, Position, Outgoing, Find Fault, Thorough, Nervous, Lazy, Relaxed, Exercise Frequency,* and *Trusting.* The r-square in step one is .22. *Gender* (beta = .18) is positively correlated with *Contingent Reward*, which suggests that women are slightly more likely than men to use *Contingent Reward* strategies as they lead employees. *Thorough* is negatively associated with *Contingent Reward*. With a beta of -.13, one may infer that the more *Thorough* the leader, the more likely he or she will use *Contingent Reward*.

The variables added in step two included *Lazy Squared, Relaxed Squared, Exercise Frequency Squared,* and *Trusting Squared*. The r-square jumped by five percent to explaining 27% of the variance in *Contingent Reward*. *Gender* is not significant in the quadratic equation (or in the cubic equation, for that matter). *Thorough*, with a beta of .22, has a positive relationship to *Contingent Reward.* The more thorough the leader, the more he or she is apt to use *Contingent Reward. Relaxed*, however, is connected to *Contingent Reward* in a quadratic relationship. The beta value of -1.27 for relaxed and the beta value of 1.15 for *Relaxed Squared* suggest that less relaxed and highly relaxed leaders use *Contingent Reward* more than do leaders at mild-to-moderate levels of feeling relaxed. Figure 35, in the Appendix, reflects this quadratic relationship. This quadratic relationship maintains consistency in step three; the beta value for *Relaxed* moved to -1.18 and stayed the same for *Relaxed Squared*.

In step three, 30% of the variance was explained by the equation, which increased by .03 from the quadratic model. As mentioned in the previous paragraph, *Relaxed* has a quadratic relationship with *Contingent Reward*. *Thorough* remains positively associated with the use of *Contingent Reward*, with a beta value of .20. *Outgoing* is also positively associated with *Contingent Reward*; the beta value of .16 suggests that the more outgoing the leader, the more heavily he or she will rely on the use of *Contingent Rewards*. *Exercise Frequency* is connected through a cubic relationship with *Contingent Reward*, with beta values of -1.17, 3.03, and -1.83 for *Exercise Frequency*, *Exercise Frequency Squared*, and *Exercise Frequency Cubed* respectively. Curve-fitting analysis shows *Contingent Reward* at its highest for those who exercise seven or more times per week.

Appendix Figure 36 displays the cubic relationship between *Contingent Reward* and *Exercise Frequency*.

Therefore, our hypotheses, which projected curvilinear relationships between PRE and *Contingent Reward* and the Big Five dimension of *Neuroticism* and *Contingent Reward*, are supported.

Management By Exception Active

The transactional leadership style that is represented by the variable *Management By Exception Active* was regressed on *Age, Gender, Race, Position, Find Fault,* and *Active Imagination* in step one of the quadratic regression equation. The r-square was .07, which suggests that 7% of the variance in *Management By Exception Active* is explained by the equation. The only independent variable with statistical significance was *Find Fault*, with a beta value of .20. The more the leader tends to find fault in others, the more likely he or she will be to employ an active management by exception leadership style.

The r-square improved by .06 in step two, rising to explaining 13% of the variance in *Management By Exception Active*. The *Find Fault* relationship is stable in step two, with the same beta value found in step one. The quadratic relationship between the leader's *Active Imagination* and *Management By Exception Active* is evident in the beta of -1.49 for *Active Imagination* and 1.57 for *Active Imagination Squared*. Lower levels of active imagination are associated with higher levels of *Management By Exception Active*; however, the curve turns at higher levels of *Active Imagination*, where more *Active Imagination* is associated with more *Management By Exception Active*. Figure 37 in the

Appendix shows this relationship, and Appendix Table 28 displays the regression results.

Therefore, the hypothesized curvilinear relationship between the Big Five dimension *Active Imagination* and *Management By Exception Active* is supported.

Management By Exception Passive

The transactional leadership style that is represented by the variable *Management By Exception Passive* was regressed on *Age, Gender, Race, Position, Lazy, Thorough,* and PRE in step one of the quadratic regression equation. The r-square was .12, which suggests that 12% of the variance in *Management By Exception Passive* is explained by the equation. *Lazy* is positively associated with *Management By Exception Passive.* A beta value of .19 implies that the lazier the leader, the more he or she will employ the *Management By Exception Passive* style. With a beta value of -.21, *Thorough* is negatively associated with *Management By Exception Passive.* The more *Thorough* the leader, the less likely he or she will use this transactional leadership style.

The r-square improved by .02 in step two, rising to explaining 14% of the variance in *Management By Exception Passive.* Both *Thorough* and *Lazy* maintained their relationships to *Management By Exception Passive,* with beta values of -.21 and .18 respectively. The quadratic relationship between *Management By Exception Passive* and PRE is evident, with the beta for PRE of .58 and for PRE *Squared* of -.56. *Management By Exception Passive* is lowest at the lowest and highest levels of the leader's PRE. Figure 38 in the Appendix presents this relationship. Shown in Appendix Table 29 are the curvilinear regression results.

Therefore, the hypothesized curvilinear relationship between PRE and *Management By Exception-Passive* is supported.

Laissez-Faire

Laissez-faire leadership was regressed on leader characteristics and their exercise habits in a three-step curvilinear regression equation. The independent variables in step one were *Age, Gender, Race, Position, Thorough, Nervous, Active Imagination, Lazy, Find Fault, Moderate Exercise Intensity,* and *Mild Exercise Intensity.* The r-square was .26, which implies that 26% of the variance in *Laissez-faire* is explained by the linear equation. *Thorough* is negatively associated with *Laissez-faire,* which suggests that more *Thorough* leaders are less likely to use a *Laissez-faire* leadership style (beta = -.26). *Moderate Exercise Intensity* was also negatively associated with *Laissez-faire* (beta = -.19). The more a leader exercises at the moderate intensity level, the less likely she or he will adopt a *Laissez-faire* leadership style. *Nervous* and *Active Imagination* are positively associated with *Laissez-faire* (betas were .28 and .23 respectively). The more nervous the leader and the higher the leader's level of active imagination, the more likely he or she will employ a *Laissez-faire* leadership style.

Three independent variables were introduced to the equation in step two: *Lazy Squared, Find Fault Squared,* and *Mild Exercise Intensity Squared*. The r-square improved in step two of the equation by .04 to explaining 30% of the variance in *Laissez-faire*. The relationships among *Thorough, Nervous, Active Imagination,* and *Moderate Exercise Intensity* and *Laissez-faire* remained intact in step two, with beta values of -.21, .18, .23, and -.16 respectively. *Find Fault* was significant in step two. With a beta value of .74, one can infer that the more the leader's tendency to find fault in others, the greater is the leader's likelihood to use a *Laissez-faire* leadership style. *Lazy* (beta = .67) and *Lazy Squared* (beta = -.77) are significantly associated with *Laissez-faire* in step two. At the highest and lowest levels of laziness, leaders are less likely to use *Laissez-faire* leadership; however, at moderate levels of laziness, *Laissez-faire* leadership will be more likely. Figure 39, in the Appendix, depicts this relationship.

In step three, the independent variable *Mild Exercise Intensity Cubed* was added to the equation. The r-square value improved slightly, moving up .01 to explaining 31% of the variance. The statistically significant relationships in this step included *Thorough* (beta = -.21), *Nervous* (beta =.18), *Active Imagination* (beta =.23), *Find Fault* (beta = .79), and *Moderate Exercise Intensity* (beta = -.16). The more thorough the leader, the less likely her or his leadership style will be characterized as *Laissez-faire*. More nervous leaders as well as leaders who find fault with others will also use more of a *Laissez-faire* style. Leaders who exercise at a moderate intensity level are less likely to adopt a *Laissez-faire* leadership style. Appendix Table 30 presents the curvilinear regression results for the dependent variable *Laissez-faire.*

Therefore, our hypothesis of a curvilinear relationship between PRE and *Laissez-faire* leadership is supported. So is our hypothesis of a curvilinear relationship between Big Five dimensions *Active Imagination* as well as *Thorough* and *Laissez-faire* leadership.

Results concerning regressions run on the three outcome variables, extra effort, effectiveness, and satisfaction are discussed in the next three sections. All three are effectiveness dimensions, against which leadership and personality styles were considered. We present the full regression tables within the text of these three sections because measures of leader effectiveness are the most important. No matter what the leadership style or personality of a leader, what matters most to organizations is effectiveness.

Extra Effort

Many variables were included in step one of the curvilinear regression of the outcome variable *Extra Effort* on *Age, Gender, Race, Position, Thorough, Nervous, Active Imagination, Lazy, Relaxed, Outgoing,* and PRE. Independent variables added in step two included *Nervous Squared, Active Imagination Squared, Lazy Squared, Relaxed Squared, Outgoing Squared,* and *PRE Squared.* In the final step, we added *Lazy Cubed, Relaxed Cubed,* and *Outgoing Cubed.* The r-square moved from .18 in step one to .24 in step two, to .31 in step three. Thirty-one percent of the variance in *Extra Effort* is explained by this curvilinear equation.

Age was significant in step one, with a negative beta of .16, which implies that younger leaders are more likely than older leaders to inspire *Extra Effort* from their employees. The beta of .18 for *Gender* in Table 31 suggests that women are more likely than men to rouse employees toward *Extra Effort.* The beta of .17 for *Relaxed* means that calmer leaders are more likely than less serene leaders to motivate followers to put forth *Extra Effort.* We found no significant results in step two. However, in step three, significant quadratic and cubic relationships resulted. A quadratic function resulted for *Active Imagination* and *Extra Effort.* With a beta of -.94 for *Active Imagination* and .95 for *Active Imagination Squared,* one may infer that at the lowest and highest levels of *Active Imagination,* the leader is more likely to inspire extra effort in his or her employees. Appendix Figure 40 displays this relationship.

A cubic relationship exists between *Extra Effort* and *Lazy,* with the betas for *Lazy, Lazy Squared,* and *Lazy Cubed* at -3.78, 7.98, -4.41 and respectively. The *Extra Effort* put forth by employees tends to be lowest for leaders who tend to be slightly or highly lazy, as depicted in Appendix Figure 41.

Similarly, we found a cubic relationship between *Extra Effort* and *Outgoing.* The betas for *Outgoing, Outgoing Squared,* and *Outgoing Cubed* are -5.01, 10.97, and -6.05 respectively. Leaders who are not outgoing as well as those who are more sociable tend to promote higher levels of extra effort from their employees, as depicted in

Carol R. Himelhoch and Mary Antonaros Raymond

Appendix Figure 42. Table 31, which follows Figure 42, presents the cubic regression results.

TABLE 31

Curvilinear Regression of Extra Effort on Leader Characteristics and Exercise Habits

Predictor					Criterion					
					Extra Effort -Total					
	Beta	B	ΔR2	R2	ΔF	F	SE	95% CI		
Step 1			.18	.18	2.889	2.889	.54			
Age	-.16*	-.08						-.17	to	.00
Gender	.18*	.23						.02	to	.43
Race	.10	.32						-.18	to	.82
Position	.12	.09						-.03	to	.20
Thorough	.09	.07						-.07	to	.22
Nervous	-.05	-.02						-.10	to	.05
Active Imag.	.01	.01						-.08	to	.10
Lazy	-.08	-.06						-.17	to	.06
Relaxed	.17*	.09						.00	to	.18
Outgoing	.00	.00						-.07	to	.07
PRE	.15	.10						.00	to	.20
Step 2			.06	.24	-.295	2.594	.53			
Age	-.13	-.07						.16	to	.01
Gender	.16	.20						.01	to	.41
Race	.12	.38						.12	to	.88
Position	.08	.06						.06	to	.18
Thorough	.05	.05						.10	to	.19
Nervous	-.65	-.31						.64	to	.02
Active Imag.	-.79	-.48						1.02	to	.07
Lazy	-.21	-.15						.67	to	.37
Relaxed	-.16	-.09						.57	to	.40
Outgoing.	-.37	-.18						.63	to	.26
PRE	-.05	-.03						.39	to	.32
Nervous Squared	.62	.05						.01	to	.11
Active Imag. Sq.	.80	.07						.01	to	.14
Lazy Squared	.15	.02						.09	to	.14
Relaxed Squared	.34	.03						.04	to	.10
Outgoing Squared	.39	.03						.04	to	.09
PRE Squared	.23	.03						.04	to	.10

(continued)

TABLE 31 (CONTINUED)

Curvilinear Regression of Extra Effort on Leader Characteristics and Exercise Habits

Predictor	Criterion										
	Extra Effort -Total										
	Beta	B	ΔR2	R2	ΔF	F	SE	95% CI			
Step 3			.07	.31	.490	3.084	.51				
Age	-.12	-.06						-.15	to	.02	
Gender	.15	.19						-.01	to	.39	
Race	.13	.41						-.07	to	.90	
Position	.09	.06						-.05	to	.18	
Thorough	.09	.07						-.07	to	.22	
Nervous	-.54	-.25						-.58	to	.07	
Active Imag.	-.94*	-.57						-1.10	to	-.04	
Lazy	-3.78*	-2.69						-5.48	to	.10	
Relaxed	-2.67	-1.41						-3.16	to	.34	
Outgoing.	-5.01**	-2.46						-4.08	to	-.83	
PRE	.05	.03						-.31	to	.37	
Nervous Squared	.48	.04						-.02	to	.10	
Active Imag. Sq.	.95*	.08						.01	to	.15	
Lazy Squared	7.98*	1.29						-.05	to	2.62	
Relaxed Squared	6.05	.47						-.09	to	1.03	
Outgoing Squared	10.97**	.79						.25	to	1.32	
PRE Squared	.13	.02						-.05	to	.09	
Lazy Cubed	-4.41*	-.18						-.37	to	.01	
Relaxed Cubed	-3.29	-.05						-.10	to	.01	
Outgoing Cubed	-6.05**	-.08						-.13	to	-.02	

*p<.05. **p<.01. ***p<.001

Therefore, our hypothesized curvilinear relationships between the Big Five dimensions *Relaxed, Outgoingness, Nervousness* and *Extra Effort* and the leader effectiveness dimension *Extra Effort* are supported.

Effectiveness

As depicted in Table 32, *Effectiveness* is an outcome variable that was regressed on *Age, Gender, Race, Position, Mild Exercise Intensity, Find Fault, Thorough, Relaxed, and Nervous* in step one of the curvilinear regression equation. Eighteen percent of the variance in *Effectiveness* was explained by the linear equation. By adding the independent variables *Find Fault Squared, Through Squared, Relaxed Squared,* and *Nervous Squared* in step two, the r-square jumped by six percent to explain 24% of the variance. *Relaxed Cubed* and *Nervous Cubed* were added in step three, and the r-square increased by 4% to explain 28% of the variance.

Gender is significant in all three steps, with beta values of .25, .21, and .23 for steps one through three. Women are more likely than men to be effective leaders. One should note that this correlation is mild, however. *Mild Exercise Intensity* is negatively associated with *Effectiveness* in steps one and two, with betas of -.17 and -.15; however, this variable was not significant in step three. *Thorough* is positively associated with *Effectiveness* in step one with a beta value of .17. However, it is significant in the linear model only. The relationship between *Effectiveness* and *Relaxed* is cubic. The beta values in step three for *Relaxed, Relaxed Squared,* and *Relaxed Cubed* are -3.94, 8.76, and -4.75 respectively. At the lowest and highest levels of relaxation, leaders are their most effective. Appendix Figure 43 shows this relationship.

Therefore, our hypothesized curvilinear relationships between the Big Five dimensions *Nervous, Relaxed, Find Fault,* and *Thoroughness* and the leader effectiveness dimension *Effectiveness* are supported. Our hypothesis that women are more effective leaders than men is supported for this *Effectiveness* dimension.

Satisfaction

Satisfaction, the final outcome variable, was regressed on Age, Gender, Race, Position, Find Fault, Relaxed, Mild Exercise Intensity, Relaxed Squared, and Mild Exercise Intensity Squared in a quadratic equation. The r-square of .09 in step one improved by step two, which explains 16% of the variance in Satisfaction. Gender, Race, and

TABLE 32

Curvilinear Regression of Effectiveness on Leader Characteristics and Exercise Habits

Predictor	Criterion									
	Effectiveness -Total									
	Beta	B	ΔR2	R2	ΔF	F	SE	95% CI		
Step 1			.18	.18	3.743	3.743	.45			
Age	-.07	-.03						-.10	to	.04
Gender	.25**	.27						.11	to	.44
Race	.03	.09						-.29	to	.47
Position	.11	.06						-.03	to	.15
Mild Ex. Inten.	-.17*	-8.41X10⁻⁵						.00	to	.00
Find Fault	-.01	.00						-.08	to	.07
Thorough	.17*	.12						.01	to	.24
Relaxed	.17*	.07						.00	to	.15
Nervous	.03	.01						-.05	to	.08
Step 2			.06	.24	-.076	3.667	.44			
Age	-.07	-.03						-.10	to	.04
Gender	.21**	.23						.06	to	.40
Race	.03	.08						-.29	to	.46
Position	.08	.05						-.04	to	.14
Mild Ex. Inten.	-.15*	-7.54X10⁻⁵						.00	to	.00
Find Fault	-.41	-.20						-.55	to	.16
Thorough	-1.12	-.82						-1.99	to	.34
Relaxed	-.37	-.16						-.57	to	.24
Nervous	-.47	-.19						-.46	to	.08
Find Fault Sq.	.39	.03						-.03	to	.10
Thorough Sq.	1.26	.11						-.03	to	.25
Relaxed Sq.	.55	.04						-.02	to	.09
Nervous Sq.	.51	.04						-.01	to	.09

(continued)

Find Fault are significant in both steps. Women are slightly more likely than men to influence job satisfaction among their employees. The beta for Gender is .18 in step one and .15 in step two. Caucasians are slightly more likely than minorities to engender satisfaction in employees, with betas of .17 both in steps one and two. Find Fault is negatively associated with Satisfaction, with a beta of -.19 in step one

Carol R. Himelhoch and Mary Antonaros Raymond

TABLE 32 (CONTINUED)

Curvilinear Regression of Effectiveness on Leader Characteristics and Exercise Habits

Predictor	Criterion									
	Effectiveness -Total									
	Beta	B	ΔR2	R2	ΔF	F	SE	95% CI		
Step 3			.04	.28	.135	3.802	.43			
Age	-.04	-.02						-.08	to	.05
Gender	.23**	.25						.08	to	.41
Race	.03	.07						-.30	to	.44
Position	.06	.04						-.05	to	.13
Mild Ex. Inten.	-.12	-6.04×10^{-5}						.00	to	.00
Find Fault	-.30	-.14						-.50	to	.21
Thorough	-1.32	-.97						-2.12	to	.18
Relaxed	-3.94*	-1.75						-3.24	to	-.26
Nervous	.82	.33						-.44	to	1.10
Find Fault Sq.	.27	.02						-.04	to	.09
Thorough Sq.	1.42	.13						-.01	to	.26
Relaxed Sq.	8.76*	.57						.09	to	1.05
Nervous Sq.	-2.49	-.18						-.50	to	.13
Relaxed Cubed	-4.75*	-.05						-.10	to	-.01
Nervous Cubed	1.73	.03						-.01	to	.06

*p<.05. **p<.01. ***p<.001

and -.18 in step two. Leaders who tend to find fault in their employees are less likely to lead employees who are satisfied with their jobs. Mild Exercise Intensity Squared is positively associated with Satisfaction, with a beta of .34. Although statistically significant, this value is too small to be meaningful.

Therefore, our hypothesized curvilinear relationships between PRE, Exercise Frequency, and Big Five dimensions with the effectiveness dimension *Satisfaction* **are not supported. Our hypothesis that women are more effective leaders than men is supported for the effectiveness dimension** *Satisfaction.* **Our hypothesis that minorities are more effective than non-minorities on the** *Satisfaction* **dimension is not supported.**

Table 33

Curvilinear Regression of Satisfaction on Leader Characteristics and Exercise Habits

Predictor	Criterion									
	Satisfaction -Total									
	Beta	B	$\Delta R2$	R2	ΔF	F	SE		95% CI	
Step 1			.09	.09	3.225	3.225	.54			
Age	-.05	-.03						-.11	to	.05
Gender	.18*	.23						.04	to	.42
Race	.17*	.52						.06	to	.97
Position	.13	.09						-.01	to	.20
Find Fault	-.19*	-.10						-.19	to	-.02
Relaxed	.12	.06						-.02	to	.14
Mild Ex. Inten.	.02	9.57×10^{-6}						.00		.00
Step 2			.07	.16	.155	3.380	.53			
Age	-.05	-.03						-.11	to	.05
Gender	.15*	.19						.00	to	.38
Race	.17*	.51						.07	to	.96
Position	.11	.08						-.03	to	.18
Find Fault	-.18*	-.10						-.18	to	-.01
Relaxed	-.59	-.31						-.77	to	.15
Mild Ex. Inten.	-.29	.00						.00		.00
Relaxed Sq.	.73	.06						-.01	to	.12
Mild Ex. Int. Sq.	.34*	2.53×10^{-8}						.00		.00

*p<.05. **p<.01. ***p<.001

Summary

The data analysis that we presented in Chapter Four covered leader/employee differences in perceptions of their leadership, finding congruence overall. We also shared the data concerning the dark side effects of too much exercise frequency and too great a level of exertion. We presented curvilinear relationships among PRE, and *Exercise Frequency* and Big Five dimension on leadership styles and leader effectiveness. In Chapter Five, we review and interpret the results, to help elucidate their relevance to practice.

[5]

CONCLUSIONS AND RECOMMENDATIONS

Few would advocate against the physical and psychological benefits of exercise. A relatively new area of study, however, addresses the questions of *how much* and *at what intensity* is exercise the most useful (Brown & Bray, 2015; Eijsvogels et al., 2016; Gay et al., 2016). Similarly, most scholars recognize that certain Big Five personality traits are associated with leadership styles that are correlated to effective leadership. Judge, Bono, Ilies, and Gerhardt (2002) conducted a meta-analysis of 222 correlations from 73 samples, and found the relevant dimensions that include extraversion, agreeableness, conscientiousness, neuroticism, and openness to experiences. Yet as with exercise, the ideal level and intensity of these traits remains an open question (Hereford, 2011). As we mention in Chapter One, trait research explains a small part of the variance in leader behavior (Jin et al., 2016). Yet, explaining 5-12% of the variance in leader behavior still provides value. Knowing even five percent is better than knowing nothing. Our research contributes to the current body of knowledge because we explored optimal levels of leisure exercise habits and personality dispositions to gain a deeper understanding of antecedents to TLB, and in doing so examined transactional and passive-avoidant leadership as well. We wanted to understand to which the intensity of exercise, and to what concentrations, personality traits are significant antecedents while factoring in leader demographics.

In this study, we sought to advance the conversation addressing why certain leaders engage in TLB, transactional, or passive-avoidant leadership. Specifically we asked, "In what ways do personality characteristics, demographic characteristics, and leisure exercise habits influence leadership styles and leader effectiveness?" We hypothesized a point of diminishing returns - a peak that could be considered extreme because it is the point at which positive exercise habits and traits have a negative effect on leadership. We applied the "dark side" hypothesis to exercise frequency, PRE, and Big Five personality dimensions in association with TLB and leader effectiveness. We based these hypotheses on assumptions that emanated from the work Avolio and Bass (2004), who began the research thread establishing TLB as the most effective, transactional as less effectual, and passive-avoidant behaviors as an ineffective leadership style.

In this final chapter, we summarize and evaluate the results of our study. We revisit our research questions to ensure that we answered them all explicitly. We reflect upon their significance to society in general and consider how the findings pertain to leaders specifically. We also make recommendations concerning practical applications of the results. Knowing that it is impossible for any researcher to achieve pure impartiality, we disclose our biases and assumptions in the section that follows applications. As all answers lead to new questions, we close with our recommendations for future research.

SUMMARY OF FINDINGS

Before pondering implications, we thought it helpful to review the key results of our research at a broad level, using a perspective that is unencumbered by numerical detail. In this section, we summarize our findings in seven sub-sections. We begin by reviewing congruence between leader and employee perceptions of leadership styles. Second, we recap significant relationships between *PRE* and leadership styles. In the third section, we recapitulate the findings on *Exercise Frequency* and leadership styles. Fourth, we revisit key curvilinear relationships between the Big Five Factors and TLB. Fifth, we re-examine the significant curvilinear associations between the Big Five Factors and transactional and passive-avoidant leadership styles. In the sixth section, we abridge the main findings in connection with the Big Five Factors and the leadership outcome variables *Extra Effort, Effectiveness,* and *Satisfaction.* Finally, we summarize the results of our curvilinear regression analyses.

Comparison of Employee/Leader Perceptions

When comparing leader and employee perceptions of leader behaviors and effectiveness, we found congruence overall. The MLQ contains 45 questions, and there were significant differences in perceptions pertaining to five dimensions only. Employees see their leaders as stronger than their leaders view themselves in helping them address work problems. Leaders believe they rely less on management-by-exception than deemed by their employees. Employees believe their leaders are more self-confident than their leaders consider themselves. Leaders think they regard their employees individually, having unique needs, abilities, and aspirations, to a greater degree than that deemed by their employees. Finally, leaders view their teams as more effective than their employees perceive them to be.

Relationship Between PRE and Leadership Styles

We found significant curvilinear relationships between *PRE,* and *Idealized Attributes,* and *PRE* and *Inspirational Motivation.* Although more strenuous exercise is best, we did find a "dark side" relationship at the most extreme intensity levels. Leaders who do not exercise at all reflect noteworthy levels of *Idealized Attributes* and *Inspirational Motivation.* Those who exercise strenuously and moderately use *Idealized Attributes* more than those who used to exercise. Leaders who participate in strenuous exercise use *Inspirational Motivation* more than those who participate in mild exercise. Those who engage in mild exercise use *Inspirational Motivation* more than those who used to exercise.

The level of *Inspirational Motivation* decreases between no exercise and mild exercise, and then increases as the leader moves toward strenuous exercise. At the highest levels of perceived strenuous exercise, there appears to be a point of diminishing returns.

Strenuous exercisers use *Individual Consideration* more than moderate exercisers, and moderate exercisers use *Individual Consideration* more those who exercised formerly. A point of diminishing returns does not apply for this dimension, however.

Relationship Between Frequency of Exercise and Leadership Styles

As with *PRE,* we found significant curvilinear relationships between *Exercise Frequency* and some leadership styles. Specifically, we found curvilinear relationships between *Exercise Frequency* and *Idealized Behaviors, Inspirational Motivation,* and *Individual Consideration.* With *PRE* there was no curvilinear relationship to *Individual Consideration;* however, we did find the connection for *Exercise Frequency.* For all three leadership styles, the point of diminishing returns appears to be exercising more than six days per week.

Another related finding was that the *Active Management By Exception* leadership style tends to be used by those who do not exercise at all.

Figure 44 provides a conceptual summary of how *PRE* and *Exercise Frequency* constructs are related to leadership styles. Thick lines represent strong relationships, and dotted lines depict weak associations.

Significant Curvilinear Relationships Between the Big Five Factors and TLB

Consistent with the Judge et al., (2002) study, we found that *Nervousness* at the highest levels is associated with *Idealized Attributes.* However, this relationship is quadratic. *Idealized Attributes* decline as the leader's *Nervousness* increases; at the highest levels of *Nervousness,* leaders reveal an increase in *Idealized Attributes.*

Active Imagination and *Idealized Attributes* also are associated through a quadratic relationship. This transformational style is highest when the leader's *Active Imagination* is at its lowest and at its highest. The same configuration holds true for the relationship between *Active Imagination* and *Idealized Behaviors* and between *Active Imagination* and *Intellectual Stimulation.* The relationship between *Active Imagination* and *Inspirational Motivation,* however, is cubic. *Inspirational Motivation* is at its highest points when *Active Imagination* is at its lowest, then declines but increases again at a moderate level. At the greatest point of Active Imagination, Inspirational Motivation begins to decline again.

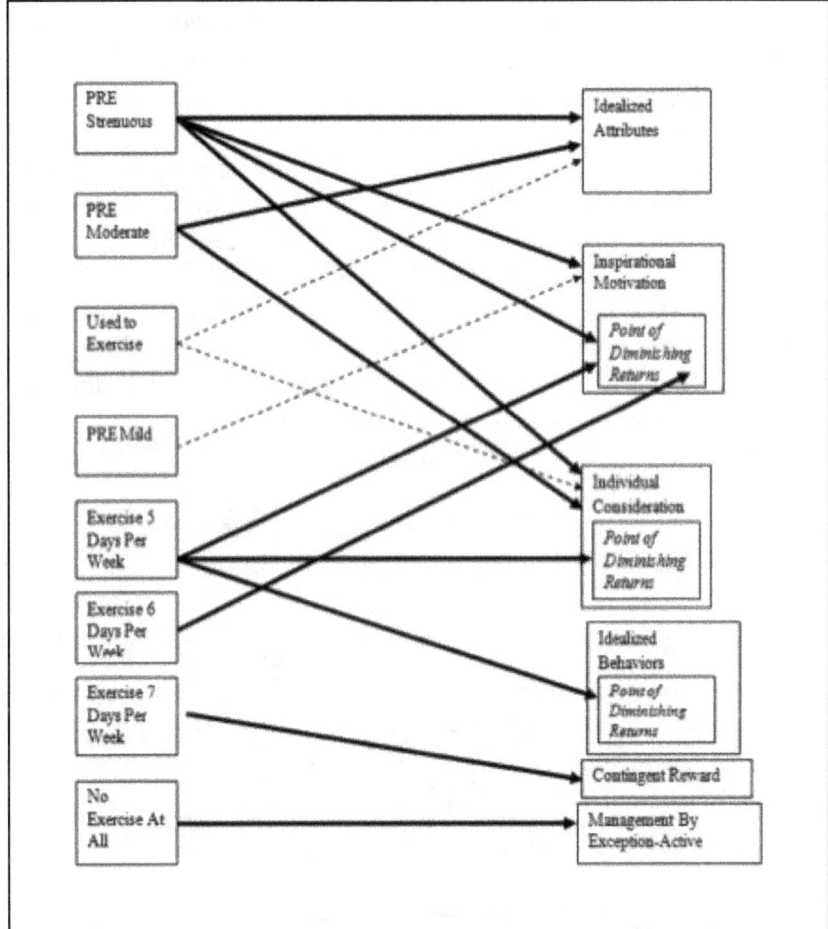

Figure 44. Conceptual representation of the relationship between PRE as well as exercise frequency and leadership styles.

Trust and Laziness are connected to Inspirational Motivation through a quadratic relationship. For both Big Five dimensions, Inspirational Motivation declines from higher points when leaders possess low levels of these traits. Inspirational Motivation increases as the leaders levels of Trust and Laziness increase.

Both Find Fault in others and Active Imagination exhibit a quadratic relationship with Individual Consideration. Mutually, Individual Consideration declines, then rises again as leaders exhibit these two personality traits in greater degrees.

Significant Curvilinear Relationships Between the Big Five Factors and Transactional and Passive-Avoidant Leader Behaviors

Leaders with the lowest levels of *Active Imagination* are prone to use the most *Management By Exception Active*. As *Active Imagination* increases, *Management By Exception Active* decreases, and then rises again at its more prominent levels. Similarly, both *Lazy* and *Find Fault* are associated with *Laissez-faire Leadership* through a quadratic connection. For both variables, *Laissez-faire Leadership* increases with stronger tendencies toward these dimensions, and then it declines at the highest levels of *Lazy* and *Find Fault* with others.

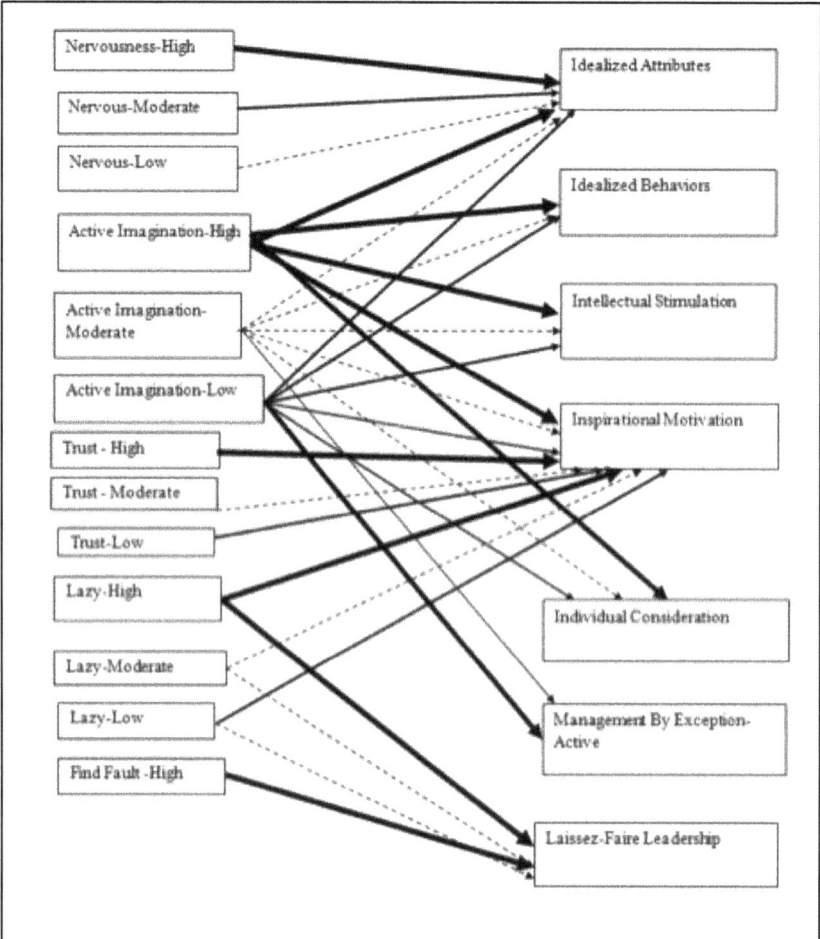

Figure 45. Conceptual connections between the significant big five dimensions and leadership styles.

Figure 45 summarizes the conceptual connections between the significant Big Five dimensions and leadership styles. The thickest arrows reflect strong relationships; medium-width arrows depict moderate relationships, and the arrows affixed to dotted lines represent the weakest relationships.

Significant Curvilinear Relationships Between the Big Five Factors and the Leadership Outcome Variables

Relaxed, Outgoingness, Nervousness, and *Active Imagination* are all associated with *Extra Effort* through cubic or quadratic relationships. With both *Relaxed* and *Outgoingness,* levels of *Extra Effort* decline, rise, and then decline again with increased levels of each, thus suggesting a "dark side" of these two positive traits. A quadratic relationship was found between both *Nervousness* and *Active Imagination* and *Extra Effort.* As levels of these two traits rise, *Extra Effort* put forth by employees declines, then rises again.

A cubic relationship exists between *Relaxed* and *Effectiveness. Effectiveness* drops, then rises, then declines again with an increase in the leader's perceived state of a relaxed demeanor, reflecting yet another "dark side" of what at first glance appears to be an exclusively positive characteristic. Quadratic relationships were found between each of the *Nervousness, Find Fault* and *Thorough* dimensions and *Effectiveness.* For all three Big Five dimensions, *Effectiveness* declines and then rises as the tendency toward these traits strengthens.

Finally, a significant quadratic relationship was found between *Relaxation* and *Satisfaction.* As the level of the leader's relaxed state increases, employee *Satisfaction* declines, and then rises again.

Figure 46 depicts a conceptual summary of the significant association between the Big Five factors and dimensions of leader effectiveness. The thickest lines represent strong relationships; lines of medium thickness correspond with moderate associations; and the dotted lines align with the weakest relationships.

REGRESSION ANALYSES

The regression analyses provided an opportunity to consider all demographic, personality, and exercise variables in connection with leadership styles concurrently. Standardized betas, shared in the regression tables in Chapter Four, permitted us to examine the relative strength of each dimension as compared to the others because the very process of calculating standardized betas creates a common unit of measure. In addition, the polynomial regression equations afforded an opportunity to see more of the variance in the relationships explained upon each step, as was evident in the increased r-square value at each iteration. In this subsection, we summarize the key findings gleaned from the final steps in all polynomial regression equations.

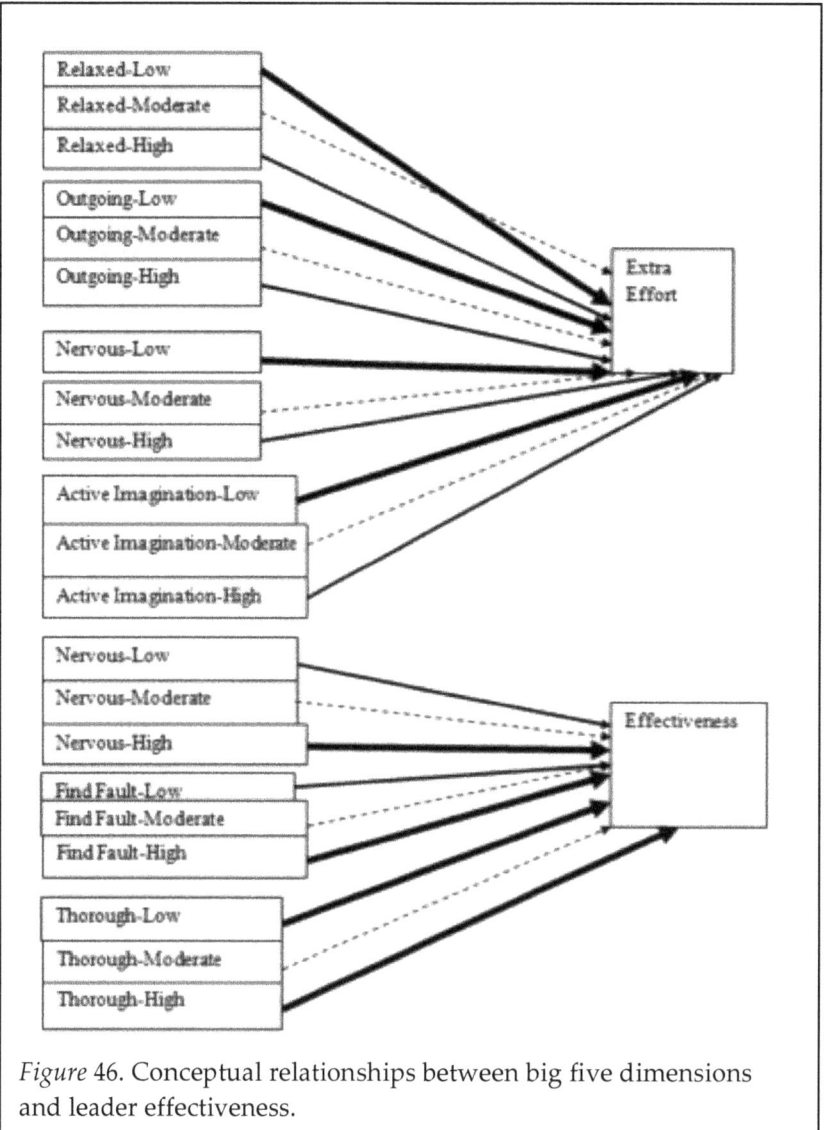

Figure 46. Conceptual relationships between big five dimensions and leader effectiveness.

Curvilinear Regression of Idealized Attributes on Leader Characteristics and Exercise Habits

Significant predictors of *Idealized Attributes* included Big Five dimensions and frequency of exercise. *Relaxed* and *Outgoing* are associated with *Idealized Attributes* through a linear positive correlation. In other words, the more relaxed and outgoing the leader, the more he or she will be perceived to have *Idealized Attributes*. We also found significant negative linear relationships between both *Nervousness* and *Idealized Attributes*. With greater levels of *Nervousness* come weaker intensities of *Idealized Attributes*.

We found a quadratic relationship between *Active Imagination* and *Idealized Attributes*. Consistent with our curve-fitting analysis, *Idealized Attributes* are highest when the leader's *Active Imagination* is at its lowest highest points. This suggests that those perceived with moderate active imagination levels are not strong on this measure of TLB.

Exercise Frequency emerged as a statistically significant but weak cubic association with *Idealized Attributes*. *Idealized Attributes* are higher among those who do not exercise than they are for people exercising up to two days per week. When leaders exercise more than two days per week, *Idealized Attributes* are more prominent. They peak at six days per week, at which point they decline again. Its significance suggests a "dark side" of exercising at the highest levels in relation to *Idealized Attributes*, such as more than six days per week. Demographic variables like age, race, gender, or position were not significant.

Curvilinear Regression of Idealized Behaviors on Leader Characteristics and Exercise Habits

Gender is the only significant demographic variable predicting *Idealized Behaviors*, with women employing this transformational leadership style more than men. *Nervousness* was found to have a linear association with *Idealized Behaviors*. The more nervous the leader, the more likely he or she is to show convey values, a sense of purpose and mission, and to consider the moral and ethical consequences of decisions. Because of a quadratic relationship, the Big Five dimension, *Active Imagination,* is highest when the leader's *Idealized Attributes* are at their lowest and at its highest. The implication is that moderate levels of *Active Imagination* do not promote this dimension of TLB. We found a cubic relationship between *Exercise Frequency* and *Idealized Behaviors*. This relationship, mentioned previously, hung together in this regression equation.

The "dark side" of exercise frequency in association with *Idealized Behaviors* appears to take effect when leaders exercise more than six days per week.

Curvilinear Regression of Inspirational Motivation on Leader Characteristics and Exercise Habits

Age was the only demographic variable associated with *Inspirational Motivation*. Younger leaders tend to use this style more than their members of older age cohorts. *Nervousness* was negatively associated with this dimension; the more nervous the leader, the less likely he or she adopt the style of *Inspirational Motivation*. The only other predictor of *Inspirational Motivation* is *PRE* through a cubic relationship. Although exercising up to a strenuous level is considered positive, there is a "dark side" of the highest levels of *PRE* as depicted in Figure 2. The point of diminishing returns is evident in the curve, just short of 4, which is the highest level of *PRE* in the survey.

Curvilinear Regression of Intellectual Stimulation on Leader Characteristics and Exercise Habits

Exercise Frequency, through a positive linear relationship, and *Moderate Exercise Intensity*, through a quadratic relationship, and *Active Imagination*, also through a quadratic relationship, were the significant predictors of *Intellectual Stimulation*. The more frequently leaders exercise, the more apt they are to use *Intellectual Stimulation* to inspire their employees. In addition to frequency, intensity of exercise matters. Moderate intensity tends to be optimal, but as leaders move toward the high end of the moderate range, they use lower amounts of *Intellectual Stimulation*. When the leader's *Active Imagination* is at its lowest and at its highest, the leader employs greater levels of *Intellectual Stimulation*.

Curvilinear Regression of Individual Consideration on Leader Characteristics and Exercise Habits

Gender and *Race* are both significant predictors of *Individual Consideration*. Women and minorities have the strongest levels of this transformational leadership style. *Thoroughness* was the only significant Big Five dimension associated with *Individual Consideration*. The more thorough the leader, the more *Individual*

Consideration he or she will exhibit in relating to employees. Leaders reporting the lowest levels of *PRE*, defined as "do not exercise," are associated with the highest levels of *Individual Consideration*. *Individual Consideration* drops at the mild level of exercise, and begins to rise again to its peak at a point just short of the most strenuous level of perceived exertion. This cubic relationship leads us to conclude a "dark side" of *PRE* in connection with *Individual Consideration*.

Curvilinear Regression of Contingent Reward on Leader Characteristics and Exercise Habits

The Big Five dimensions *Relaxed, Thorough,* and *Outgoing* are associated with the transactional leadership style *Contingent* Reward. *Relaxed* has a quadratic relationship with *Contingent Reward*. At the very lowest and highest levels of *Relaxed*, leaders tend to use *Contingent Reward* more. *Thorough* is associated positively with the use of *Contingent Reward*, as is *Outgoing*. The more outgoing and thorough the leader, the more heavily he or she will rely on this transactional style. *Exercise Frequency* is connected through a cubic relationship to *Contingent Reward*, with the use of this transactional style highest among those who exercise seven or more days per week.

Curvilinear Regression of Management by Exception Active on Leader Characteristics and Exercise Habits

Find Fault and *Active Imagination* are associated with *Management By Exception Active*. Of all the significant antecedents, none is correlated with exercise. The association between *Find Fault* and *Management By Exception Active* is linear and positive. The tendency for the leader to find fault in others is associated with using this transactional style. Leaders with the lowest levels of *Active Imagination* are prone to use the most *Management By Exception Active*. As *Active Imagination* increases, *Management By Exception Active* decreases. This transactional leadership style increases again when *Active Imagination* is at its more prominent levels.

Curvilinear Regression of Management by Exception Passive on Leader Characteristics and Exercise Habits

The passive-avoidant leadership style *Management By Exception-Passive* is influenced by the level of the leader's laziness, thoroughness, and PRE. The lazier the leader, the more likely she or he will use this style. Leaders who tend to be more thorough are less likely to apply *Management By Exception-Passive*. The relationship between *PRE* and *Management By Exception-Passive* is quadratic. This passive-avoidant leadership style is highest at moderate levels of perceived exertion, and is least likely at the lowest and highest levels of *PRE*.

Curvilinear Regression of Laissez-Faire on Leader Characteristics and Exercise Habits

Three Big Five dimensions and one exercise intensity dimension influences *Laissez-faire Leadership*. More *Thorough* leaders are less likely to use this passive-avoidant style. Leaders with strong active imaginations and who tend to find fault in others are also prone to use laissez-faire leadership. Finally, the only exercise intensity associated with laissez-faire leadership is that performed moderately. The association is negative, so the more the leader participates in moderate exercise, the less likely she or he will be a laissez-faire leader.

Curvilinear Regression of Extra Effort on Leader Characteristics and Exercise Habits

Many factors were significantly associated with *Extra Effort*. However, none is connected to the leader's leisure exercise habits. As *Active Imagination* levels increase, *Extra Effort* decreases and then rises again. *Lazy* is connected through a cubic relationship. At low levels, there is a moderate degree of *Extra Effort*. However, as the leader moves away from lazy, employees' *Extra Effort* rises. However, there is a "dark side" to this dimension. At the highest levels, when the leader is the least lazy, *Extra Effort* declines again.

Outgoing is also connected to this outcome variable through a cubic relationship. *Extra Effort* is highest at the lowest and moderate levels of leader sociability. It drops at moderate levels, then increases to its peak when the *Outgoing* dimension is strong. However, at the uppermost level of *Outgoing*, *Extra Effort* declines again. *Outgoing* is one of those "dark side" dimensions of *Extra Effort*. *Active Imagination* and *Extra Effort* unite through a quadratic relationship. When the leader's active imagination is weak, *Extra Effort* is strong. However, at stronger levels of *Active Imagination, Extra Effort* declines.

Curvilinear Regression of Effectiveness on Leader Characteristics and Exercise Habits

Only two variables were significant in relationship to *Effectiveness*, and none is related to exercise. *Gender* is a significant dimension, with women more likely than men to be achieve the effectiveness outcome. *Relaxed* was the only other significant variable, and its relationship to *Effectiveness* is cubic. *Effectiveness* drops, rises, and then drops again as the leader's perceived relaxed state increases. *Relaxed* is yet another positive trait with a "dark side" in its connection to *Effectiveness*.

Curvilinear Regression of Satisfaction on Leader Characteristics and Exercise Habits

Gender, Race, Find Fault, and *Mild Exercise Intensity Squared* influence the final outcome variable, *Satisfaction*. Women are more liable to influence *Satisfaction* than men. Caucasians influence high *Satisfaction* levels more than minorities. The tendency to *Find Fault* in employees is negatively associated with this outcome variable. The statistically significant relationship between mild exercise intensity and *Satisfaction* is too small to be noteworthy on a practical level.

Evaluation of Findings as Compared to the Literature

At the conclusion of any research, it is helpful to assess the findings in the context of related investigations conducted by established scholars. In this section, we examine how our data compare to existing studies. We begin by evaluating the congruence in leader-employee ratings. Next, we discuss the curvilinear relationships between the Big Five dimensions and our outcome variables. We follow with a discussion of the curvilinear connections between exercise and leadership. Finally, we evaluate how our analysis of demographic variables compares to that in the literature.

Similar Employee/Leader Ratings

We were not surprised to find consistency between leader and employee perceptions of leadership styles on the MLQ. Taylor, Wang, and Yujie (2012) conducted a study in which leaders were asked to predict how their employees would rate them on a number of dimensions. They found that the most effective leaders were the most accurate in their predictions. Atwater and Yammarino (1992) established a connection between the leader's self-awareness and strong performance. Our study did not measure the accuracy of leader predictions of employee ratings. However, we wondered whether or not there are significant relationships between leaders who granted us permission and *Extra Effort, Effectiveness,* or *Satisfaction.* We ran Pearson r correlations and one-way ANOVAs, but found no significant relationships. Regardless, the employees who participated provided ratings that are congruent with those of their leaders' self-assessments. This similarity aligns with prior research.

The Goldilocks Paradox - How Much of a Trait is "Just Right?"

Lord, DeVader, and Alliger (1986) uncovered flaws in methodology that led prior researchers to dismiss the relationship between personality and leadership styles. Building on their work, our study assumed curvilinear relationships that were missed in earlier examinations. Our research demonstrated several paradoxes, which are consistent with other recent investigations. In particular, extreme levels of *Relaxed* have a detrimental influence on *Effectiveness.* This measure of emotional stability aligns with prior research that suggests moderate levels are better than extremes. The same holds for *Extra Effort* and *Extraversion* in moderate levels.

As discussed below, our data diverged from other research in that we did not find moderate levels of personality scales optimal for several Big Five factors. We learned that transformational leadership behaviors are strongest when several Big Five personality strengths are either low or high, not moderate. For example, *Idealized Attributes, Idealized Behaviors, Intellectual Stimulation, Inspirational Motivation,* and *Extra Effort* are highest at the lowest levels of *Active Imagination,* but rise again when *Active Imagination* is at its strongest intensity. *Inspirational Motivation* is strongest at the lowest and highest levels of leader *Trust. Extra Effort is* more common when *Relaxed* and *Outgoingness* are weak and strong. *Extra Effort* is also enhanced when the leader is low and high on the *Lazy* dimension, a Big Five factor many would not consider a strength. Yet, in this context it is a strength because *Extra Effort* drops when the leader is the least *Lazy*, (on the conscientiousness continuum) the point of extreme for this personality dimension. *Satisfaction* is greatest when *Relaxed* (a dimension of emotional stability) is at its highest and lowest. Although not transformational, *Contingent Reward,* an active transactional style associated with favorable outcomes (Harris & Russell, 2013), is found most when leaders are either very *Relaxed* or not *Relaxed* at all.

Some transformational leadership styles are associated with the highest levels of undesirable personality traits. For example, *Idealized Attributes, Extra Effort,* and *Effectiveness* decline when the leader's nervousness (emotional stability scale) increase, but at the most intense levels of leader nervousness, *Idealized Attributes* are the greatest. *Inspirational Motivation* is strongest when leaders are very low or very high on the *Lazy* (on the conscientious scale) dimension. *Laissez-faire* leadership is seen more when leaders are low or high on the *Lazy* and *Find Fault* (emotional stability) dimensions. Although perhaps puzzling at first glance, our paradoxical findings are consistent with recent research.

Judge, Piccolo, and Kosalka (2009) discuss correlations between effectiveness and extraversion, conscientiousness, emotional stability, and openness to experience. Using a social-Darwinism-type of paradigm, they argued that traits leading to "fitness" [not physical fitness, but fitness for survival] under one condition might be disadvantageous under others. They posited a natural linkage from traits to outcomes that emerge naturally from the leader's characteristics. For example, the "conscientious, extraverted, and emotionally stable ... individual may be more motivated to get ahead, extraverted and agreeable individuals may be more likely to go along..., more speculatively, open, intelligent, and charismatic individuals may be more likely to provide meaning for their compatriots" (p. 863). They also suggested that a situational lens applies to traits. For example, "bright" traits are counterproductive if employees believe the tendencies will impede group survival. A Goldilocks paradox appears to describe the correlations between moderate levels of most traits and effectiveness.

> *Similar countervailing effects of bright and dark traits based on the intensity of one's trait disposition, whereby modest levels of a bright trait (e.g., extraversion) are attractive, desirable, and functional for leadership and group effectiveness, but extreme cases*

of extraversion, characterized in part by risk taking and self-serving pursuit of adventure, might threaten the stability and survival of a particular group. (Judge, Piccolo, & Kosalka, 2009, p. 864)

Judge and colleagues argue that socially desirable traits are typically associated with favorable outcomes just as socially undesirable traits correlate with unfavorable results. However, at extreme levels, their effects reverse. Figure 47 presents their conceptual framework, in which they provide examples of benefits and drawbacks of socially desirable traits under normal and extreme conditions.

DeRue, Nahrgang, Wellman, and Humphrey (2011) conducted a meta-analysis of the Five Factor model and the alignment between personality and careers. They found associations between the interpersonally-oriented traits, agreeableness and extraversion, with individual consideration. They also found associations between task-oriented traits, like conscientiousness, and leader behaviors that focus on contingent reward and management by exception-active. Traits that are change-oriented, like openness, are associated with TLBs, according to their study.

Kaiser and Hogan (2011) corroborated the work of Judge et al. (2009). They studied 126 executives, and concluded that, "both high and low scores on personality dimensions can compromise performance through an association with excessive behavior" (p. 219). They revealed that ambition was the key component of extraversion most highly correlated with leader effectiveness. The other sociability components of extraversion are less significant. They established that adjustment, the measure they used to represent emotional stability, was associated with "forceful and enabling leadership" (p. 235). Kaiser and Hogan stated also that Conscientiousness is not associated with the sociability facets of leader effectiveness. They speculate that leaders who are overly detail-oriented are susceptible to micro-management.

However, *Conscientiousness* at higher levels promotes more effectiveness when the leader is focusing on technical operational details. However, leaders with high levels of *creativity* are less effectual with technical operational details. Strategic leadership, defined by Kaiser and Hogan, is "positioning the organization or unit or team to be competitive in the future, and includes setting direction, expanding capability, and supporting innovation" (p. 222). These authors suggested that strategic leadership is enhanced by creativity and intellectual curiosity, but that *Conscientiousness* detracts from it.

Framework for discussion of implications of personality traits for leader effectiveness.		
Social	Actual effects in specific context or situation	
Desirability	Bright	Dark
Bright	Socially desirable trait has positive implications for leaders and stakeholders *Example:* Conscientious leader displays high ethical standards in pursuing agenda in long-term interest of organization.	Socially desirable trait has negative implications for leaders and stakeholders *Example:* Self-confident (high CSE) leader pursues risky course of action built on overly optimistic assumptions.
Dark	Socially undesirable trait has positive implications for leaders and stakeholders *Example:* Dominant leader takes control of ambiguous situation, and assumes responsibility for the outcome.	Socially undesirable trait has negative implications for leaders and stakeholders *Example:* Narcissistic leader manipulates stock price to coincide with exercise of personal stock options
Note. CSE = core self-evaluation.		

Figure 47. Implications for bright- and dark-side traits. Adapted from Judge et al., 2009, p. 865.

Kaiser and Hogan noted also that the "curvilinear relationship between personality and performance is moderated by excessive behavior—for example, highly assertive managers degrade the morale of their employees ... because they are too forceful: overly controlling, dictatorial, and aggressive" (p. 236). They also found that "Each FFM [Five Factor Model] dimension was associated with overdoing some leader behavior. This highlights a robust role for personality in taking otherwise desirable behaviors and skills to counterproductive extremes" (p. 236).

Interestingly, we found linear, not curvilinear, relationships among a few of our dimensions. For example, thoroughness had a linear relationship with *Individual Consideration,* and *thorough* and *outgoing* had a linear relationship with *Contingent Reward. Thorough* leaders are unlikely to use *Laissez-faire* leadership. *Laissez-faire* leadership is used more by those inclined to *Find Fault* in others. *Satisfaction* is found more when leaders are less inclined to find fault. *Relaxed* and *Outgoing* both have linear relationships in connection with *Idealized Attributes.* The leader's tendency to *Find Fault* is directly associated with greater levels of *Management By Exception-Active. Nervous* leaders tend to use *Idealized Behaviors* but are less likely to use *Inspirational Motivation.*

Bono and Judge (2004) found several Big Five traits with linear relationships with transactional and passive-avoidant leadership. Agreeableness was the strongest predictor of contingent reward; they found neuroticism negatively associated with management-by-exception-passive; agreeableness, extraversion, and conscientiousness were negatively correlated with passive leadership. All these traits had weak correlations, as did ours. Bono and Judge (2004) postulate that both transformational and transactional leadership behaviors "are more malleable, more transient, and less trait-like than one might otherwise believe" (p. 906), because MBA and other training programs often focus on transactional behaviors, which may weaken the behavioral influences of traits. Judge and Bono (2002) did find a moderate correlation of .48 between all Big Five factors and leadership, which suggests that the linear relationships explain only 48% of the variance. We suspect that curvilinear relationships explain much of the 52% that is unexplained. Clearly, more research is needed.

The Goldilocks Paradox - How Much Exercise is "Just Right" for Leaders?

We found paradoxical relationships between exercise and leadership. As expected, significant numbers of executives who do not exercise at all are effective leaders. We learned that the absence of regular leisure exercise habits is associated with effective leadership styles, including *Idealized Attributes, Idealized Behaviors, Inspirational Motivation, Individual Consideration,* and *Contingent Reward.* When any research explains a percentage of variance in relationships, the portion unexplained is attributable to factors that were unexplored. Such is the case with no exercise participation in this study. In striving to understand antecedents to TLB, transactional and passive-avoidant leadership, numerous factors unidentified by us play a role. Without question, exercise habits comprise a small part of the variance in leadership styles; therefore, it is entirely possible for a leader with a sedentary lifestyle to be highly effective.

We also found optimal levels of *Exercise Frequency* and *PRE* for dimensions of leadership associated with effectiveness. *Idealized Attributes* and *Idealized Behaviors* peak at six days per week of exercise. If a leader exercises more frequently than six days per week, these transformational leadership behaviors decline. Seven days per week is the optimal exercise frequency *Contingent Reward* behaviors. Beyond seven days, that behavior declines. The relationship between *Exercise Frequency* and *Intellectual Stimulation*, however, was linear. The more the leader exercises, the greater will be his or her *Intellectual Stimulation* levels. Regarding *PRE*, *Inspirational Motivation* increases with greater intensities of perceived exertion (excluding leaders who do not exercise); however, the point of diminishing returns is just shy of *PRE* at its highest.

We were unable to find research that connects optimal exercise levels to leadership. However, several studies explore curvilinear relationships between exercise and a variety of outcome variables, such as cardiovascular events (Eijsvogels et al., 2016), inflammatory biomarkers (Balakrishnan, Scott, & Oliver, 2016), and fertility (Stephenson, 2006), and found that moderate activity levels are best. The dearth of research on the effects of exercise on leadership may emanate from the assumption that traits explain only a small variance in leadership styles. Perhaps as more scholars explore curvilinear associations between personality traits and leadership, measures of physical and psychological health will receive consideration. Certainly, exercise habits are not traits; they are behaviors. Moreover, exercise as a routine behavioral pattern is associated with psychological well-being (McAuley, Elavsky, Jerome, Konopack, & Marquez, 2005). McAuley et al., (2005) found that self-efficacy was predicted by increases in physical activity and well-being.

Demographic Antecedents

Gender surfaced as a significant predictor of leadership behaviors. Women are more likely than men to use *Idealized Behaviors, Individual Consideration,* and for their leadership to influence *Effectiveness* and *Satisfaction.* This is consistent with the meta-analyses of 45 leadership studies conducted by Eagly, Johannesen-Schmidt, and Van Engen (2003), which concluded that women were more transformational leaders than men. Their study also found that women used *Contingent Reward* more than men, a result that did not emerge from our data.

Results indicate that minorities are more apt than Whites to use *Individual Consideration.* However, Caucasians influence *Satisfaction* more than minorities do. The research of Gundemir, Homan, Dreu, and Vugt (2014) may help explain why minorities are rated as less effective than Caucasians on this effectiveness measure. Their research uncovered a "pro-White" bias, which they surmise accounts for the under-representation of minorities in leadership positions. Finally, the younger the leader, the greater the association is with *Inspirational Motivation.* Most studies that address the age variable concern the effects of leadership on employees belonging to different age cohorts (Myers & Sadaghiani, 2010; Schneid, Isidor, Steinmetz, & Kabst, 2016). However, one study by Zacher, Rosing, Henning, and Frese (2011) found similar connections for more youthful leaders, but rather than a connection to *Inspirational Motivation,* the association was between the age of the leader and follower perceptions of leader effectiveness and extra effort. A final study (Barbuto, Fritz, Matkin, & Marx; 2007) found that younger leaders were more likely to use TLB.

Answering each Research Question

Answers to our main research question emerged from the data. We asked, "In what ways do personality characteristics, demographic characteristics, and leisure exercise habits influence leadership styles?" The answers to all sub-questions, aggregated together, establish an assessment. We provide explicit answers for each in the four subsections that follow.

1. In what ways does a leader's perceived rate of exertion and his or her leisure exercise frequency influence leadership style and leader effectiveness?

Our data suggest that the optimal *PRE* to promote *Inspirational Motivation* is strenuous exercise at just below the maximum perceived intensity. The most advantageous number of days per week to exercise to advance *Idealized Attributes* and *Idealized Behaviors* is six. Seven days per week is the most favorable regularity associated with *Contingent Reward.* Relationships between exercise and other facets of transformational, transactional, or passive-avoidant leadership styles are not salient. Moreover, leaders who do not exercise at all are competent across leadership dimensions associated with effectiveness, including *Idealized Attributes, Idealized Behaviors, Inspirational Motivation, Individual Consideration,* and

Contingent Reward although at slightly lower levels than their counterparts who exercise. Other factors contribute to effective leadership, although exercise does play a role.

2. How do the Big Five personality dimensions influence leadership style and leader effectiveness?

The Big Five Factors go beyond explaining the perceptions held by leaders. They also influence how leadership is executed. The Big Five factors, in relation to their influence on leadership styles and leader effectiveness, are paradoxical. Those normally considered strengths may be weaknesses, while those considered liabilities may be assets under certain conditions. Certainly, there is modest correlation between many of the individual factors and leadership styles. However, when taken together, the bivariate dimensions of openness (*Active Imagination*), agreeableness (*Trust*), extraversion (*Outgoingness*), conscientiousness (*Lazy*), and emotional stability (*Relaxed*) contribute to a multivariate effect to the leadership styles and effectiveness variables that is noteworthy. These dimensions do influence the exercise of *Idealized Attributes, Idealized Behaviors, Intellectual Stimulation, Inspirational Motivation, Extra Effort, Satisfaction*, and *Contingent Reward*.

3. In what ways do demographic factors like supervisory level (firstline, middle, senior manager), age, gender, race, and income influence leadership style and leader effectiveness?

Income does not influence leadership style or leader effectiveness. Managerial level does have a linear association. The other demographic variables have modest correlations. Women, more than men, are likely to behave consistently with the *Behaviors,* and *Individual Consideration* dimensions. Women also perform better than men on *Effectiveness and Satisfaction* factors. Minorities use *Individual Consideration* more than Whites, but Whites affect *Satisfaction* more than minorities do. Younger leaders use more *Inspirational Motivation,* inspiring enthusiasm for accomplishing future goals and realizing the organizational vision.

4. In what ways do the perceptions of leader effectiveness and leadership style differ between leaders and their employees?

Employee and leader perceptions concerning leadership styles and leader effectiveness are congruent when examined across most of the 45 MLQ dimensions. This was expected because we assumed that successful leaders tend to have accurate self-assessments. The congruence aligns with the association between self-awareness and performance, established through the research of Atwater and Yammarino (1992).

SIGNIFICANCE OF AND RECOMMENDATIONS FOR APPLICATION

Caution is warranted whenever physical characteristics are discussed in connection with leadership. Prior research has demonstrated followers' preferences for physically formidable leaders, either in association with height, weight, body mass index, gender, and physical strength (Murray, 2014), "because of evolutionary adaptations derived from humans' violent ancestral environment" (p. 33). This innate preference implies a predilection toward discrimination, which is a dangerous and detrimental bias harmful to both organizations and society. Diversity provides critical benefits. For example, through simultaneous equation modeling, Isidro and Sobral (2015) found that "Women on the board [of directors] are positively related with financial performance (measured in terms of return on assets and return on sales) and with ethical and social compliance, which in turn are positively related with firm value" (p. 1). Moreover, upcoming leaders, albeit children currently in school, recent college graduates, or employees wishing to advance into management, need role models to give credibility to their belief in promising career paths. Therefore, any discussions of leader fitness and health should be bounded by two assumptions. The first is that any recommendation begins with a diverse workforce. Second, exercise is one of many methods one may use to reduce stress, improve well-being, and in the circumstances found herein, advance leadership styles that align with the demands of the business environment.

    Some companies use assessments, such as the Big Five inventory, in both selection and training. Decision makers should remain open to the connections between the strength of each dimension in association with the desired leadership styles and leader effectiveness dimensions. Unknown is the extent to which a desired behavioral change associated with personality is attainable. According to Costa and McCrea (2002), personality is mostly set in later life; however, Roberts (2006) found that "personality traits have to develop and can change, even in adulthood" (p. 5). Roberts' conceptual model posits that several factors influence personality change in maturity, including genes, motives and values, abilities, narratives ("significant memories, scripts, and stories"), identity ("self-reports and conscious, subjective experience"), reputation, roles ("status and belongingness"), and culture (p. 6). However, training in self-regulation provides a path to changes in traits that are associated with desired behavioral outcomes. Baumeister, Muraven, and Tice (2000) suggest that, "Human beings are set apart from all other earthly creatures by the high extent of their exceptional capacity to control and regulate their own behavior" (p. 131). Shiffrin and Schneider (1977) proposed a method for teaching self-regulation, which involves learning how to interfere with automatic responses through controlled processing to focus attention on a desired behavior.

It makes sense to select and develop leaders so their traits match the demands of the situation. Judge et al., (2009) said, "We recognize the interplay of traits and context, describing both the positive and negative consequences of socially desirable (and undesirable) traits" (p. 871). For example, conscientiousness (the *Thorough* variable in our study) is observed in leaders who are self-disciplined in working to achieve goals, efficient in how they approach their work, "detailed-oriented, deliberate in their decision-making, and polite in most interpersonal interactions" (Judge et al., 2009, p. 865-865). Since clearly defined goals and role expectations are communicated by conscientious leaders, there is a natural alignment with *Contingent Reward* behaviors. Extraversion (the construct represented by our *Outgoing* variable) was also associated with *Contingent Reward*, which aligns well with the act of communicating goals and expectations clearly. In business situations that dictate *Contingent Reward* behaviors, such as the need to emphasize technical operational details, it is prudent to select leaders with these traits and/or develop more of these traits through self-regulation. It follows that leaders with high *Creativity* levels may not fit these circumstances.

In other situations, such as those in which innovation and creativity are demanded, leaders with strategic planning and visioning capabilities should be selected or developed through training that emphasizes self-regulation. Selecting and developing creative leaders under the assumption of a dynamic external environment would be a better fit. Research suggests that transformational leaders are best suited to environments perceived to face high environmental uncertainty (Waldman, Ramirez, House, & Puranam, 2001). As such, the Big Five traits that align with the transformational leadership style are best. All passive-avoidant leadership styles are less desirable. As such, it would be wise to avoid hiring leaders with personality characteristics associated with *Laissez-faire* and *Management By Exception-Passive* styles. If current leaders possess these traits (i.e., lazy, little creativity, find fault in others), we suggest training in self-regulation to reduce them plus developing those traits associated with the styles dictated by the situation. The recruitment and development plan should align with the business situation.

Turning to exercise, we do not recommend hiring or training leaders based on physical fitness or their leisure conditioning routines. Such actions would be immoral and discriminatory. Moreover, our data show that many successful leaders do not exercise at all. However, we do propose that organizations make formal efforts to promote and encourage exercise, because we found correlations between exercise at specific levels (i.e., six days or seven days per week depending on the desired leadership style and effectiveness measure) and desired leadership styles and effectiveness outcomes. Organizations could provide employee benefit packages that include gym memberships, or even build workout facilities onsite, for example. Flexible schedules, which encourage making time to tend to fitness needs, could become the norm in many organizations. Finally, organizations could educate leaders and employees concerning optimal levels of *PRE,* and encourage their consultation with medical professionals to determine the intensity best suited to their individual needs and circumstances.

RESEARCHER REFLECTIONS (BIASES AND ASSUMPTIONS)

Both of us have participated in strenuous exercise for years, albeit running, hot yoga, or CrossFit®. We both also enjoy mild exercise, such as distance walking. Regardless, we believe that regular exercise routines lead to physical and psychological benefits, which is a bias we brought to the study. Despite our personal preferences, our research methods were sound. The data presented some relationships that challenged us to remain impartial. For example, the strength of relationships among exercise and favorable leadership behaviors was significant, but modest. Many of the best leaders, as measured by *Effectiveness, Satisfaction,* and *Extra Effort,* do not exercise at all. Notwithstanding our biases, we learned from our findings and embrace the knowledge uncovered through our study.

Suggestions for Future Research

Our research offered initial answers to our questions. However, certain relationships between Big Five factors and transformational leadership behaviors were perplexing, and deserve further study. We would like to see exploratory research that examines the "why" question behind some unexpected findings. For example, future studies could explore why *Idealized Attributes* is observed when the leader's *Active Imagination* is low. It is more intuitive to see more intensity of *Idealized Attributes* at higher levels of *Active Imagination*, but it mystified us to learn that low levels are associated with this desired leadership behavior. Although *Extra Effort* is highest when *Active Imagination* is also at its highest point, it is confusing to know that *Extra Effort* decreases as *Active Imagination* increases toward its highest point. Another interesting question is to uncover the reasons why higher levels of neuroticism are associated with *Idealized Behaviors*, or why when leaders are very relaxed they use more *Contingent Reward*. We wonder whether situational conditions factor into these relationships, and/or if there are components of each Big Five construct that dominate the influence each has on these relationships.

Much of the variance in how demographics, exercise habits, and personality traits relate to leadership styles and leader effectiveness remains unexplained. We would like to see scholars identify and investigate unknown predictors of the dependent variables. More research is needed also on how organizations can better train leaders to behave consistent with leadership styles dictated by business conditions. Repeating our current study with a larger sample size may uncover nuanced relationships that a smaller sample cannot uncover. We would like to see a larger minority representation included in the sample also, to tease out nuanced differences among all minority groups. Moreover, research that delves deeper into exploring why and what about traits and exercise makes a connection to leadership salient could offer new perspectives. Research on leaders across multiple cultures could help determine the extent to which our findings are specific to the United States' and Western cultures. Finally, we would like to see future studies explore isolated and specific types of exercise, through large samples of each exercise form, and at a range of frequencies and intensities that influence leadership styles.

SUMMARY AND CONCLUSION

We intended to learn mostly about antecedents to transformational, transactional, and passive-avoidant leadership. We hypothesized curvilinear relationships between leisure exercise habits, Big Five personality dimensions, and leadership styles and leader effectiveness. We also surmised linear relationships between demographic characteristics and the outcome variables. The data supported most of our hypotheses. Comparing our data to the findings in related studies piqued our interest in examining the importance of situational leadership on our outcomes variables. Aligning leadership styles to the conditions dictated by the external environment is important because TLB is not the most effective leadership style all the time. When the focus should be on technical operational details, transactional leadership makes sense. In dynamic, rapidly changing conditions, transformational leadership is a better fit. We are hard-pressed to find conditions in which passive-avoidant leadership is recommended. Regardless, we learned the complex relationships between personality, exercise habits, demographics, and leadership behaviors and leader effectiveness. We offered recommendations for application, which included selection and training strategies that involve self-regulation and self-monitoring. We hope all interested scholars carry our research agenda forward.

[6]

FURTHER READING

We ask the authors of our mini-monographs to provide a minimum of three titles of supplementary materials they consider essential reading pertaining to the subject they wrote about. It is hoped that the title you just read sparked your curiosity and interest in further study. Dr. Himelhoch and Dr. Raymond suggest the following papers and books.

Suggested Reading

Dossey, L. (2000). *Reinventing medicine: Beyond mind-body to a new era of healing*. San Francisco, CA: HarperOne.

Himelhoch, C. R. (2014). *Transformational leadership and high-intensity interval training*. Spring Lake, MI: MindBodyMed Press.

Pearce, C. L. (2007). The future of leadership development: The importance of identity, multi-level approaches, self-leadership, physical fitness, shared leadership, networking, creativity, emotions, spirituality and on-boarding processes. *Human Resource Management Review, 17*(4), 355–359.

Tabrizi, B. & Terrell, M. (2013). The inside-out effect: A practical guide to transformational leadership. Ashland, OH: Evolve Publishing, Inc.

Essential Reading

Ames, D., Flynn, F., & Carver, Charles S. (2007). What breaks a leader: The curvilinear relation between assertiveness and leadership. *Journal of Personality and Social Psychology*, 92(2), 307-324.

Bass, B. M. (1996). *A new paradigm for leadership: An inquiry into transformational leadership.* Alexandria, VA: U.S. Army Research Institute for the Behavioral and Social Sciences.

Chang, Y.K, Labban, J.D., Gapin, J.I., & Etnier, J.L. (2012). The effects of acute exercise on cognitive performance: A meta-analysis. *Brain Research*, 1453, 87-101.

Eisenbeiß, S., & Boerner, S. (2010). Transformational leadership and R&D innovation: Taking a curvilinear approach. *Creativity and Innovation Management*, 19(4), 364-372.

Goleman, D., Boyatzis, R. E., & McKee, A. (2002). *The new leaders: Transforming the art of leadership into the science of results.* London, GB: Little, Brown.

Hwang, J., Brothers, R. M, Castelli, D.M, Glowacki, E.M., Chen, Y.T., Salinas, M.M, Kim, J., Yeonhak, J., & Calvert, H.G. (2016). Acute high-intensity exercise-induced cognitive enhancement and brain-derived neurotrophic factor in young, healthy adults. *Neuroscience Letters*, 630(C), 247-253.

Kaiser, R., LeBreton, J., & Hogan, J. (2015). The dark side of personality and extreme leader behavior. *Applied Psychology*, 64(1), 55-92.

Yucel, I., McMillan, A., & Richard O.C. (2014). Does CEO transformational leadership influence top executive normative commitment? *Journal of Business Research*, 67(6), 1170-1177.

Yukl, G. (1989). Managerial leadership: A review of theory and research. *Journal of Management*, 15(2), 251-289.

[7]

REFERENCES

Ames, D. R., & Flynn, F. J. (2007). What breaks a leader: the curvilinear relation between assertiveness and leadership. *Journal of personality and social psychology*, 92(2), 307.

Antonaros, M.E. (2010). Gender differences in leadership style: A study of leader effectiveness in higher education. Retrieved from ProQuest. (AAI3406225).

Astin, H.S., & Leland, C. (1991). *Women of influence, women of vision: A cross-generational study of leaders and social change.* San Francisco, CA: Jossey-Bass.

Atwater, L.E., Dionne, S.D., Camobreco, J.F., Avolio, B.J., & Lau, A. (1998). Individual attributes and leadership style: Predicting the use of punishment and its effects. *Journal of Organizational Behavior*, 19(6), 559-576.

Atwater, L. E., & Yammarino, F. J. (1992). Does self-other agreement on leadership perceptions moderate the validity of leadership and performance predictions? *Personnel Psychology*, 45(1), 141-164.

Atwater, L.E. & Yammarino, F.J. (1993). Personal attributes as predictors of superiors' and subordinates' perceptions of military academy leadership. *Human Relations*, 46, 645-668.

Avolio, B.J. (2011). *Full range leadership* (2nd ed.). Thousand Oaks, CA: Sage.

Avolio, B.J., & Bass, B.M. (2004). Multifactor leadership questionnaire (MLQ, 3rd ed.) [Manual and sample set]. Menlo Park, CA: Mind Garden, Inc.

Avolio, B., & Bass, B.M. (1988). *Transformational leadership, charisma and beyond.* In J. G. Hunt, B. R. Balaga, H. P. Dachler, & C. Schriesheim (Eds.), Emerging Leadership Vistas (pp. 29-50). Elmsford, NY: Pergamon.

Avolio, B.J., Bass, B.M., & Jung, D.I. (1999). Re-examining the components of transformational and transactional leadership questionnaire. *Journal of Occupational and Organizational Psychology*, 72(4), 441-462.

Balakrishnan, K., Scott, P., & Oliver, L. (2016). A confluence of circumstances: A case of IVF, extreme exercise and spontaneous coronary artery dissection. *International Journal of Cardiology*, 23, 76-77.

Barbuto, J. E., Fritz, S. M., Matkin, G. S., & Marx, D. B. (2007). Effects of gender, education, and age upon leaders' use of influence tactics and full range leadership behaviors. *Sex Roles*, 56(2), 71-83.

Barling, J., Lys, R., Bergenwall, A., Byren, A., Dioniski, A., Dupre, K., Robertson, J., & Wylie, J. (2012, March 23). *Being well, leading well? Leaders' psychological distress predicts leadership behaviors.* Paper presented at The University of Michigan, Interdisciplinary Committee on Organizational Studies, Ann Arbor, MI.

Bass, B.M. (1985). *Leadership and performance beyond expectations.* New York, NY: Free Press.

Bass, B.M., Waldman, D. A., Avolio, B.J., & Bebb, M. (1987). Transformational leadership: The falling dominoes effect. *Group and Organization Studies*, 24, 73-87.

Bass, B.M. & Bass, R. (2008). *The Bass handbook of leadership: Theory, research, and managerial applications* (4th ed.). New York, NY: Free Press.

Bass, B.M. (1990). *Bass & Stogdill's handbook of leadership: Theory, research, & managerial applications* (3rd ed.). New York, NY: Free Press.

Bass, B.M. (1997). Does the transactional-transformational leadership paradigm transcend organizational and national boundaries? *The American Psychologist*, 52(2), 130-139.

Basu, R., & Green, S.G. (1997). Leader-member exchange and transformational leadership: An empirical examination of innovative behaviors in leader-member dyads. *Journal of Applied Social Psychology*, 27, 477–499.

Baumeister, R. F., Muraven, M., & Tice, D. M. (2000). Ego depletion: A resource model of volition, self-regulation, and controlled processing. *Social Cognition*, 18, 130–150. doi:10.1521/soco.2000.18.2.130

Belcher, B. M., Rasmussen, K. E., Kemshaw, M. R., & Zornes, D. A. (2016). Defining and assessing research quality in a transdisciplinary context. *Research Evaluation*, 25(1), 1-17.

Beng-Chong, L., & Ployhart, R.E. (2004). Transformational leadership: Relations to the Five-Factor Model and team performance in typical and maximum contexts. *Journal of Applied Psychology*, 89(4), 610-621.

Bensimon, E.M. & Neumann, A. (1993). *Redesigning collegiate leadership: Teams and teamwork in higher education*. Baltimore, MD: The Johns Hopkins University Press.

Bensimon, E., Neumann, A. & Birnbaum, R. (1989). Making sense of administrative leadership: The "L" word in higher education. ASHE-ERIC Higher Education Report 1. Washington, D.C.: School of Education and Human Development, George Washington University.

Billing, Y.D., & Alvesson, M. (1994). *Gender, managers, and organizations*. Berlin, Germany: de Gruyter.

Birnbaum, R. (1989). The implicit leadership theories of college and university presidents. *The Review of Higher Education*, 12(2), 125-136.

Bono, J.E., & Judge, T.A. (2004). Personality and transformational and transactional leadership: A meta-analysis. *Journal of Applied Psychology*, 89, 901-910.

Bommer, W. H., Rubin, R. S., & Baldwin, T. T. (2004). Setting the stage for effective leadership: Antecedents of transformational leadership behavior. *Leadership Quarterly*, 15,195-210.

Bowen, W.G., & Shapiro, H.T. (1998). *Universities and their leadership*. Princeton, NJ: Princeton University Press.

Burns, J.M. (1978). *Leadership*. New York, NY: Harper & Row.

Bushman, B. A. (2016). Finding the Balance Between Overload and Recovery. *ACSM's Health & Fitness Journal*, 20(1), 5-8.

Brown, D. M., & Bray, S. R. (2015). Isometric exercise and cognitive function: an investigation of acute dose-response effects during submaximal fatiguing contractions. *Journal of Sports Sciences*, 33(5), 487-497.

Cable, D.M., & Judge, T.A. (2003). Managers' upward influence tactic strategies: The role of manager personality and supervisor leadership style. *Journal of Organizational Behavior*, 24(2), 197-214.

Cantor, D., & Bernay, T. (1992). *Women in power*. New York, NY: Houghton Mifflin.

Camps, S. G., Verhoef, S. P., & Westerterp, K. R. (2016). Physical activity and weight loss are independent predictors of improved insulin sensitivity following energy restriction. *Obesity*, 24(2), 291-296. doi: 10.1002/oby.21325

Cattell, R. B. (1943). The description of personality: Basic traits resolved into clusters. *Journal of Abnormal and Social Psychology*, 38, 476-506.

Chaplin, W.F., John, O.P., & Goldberg, L.R. (1988). Conceptions of states and traits: Dimensional attributes with ideals as prototypes. *Journal of Personality and Social Psychology*, 54, 541-557.

Colbert, A.E., Kristof-Brown, A.L., Bradley, B.H., & Barrick, M.R. (2008). CEO transformational leadership: The role of goal importance congruence in top management teams. *The Academy of Management Journal*, 51(1), 81-96.

Clark, K.D. & Waldron, T. (2016). Early career white-collar professionals: The roles of personal characteristics and career context. *Journal of Leadership and Organizational Studies*, 23(1), 27-38. doi: 10.1177/1548051815587759

Conger J.A, & Kanungo, R.N (1987). Toward a behavioral theory of charismatic leadership in organizational settings. *Academy of Management Review*, 12, 637–647.

Costa, P. T., Jr., & McCrae, R. R. (2002). *Looking backward: Changes in the mean levels of personality traits from 80 to 12*. In D. Cervone & W. Mischel (Eds.), Advances in personality science (p. 219–237). New York, NY: Guilford Press.

Creswell, J. W. (2009). *Research design: Qualitative, quantitative, and mixed method approaches* (3rd ed.). Los Angeles, CA: Sage.

Dansereau, F., Yammarino, F.J., & Markham, S.E. (1995). Leadership: The multiple-level approaches. *Leadership Quarterly*, 6, 97–110.

De Hoogh, A.H.B., Hartog, D.N.D., & Koopman, P.L. (2005). Linking the Big-Five factors of personality to charismatic and transactional leadership; perceived dynamic work environment as a moderator. *Journal of Organizational Behavior*, 26(7), 839-865.

DeRue, D. S., Nahrgang, J. D., Wellman, N., & Humphrey, S. E. (2011). Trait and behavioral theories of leadership: A meta-analytic test of their relative validity. *Personnel Psychology*, 64, 7–52. doi:10.1111/j.1744-6570.2010.01201.x

Eagly, A. H., Johannesen-Schmidt, M. C., & van Engen, M. L. (2003). Transformational, transactional, and laissez-faire leadership styles: A meta-analysis comparing women and men. *Psychological bulletin*, 129(4), 569.

Eagly, A.H., Karau, S.J. & Makhijani, M.G. (1995). Gender and the effectiveness of leaders: A meta-analysis. *Psychological Bulletin*, 117, 125-145.

Eagly, A.H., Makhijani, M.G., & Klonsky, B.G. (1992). Gender and the evaluation of leaders: A meta-analysis. *Psychological Bulletin*, 111, 3-22.

Eijsvogels, T. M., Molossi, S., Lee, D. C., Emery, M. S., & Thompson, P. D. (2016). Exercise at the extremes: The amount of exercise to reduce cardiovascular events. *Journal of the American College of Cardiology*, 67(3), 316-329.

Female executives say participation in sport helps accelerate leadership and career potential. (2014, October 10). Retrieved from the Women Athletes Business Network website at https://www.prnewswire.com/news-releases/female-executives-say-participation-in-sport-helps-accelerate-leadership-and-career-potential-278614041.html

Foels, R., Driskell, J.E., Mullen, B., & Salas, E. (2000). The effects of democratic leadership on group member satisfaction: Integration. *Small Group Research*, 31, 676-701.

Foster, C. (1998). Monitoring training in athletes with reference to overtraining syndrome. *Medicine and Science in Sports and Exercise*, 30(7), 1164-1168.

Furtner, M.R., Baldegger, U., & Rauthmann, J.F. (2013). Leading yourself and leading others: Linking self-leadership to transformational, transactional, and laissez-faire leadership. *European Journal of Work and Organizational Psychology*, 22(4), 436-449.

Gastil, J. (1994). A meta-analytic review of the productivity and satisfaction of democratic and autocratic leadership. *Small Group Research*, 25, 384-410.

Gay, J.L., Buchner, D.M. & Schmidt, M.D. (2016 in press). Dose-response association of physical activity with HbA1c: Intensity and bout length. *Preventative Medicine*. doi:10.1016/j.ypmed.2016.01.008.

Goldberg, L. R. (1993). The structure of phenotypic personality traits. *American Psychologist* 48: 26–34. doi:10.1037/0003-066x.48.1.26

Giuli, C., Papa, R., Marcellini, F., Boscaro, M., Faloia, E., Lattanzio, F., ... & Bevilacqua, R. (2016). The role of psychological well-being in obese and overweight older adults. *International Psychogeriatrics*, 28(01), 171-172.

Gundemir, S., Homan, A.C., Dreu, K.W., & Vugt, M.V. (2014). Think leader, think white? Capturing and weakening an implicit pro-white leadership bias. *PLOS One*, 9(1), e83915, doi:10.1371/journal.pone.0083915.

Harms, P.D., & Credé, M. (2010). Emotional intelligence and transformational and transactional leadership: A meta-analysis. *Journal of Leadership and Organizational Studies*, 17(1), 5-17.

Harris, K. J., & Russell, L. M. (2013). An Investigation of the Curvilinear Effects of Contingent Reward Leadership on Stress-Related and Attitudinal Outcomes. *International Journal of Business and Social Science*, 4(10).

Heck, R.H., & Marcoulides, G.A. (1996). School culture and performance: Testing the invariance of an organizational model. *School Effectiveness and School Improvement*, 7(1), 76-95.

Harolds, J. A. (2016). Quality and Safety in Health Care, Part VII: Lower Costs and Higher Quality. *Clinical Nuclear Medicine*, 41(2), 134-136.

Hereford, J.M. (2012). Enough is enough: The curvilinear relationship between personality and leadership (Doctoral Dissertation). Retrieved from ProQuest Dissertations and Theses. (Accession 3503991).

Himelhoch, C.R. (2014). *Transformational leadership and high-intensity interval training.* Spring Lake, MI: MindBodyMed Press, LLC.

Howell, J.M., & Avolio, B.J. (1993). Transformational leadership, transactional leadership, locus of control, and support for innovation: Key predictors of consolidated-business-unit performance. *Journal of Applied Psychology*, 78(6), 891-902.

Helgesen, S. (1995). *The web of inclusion.* New York, NY: Currency/Doubleday.

Hughes, R.L., Ginnett, R.C, & Curphy, G.J. (1999). *Leadership: Enhancing the lessons of experiences.* Sydney, Australia: McGraw-Hill.

Hunt, J.G. & Conger, J.A. (1999). From where we sit: An assessment of transformational and charismatic leadership research. *The Leadership Quarterly*, 10, 335–343.

Isidro, H. & Sobral, M. (2015). The effects of women on corporate boards on firm value, financial performance, and ethical and social compliance. *Journal of Business Ethics*, 132, 1-19. doi: 10.1007/s10551-014-2302-9.

Jette, M., Sidney, K., & Blümchen, G. (1990). Metabolic equivalents (METS) in exercise testing, exercise prescription, and evaluation of functional capacity. *Clinical cardiology*, 13(8), 555-565.

Jin, S., Seo, M.G., & Shapiro, D.L. (2016). Do happy leaders lead better? Affective and attitudinal antecedents of transformational leadership. *The Leadership Quarterly*, 27(1), 64-84.

John, O. P., & Srivastava, S. (1999). *The Big-Five trait taxonomy: History, measurement, and theoretical perspectives*. In L. A. Pervin & O. P. John (Eds.), Handbook of personality: Theory and research (Vol. 2, p. 102–138). New York, NY: Guilford Press.

Judge, T. A., Bono, J. E., Ilies, R., & Gerhardt, M. W. (2002). Personality and leadership: a qualitative and quantitative review. *Journal of Applied Psychology*, 87(4), 765.

Judge, T. A., Piccolo, R. F., & Kosalka, T. (2009). The bright and dark sides of leader traits: A review and theoretical extension of the leader trait paradigm. *Leadership Quarterly*, 20, 855–875. doi:10.1016/j.leaqua.2009.09.004

Judge, T.A., & Piccolo, R.F. (2004). Transformational and transactional leadership: A meta-analytic test of their relative validity. *Journal of Applied Psychology*, 89(5), 755-768.

Jung, D.I., & Avolio, B.J. (2000). Opening the black box: An experimental investigation of the mediating effects of trust and value congruence on transformational and transactional leadership. *Journal of Organizational Behavior*, 21(8), 949-964.

Kaiser, R. B., & Kaplan, R. E. (2005). Overlooking overkill? Beyond the 1-to-5 rating scale. *Human Resources Planning*, 28, 7–11.

Kernan, M. C., Racicot, B. M., & Fisher, A. M. (2016). Effects of Abusive supervision, psychological climate, and felt violation on work outcomes: A moderated mediated model. *Journal of Leadership & Organizational Studies*, 23(3), 309–321. https://doi.org/10.1177/1548051815627358

Kezar, A. (2000). Pluralistic leadership: Incorporating diverse voices. *Journal of Higher Education*, 71(6), 722-743.

Kim, S. & Yoon, G. (2015). An innovation-driven culture in local government: Do senior manager's transformational leadership and the climate for creativity matter? *Public Personnel Management,* 44(2), 147-168.

Kuhn, P., & Weinberger, C. (2005). Leadership skills and wages. *Journal of Labor Economics*, 23(2), 395-436.

Jin. S., Seo, M.G. & Shapiro, D.L. (2016). Do happy leaders lead better? Affective and attitudinal antecedents of transformational leadership. *The Leadership Quarterly*, 27(1), 64-84.

Kaiser, R.B., Hogan, J. (2011). Personality, leader behavior, and overdoing it. *Consulting Psychology Journal: Practice and Research*, 63 (4), 219-242.

Lawler, E. E. (2008). *Make human capital a source of competitive advantage* (Working paper No. MOR 16-09). Los Angeles, CA: USC-Marshall School of Business. Retrieved from http://www.ssrn.com/abstract=1311431

Levine, K.J., Muenchen, R.A., & Brooks, A.M. (2010). Measuring transformational and charismatic leadership: Why isn't charisma measured? *Communication Monographs,* 77(4), 576-591.

Lowe, K. B., Kroeck, K. G., & Sivasubramaniam, N. (1996). Effectiveness correlates of transformation and transactional leadership: A metaanalytic review of the MLQ literature. *Leadership Quarterly*, 7, 385- 425.

Lord, R. G., DeVader, C. L., & Alliger, G. (1986). A meta-analysis of the relation between personality traits and leader perceptions. *Journal of Applied Psychology*, 71, 402–410. doi:10.1037/0021-9010.71.3.402

Martin, J., & Samels, J.E. (1997). *First among equals: The role of the chief academic officer.* Baltimore, MD: Johns Hopkins University Press.

McAuley, E., Elavsky, S., Jerome, J.J., Konopack, J.F., & Marquez, D.X. (2005). Physical activity-related well-being in older adults: Social cognitive influences. *Psychology and Aging,* 20(2), 295.

McDowell-Larsen, S.L., Kearney, L., & Campbell, D. (2002). Fitness and leadership: Is there a relationship? Regular exercise correlates with higher leadership ratings in senior-level executives. *Journal of Managerial Psychology*, 17(4), 312-324.

Marcoulides, G.A. & Heck, R.H. (1993). Examining administrative leadership behavior: A comparison of principals and assistant principals. *Journal of Personnel Evaluation in Education*, 7(1), 81-94.

Murray, G.R. (2014). Evolutionary preferences for physically formidability in leaders. *Politics and the Life Sciences*, 33(1), 33-53.

Myers, K.M & Sadaghiani, K. (2010). Millennials in the workplace: A communication perspective on Millennials' organizational relationships and performance. *Journal of Business and Psychology*, 25(2): 225–238. https://doi.org/10.1007/s10869-010-9172-7

Nanjundeswaras, T.S., & Swamy, D.R. (2014). Leadership styles. *Advances in Management* 7(2), 57-62.

Neuman, W. L. (2006). *Social research methods: Qualitative and quantitative methods* (6th ed.). Boston, MA: Pearson.

Omar, A., & Davidson, M.J. (2001). Women in management: A comparative cross-cultural overview, *International Journal of Cross Cultural Management*, 8(3/4), 35-67.

Oshagbemi, T. (2004). Age influences on the leadership styles and behavior of managers. *Employee Relations*, 26(1/2), 14-29.

Pike, G.R. (1994). *Applications of generalizability theory in higher education assessment research.* In J.C. Smart (Ed.), Higher education: Handbook of theory and research (Vol. 10, p. 45-87). New York, NY: Agathon Press.

Pitner, N.J. (1988). *The study of administrator effects and effectiveness.* In N. Boyan (Ed.), The handbook of research in educational administration (p. 99-122). New York, NY: Longman.

Pinto-Bastos, A., Ramalho, S. M., Conceição, E., & Mitchell, J. (2016). *Disordered Eating and Obesity. Obesity* , 309-319.

Ployhart, R. E., Lim, B., & Chan, K. (2001). Exploring relations between typical and maximum performance ratings and the Five-Factor Model of personality. *Personnel Psychology*, 54, 809-843.

Rammstedt, B. & John, O.P. (2007). Measuring personality in one minute or less: A 10-item short version of the Big Five Inventory in English and German. *Journal of Research in Personality*, 41, 203-212.

Rice, R., Yoder, J., Adams, J., Priest, R. and Prince, H. (1984). Leadership ratings for male and female military cadets. *Sex Roles*, 10, 885-901.

Roberts, B. W. (2006). Personality development and organizational behavior. In B. M. Staw (Ed.), *Research in organizational behavior: An annual series of analytical essays and critical reviews* (1st ed., Vol. 27, pp. 1–41). Amsterdam, NL: JAI Press. Retrieved from http://site.ebrary.com/id/10186132

Rosener, J.B. (1990). Ways women lead. *Harvard Business Review*, 68(6), 119-125.

Ross, S.M., & Offermann, L.R. (1997). Transformational leaders: Measurement of personality attributes and work group performance. *Personality and Social Psychology Bulletin*, 23, 1078-1086.

Rosser, V.J. (2003). Faculty and staff members' perceptions of effective leadership: Are there differences between women and men leaders? *Equity and Excellence in Education*, 36(1), 71-81.

Schneid, M., Isidor, R., Steinmetz, H., & Kabst, R. (2016). Age diversity and team outcomes: a quantitative review. *Journal of Managerial Psychology*, 31(1).

Shakeshaft, C. (1987). *Women in educational administration*. Newbury Park, CA: Sage.

Shakeshaft, C. (1999). The struggle to create a more gender inclusive profession. In J. Murphy, & K.S. Louis, & American Educational Research Association (Eds.), *Handbook of research on educational administration: A project of the American Educational Research Association* (2nd ed., pp. 99-118). San Francisco, CA: Jossey-Bass Publishers.

Shamir, B., House, R.J., & Arthur, M.B. (1993). The motivational effects of charismatic leadership: A self-concept based theory. *Organization Science*, 4(4), 577-594.

Shamir, B. & Howell, J.M. (1999). Organizational and contextual influences on the emergence and effectiveness of charismatic leadership. *The Leadership Quarterly*, 10, 257–283.

Shiffrin, R. M., & Schneider, W. (1977). Controlled and automatic human information processing: II. Perceptual learning, automatic attending, and a general theory. *Psychological Review*, 84, 127–190. doi:10.1037/0033-295X.84.2.127

Smith, K. B., & Smith, M. S. (2016). Obesity statistics. *Primary Care: Clinics in Office Practice*, 43(1), 121-135. doi:10.1016/j.pop.2015.10.001

Sauermann, H., & Roach, M. (2013). Increasing web survey response rates in innovation research: An experimental study of static and dynamic contact design features. *Research Policy*, 42(1), 273-286.

Sparks, J.R., & Schenk, J.A. (2001). Explaining the effects of transformational leadership: An investigation of the effects of higher-order motives in multilevel marketing organizations. *Journal of Organizational Behavior*, 22(8), 849-869.

Stephenson, J. (2006). Extreme exercise and fertility. *JAMA*, 296(19), 340-346.

Statham, A. (1987). The gender model revisited: Differences in the management styles of men and women. *Sex Roles*, 16(7-8), 409-430.

Taylor, S. N., Wang, M., & Zhan, Y. (2012). Going beyond self-other rating comparison to measure leader self-awareness. *Journal of Leadership Studies*, 6(2), 6–31. https://doi.org/10.1002/jls.21235

Vroom, V.H., & Yetton, P.W. (1973). *Leadership and decision-making*. Pittsburgh, PA: University of Pittsburgh Press.

Waldman, D. A., Ramirez, G. G., House, R. J., & Puranam, P. (2001). Does leadership matter? CEO leadership attributes and profitability under conditions of perceived environmental uncertainty. *Academy of Management Journal*, 44(1), 134-143.

Waldman, D.A., & Yammarino, F.J. (1999). CEO charismatic leadership: Levels-of-management and levels-of-analysis effects. *The Academy of Management Review*, 24(2), 266-285.

Walter, F., & Bruch, H. (2009). An affective events model of charismatic leadership behavior: A review, theoretical integration, and research agenda. *Journal of Management*, 35(6), 1428-1452.

White, J. (2014, Feb. 14). CrossFit® calories burned. Retrieved from http://creationbasedhealth.com/crossfit-calories-burned/.

Yukl, G. (2006). *Leadership in organizations*. 6th edition. Upper Saddle River, NJ: Pearson Prentice Hall.

Zacher, H., Rosing, K., Henning, T., & Frese, M. (2011). Establishing the next generation at work: leader generativity as a moderator of the relationships between leader age, leader-member exchange, and leadership success. *Psychology and Aging*, 26(1), 241.

[8]

APPENDIX

TABLE 2

Participants' Gender by Position

Position	Male/Percent	Female/Percent	Total/Percent
First-Line Supervisor	28/62%	17/38%	45/26%
Middle Manager	43/74%	15/26%	58/33%
Senior Manager	53/75%	18/25%	71/41%
Totals (N = 173)	124/71%	50/29%	174/100%

TABLE 3

Participants' Age by Position

Position	18-24	25-34	35-44	45-54	55-64	65-74	75 +	Total
First-Line Supervisor	1	7	13	9	12	2	1	45
Middle Manager	1	7	14	17	16	1	1	57
Senior Manager	0	1	5	30	34	2	0	71
Totals/ Percent (N = 173)	2/1%	15/9%	32/18%	55/32%	62/36%	5/3%	2/1%	174/100%

Carol R. Himelhoch and Mary Antonaros Raymond

TABLE 4

Participants' Race by Position

Position	White/Percent	Black or African American/ Percent	From Multiple Races/ Percent	Total/Percent
First-Line Supervisor	44/98%	1/2%	0/0%	45/26%
Middle Manager	55/95%	1/2%	2/3%	58/34%
Senior Manager	68/96%	3/4%	0/0%	71/40%
Totals (N = 173)	167/96%	5/3%	2/1%	174/100%

TABLE 5

Work-Site Location of Leaders Surveyed

Location	Frequency	Percent
Alabama	1	1%
All of the United States	8	5%
Arkansas	1	1%
California	4	2%
Connecticut	4	2%
Florida	2	1%
France	1	1%
Illinois	20	12%
Indiana	12	7%
Italy	1	1%
Kansas	1	1%
Massachusetts	3	2%
Maryland	1	1%
Michigan	44	25%
Nebraska	1	1%
Missouri	8	5%
North Carolina	11	6%
New Jersey	2	1%
Ohio	21	12%
Oregon	1	1%
Pennsylvania	18	11%
Texas	3	2%
Virginia	1	1%
Wisconsin	1	1%
Worldwide	1	1%
Total	171	100%

TABLE 6

Industries Employing Leaders in the Survey

Industry	Frequency	Percent
Administration of Economic Programs	1	.6
Administration of Environmental Quality and Housing Programs	1	.6
Administration of Human Resource Programs	2	1.1
Amusement and Recreation Services	5	2.9
Apparel, Finished Prdcts from Fabrics & Similar Materials	1	.6
Automotive Dealers and Gasoline Service Stations	1	.6
Building Construction -General Contractors & Operative Builders	2	1.1
Business Services, Marketing, Advertising	9	5.1
Chemicals and Allied Products	5	2.9
Communications	1	.6
Construction - Special Trade Contractors	2	1.1
Depository Institutions	1	.6
Eating and Drinking Places	3	1.7
Educational Services	6	3.4
Electric, Gas and Sanitary Services	2	1.1
Electronic, Elctrcl Eqpmnt & Cmpnts, Excpt Computer Eqpmnt	5	2.9
Engineering, Accounting, Research, Management & Related Svcs	11	6.3
Executive, Legislative & General Government, Except Finance	2	1.1
Fabricated Metal Prdcts, Except Machinery & Transport Eqpmnt	4	2.3
Food and Kindred Products	5	2.9
Furniture and Fixtures	2	1.1
General Merchandise Stores	1	.6
Health Services	23	12.6
Heavy Construction	1	.6
Holding and Other Investment Offices	1	.6
Hotels, Rooming Houses, Camps, and Other Lodging Places	6	3.4
Industrial and Commercial Machinery and Computer Equipment	5	2.9
Insurance Agents, Brokers and Service	1	.6
Insurance Carriers	1	.6
Justice, Public Order and Safety	8	4.6
Legal Services	2	1.1

(continued)

TABLE 6 (CONTINUED)

Industries Employing Leaders in the Survey

Industry	Frequency	Percent
Membership Organizations	3	1.7
Mesr/Anlyz/Cntrl Instrmnts; Photo/Med/Opt Gds; Watchs/Clocks	3	1.7
Miscellaneous Manufacturing Industries	5	2.9
Miscellaneous Repair Services	1	.6
Miscellaneous Retail	3	1.7
Museums, Art Galleries and Botanical and Zoological Gardens	2	1.1
National Security and International Affairs	2	1.1
Nonclassifiable Establishments	1	.6
Paper and Allied Products	1	.6
Personal Services	3	1.7
Petroleum Refining and Related Industries	1	.6
Primary Metal Industries	2	1.1
Printing, Publishing and Allied Industries	2	1.1
Public Finance, Taxation and Monetary Policy	1	.6
Real Estate	4	2.3
Rubber and Miscellaneous Plastic Products	3	1.7
Social Services, Nonprofits	6	3.4
Stone, Clay, Glass, and Concrete Products	1	.6
Textile Mill Products	1	.6
Tobacco Products	1	.6
Transportation by Air	1	.6
Transportation Equipment	2	1.1
Transportation Services	1	.6
Water Transportation	1	.6
Wholesale Trade - Durable Goods	4	2.3
Wholesale Trade - Nondurable Goods	1	.6
Total	176	100

TABLE 7

Participants' Exercise Frequency by Age

Exercise Frequency	18-24	25-34	35-44	45-54	55-64	65-74	75 or older	Total/%
None at all	0	1	2	1	3	1	0	8/5%
Used to Exercise	1	2	1	0	2	0	0	6/3%
One day a week	0	1	2	4	3	0	1	11/6%
Two days a week	0	3	4	14	9	1	1	32/18%
Three days a week	0	0	5	1	7	1	0	14/8%
Four days a week	1	4	5	15	15	0	0	40/23%
Five days a week	0	2	9	16	15	1	0	43/24%
Six days a week	0	1	3	4	4	0	0	12/7%
Seven or more days a week	0	1	2	3	4	1	0	11/6%
Totals/ Percent (N = 173)	2/1%	15/9%	33/19%	57/32%	62/35%	5/3%	2/1%	177/100%

TABLE 8

Types of Exercises in which Respondents Engage

Exercise Name	Frequency	Percent
Basketball	4	1%
Bicycling	11	3%
Boot Camp	3	1%
Bowling	2	1%
Boxing	2	1%
Calisthenics	2	1%
Combination Cardio and Strength	22	7%
Core Performance	1	0%
CrossFit®	8	2%
Elliptical	6	2%
Fishing	3	1%
Golf	25	8%
HIIT	9	3%
Hockey	1	0%
Horseback Riding	1	0%
Housework	3	1%
Jogging	15	5%
Kettle bell	2	1%
Martial Arts	4	1%
Multiple Cardio Forms	31	9%
P90X	1	0%
Pilates	1	0%
Playing with Kids	1	0%
Private Training	2	1%
Racquetball	1	0%
Rock Climbing	2	1%
Running	24	7%

(continued)

TABLE 8 (CONTINUED)

Types of Exercises in which Respondents Engage

Exercise Name	Frequency	Percent
Snowmobiling	2	1%
Softball	1	0%
Spinning	2	1%
Squash	1	0%
Swimming	4	1%
Tennis	2	1%
Volleyball	3	1%
Walking	88	27%
Weight Training	35	11%
Yard Work	5	2%
Yoga	1	0%
Zumba	1	0%
Total	332	100%

TABLE 9

Participants' Perceived Rate of Exertion

Perceived Rate of Exertion	Frequency	Percent	Valid Percent	Cumulative Percent
Do not exercise	6	3.2	3.2	3.2
Used to exercise	6	3.2	3.2	6.4
Partake in mild exercise	27	14.3	14.4	20.7
Partake in moderate exercise	110	58.2	58.5	79.3
Partake in strenuous exercise	39	20.6	20.7	100.00
Total	189	99.5	100.0	

Table 10

METS Values Assigned to Exercises

Exercise Name	METS Values	
Basketball	11.10	
Bicycling	4.8	9.8
Bootcamp	5.00	8.00
Bowling	2.00	4.00
Boxing	13.4	
Calisthenics	2.00	6.00
Combination Cardio and Strength	4.80	14.60
Core Performance	7.00	9.00
CrossFit®	11.00	
Elliptical	8.00	10.50
Fishing	2.00	3.00
Golf	2.50	5.10
HIIT	5.00	8.00
Hockey	10.30	
Horseback Riding	3.20	8.60
Housework	4.00	
Jogging	8.80	10.50
Kettle bell	9.80	
Martial Arts	8.00	10.50
Multiple Cardio Forms	5.50	14.60
P90X	6.70	10.80
Pilates	3.00	
Playing with Kids	4.70	
Private Training	10.90	
Racquetball	8.00	12.00
Rock Climbing	11.0	
Running	12.90	14.60

(continued)

TABLE 10 (CONTINUED)

METS Values Assigned to Exercises

Exercise Name	METS Values	
Snowmobiling	2.00	3.00
Softball	3.00	6.00
Spinning	7.50	15.00
Squash	8.00	12.00
Swimming	4.30	13.60
Tennis	6.80	
Volleyball	6.00	
Walking	1.80	5.30
Weight Training	10.90	
Yard Work	5.00	7.00
Yoga	3.20	
Zumba	6.50	7.30

TABLE 11

Crosstab of Total Exercise Intensity Per Week by Position

Total Exercise Intensity	First-Line Supervisor	Middle Manager	Senior Manager	Total
0	3	6	4	13
36	1	1	0	2
54	1	0	0	1
90	0	1	0	1
96	0	1	0	1
121.50	0	1	0	1
157.5	0	0	1	1
197.70	0	1	0	1
210	1	0	0	1
252	0	0	1	1
262.50	0	0	2	2
264	0	1	0	1
270	1	2	0	3
315	0	1	0	1
324	2	0	0	2
327	0	0	1	1
360	0	1	0	1
380	0	0	1	1
409.50	0	1	0	1
416	1	0	0	1
420	0	0	1	1
423	0	0	1	1
472.5	1	0	0	1
562.5	0	0	1	1
600	0	0	1	1
624	0	0	1	1
630	0	1	0	1
660	0	1	0	1
693.75	1	0	0	1
720	0	0	1	1
798.75	0	1	0	1
810	1	0	0	1
822	1	0	0	1
851.25	0	0	1	1
880	0	0	1	1
909	0	0	1	1
918.75	0	0	1	1
924	0	1	0	1

(continued)

TABLE 11 (CONTINUED)

Crosstab of Total Exercise Intensity Per Week by Position

Total Exercise Intensity	First-Line Supervisor	Middle Manager	Senior Manager	Total
1003.50	0	0	1	1
1008	0	0	1	1
1012	0	0	1	1
1032	0	1	0	1
1057.50	1	0	0	1
1092	0	0	1	1
1095	0	0	1	1
1107	0	1	0	1
1134	0	1	0	1
1140	0	0	1	1
1150	0	1	0	1
1188	0	1	0	1
1191	1	0	0	1
1122.50	1	0	0	1
1224	0	1	0	1
1245	1	0	0	1
1305	0	0	1	1
1312.50	1	0	0	1
1332	0	1	0	1
1350	0	0	1	1
1368	0	1	0	1
1437.50	1	0	0	1
1440	0	2	0	2
1470	0	1	0	1
1506	0	1	0	1
1632	0	0	1	1
1645.50	0	0	1	1
1650	0	1	0	1
1674	0	1	0	1
1676.25	0	0	1	1
1686	0	1	0	1
1710	0	0	1	1
1728	0	1	0	1
1736	0	1	0	1
1752	0	0	1	1
1805	1	0	0	1
1810	1	0	0	1
1827	0	1	0	1
1842	0	1	0	1
1860	0	0	1	1
1890	1	0	0	1

(continued)

Carol R. Himelhoch and Mary Antonaros Raymond

TABLE 11 (CONTINUED)

Crosstab of Total Exercise Intensity Per Week by Position

Total Exercise Intensity	First-Line Supervisor	Middle Manager	Senior Manager	Total
1893.75	1	0	0	1
1908	0	0	1	1
1918.50	0	1	0	1
1920	0	0	1	1
1935	1	0	0	1
1954	0	0	1	1
1980	0	2	0	2
2010	0	0	1	1
2013.75	1	0	0	1
2100	1	0	1	2
2106	0	0	1	1
2160	1	0	0	1
2275	0	0	1	1
2283.75	1	0	0	1
2340	0	0	1	1
2358.75	1	0	0	1
2393.25	0	0	1	1
2394	0	1	0	1
2400	1	0	0	1
2412	1	0	0	1
2460	0	1	0	1
2467.50	0	0	1	1
2497.50	0	1	0	1
2520	0	0	1	1
2563.88	0	0	1	1
2602.50	0	0	1	1
2776.50	1	0	0	1
2810	0	1	0	1
2925	0	1	0	1
3060	0	0	1	1
3090	0	0	1	1
3123	0	1	0	1
3132	0	1	0	1
3140	0	1	1	2
3150	1	0	0	1
3163.50	1	0	0	1
3174	1	0	0	1
3189.38	0	1	0	1
3204	0	0	1	1
3226	0	0	1	1
3240	0	1	0	1

(continued)

TABLE 11 (CONTINUED)

Crosstab of Total Exercise Intensity Per Week by Position

Total Exercise Intensity	First-Line Supervisor	Middle Manager	Senior Manager	Total
3280	0	0	1	1
3315	0	1	0	1
3356.25	0	0	1	1
3392.50	1	0	0	1
3408	1	0	0	1
3600	0	0	1	1
3976.88	0	0	1	1
3993	0	1	0	1
4134	0	1	0	1
4158	0	0	1	1
4207.13	0	0	1	1
4341	0	0	1	1
4554	0	0	1	1
4662	1	0	0	1
4710	0	0	1	1
5160	0	0	1	1
5292	1	0	0	1
5484	1	0	0	1
5553	1	0	0	1
5649	0	0	1	1
5740	1	0	0	1
5827.50	0	1	0	1
6228	0	0	1	1
6786	1	0	0	1
7290	0	0	1	1
7526.25	0	0	1	1
7218	0	0	1	1
8700	0	0	1	1
9816	1	0	0	1
11556.75	0	0	1	1
12840	0	0	1	1
43816.50	1	0	0	1
Total/%	45/25.9%	58/33.1%	72/41.1%	175/100%

Carol R. Himelhoch and Mary Antonaros Raymond

TABLE 12

Confirmatory Factor Analysis of Leadership Style Variables in the MLQ

Variables (Question No.)	Factors								
	IIA*	IIB*	IM*	IS*	IC*	CR*	MBEA*	MBEP*	LF*
I instill pride in others for being associated with me (10)	.79								
I go beyond self interest for the good of the group (18)	.59								
I act in ways that build others' respect for me (21)	.78								
I display a sense of power and confidence (25)	.66								
I talk about my most important values and beliefs (6)		.72							
I specify the importance of having a strong sense of purpose (14)		.80							
I consider the moral and ethical consequences of decisions (23)		.50							
I emphasize the importance of having a collective sense of mission (34)		.73							
I talk optimistically about the future (9)			.66						

(continued)

TABLE 12 (CONTINUED)

Confirmatory Factor Analysis of Leadership Style Variables in the MLQ

Variables (Question No.)	Factors								
	IIA*	IIB*	IM*	IS*	IC*	CR*	MBEA*	MBEP*	LF*
I talk enthusiastically about what needs to be accomplished (13)			.81						
I articulate a compelling vision of the future (26)			.78						
I express confidence that goals will be achieved (36)			.67						
I reexamine critical assumptions to question whether they are appropriate (2)				.45					
I seek differing perspectives when solving problems (8)				.70					
I get others to look at problems from many different angles (30)				.80					
I suggest new ways at how to complete assignments (32)				.66					
I spend time teaching and coaching (15)					.72				

(continued)

Carol R. Himelhoch and Mary Antonaros Raymond

TABLE 12 (CONTINUED)

Confirmatory Factor Analysis of Leadership Style Variables in the MLQ

Variables (Question No.)	IIA*	IIB*	IM*	IS*	IC*	CR*	MBEA*	MBEP*	LF*
				Factors					
I treat others as individuals rather than just as members of the group (19)					.63				
I consider an individual as having different needs, abilities, and aspirations from others (29)					.61				
I help others to develop their strengths (31)					.71				
I provide others assistance in exchange for their efforts (1)						.46			
I discuss in specific terms who is responsible for achieving performance targets (11)						63			
I make clear what one can expect to receive when performance goals are achieved (16)						.75			
I express satisfaction when others meet expectations (35)						.64			

(continued)

TABLE 12 (CONTINUED)

Confirmatory Factor Analysis of Leadership Style Variables in the MLQ

	Factors								
Variables (Question No.)	IIA*	IIB*	IM*	IS*	IC*	CR*	MBEA*	MBEP*	LF*
I focus attention on irregularities, mistakes, exceptions, and deviations from standards (4)							.75		
I concentrate my full attention on dealing with mistakes, complaints, and failures (22)							.79		
I keep track of all mistakes (24)							.70		
I direct my attention toward failures to meet standards (27)							.80		
I fail to interfere until problems become serious (3)								.73	
I wait for things to go wrong before taking action (12)								.80	
I show that I am a firm believer in "if it ain't broke don't fix it" (17)								.54	
I demonstrate that problems must be chronic before taking action (20)								.79	

(continued)

Carol R. Himelhoch and Mary Antonaros Raymond

TABLE 12 (CONTINUED)

Confirmatory Factor Analysis of Leadership Style Variables in the MLQ

Variables (Question No.)	Factors								
	IIA*	IIB*	IM*	IS*	IC*	CR*	MBEA*	MBEP*	LF*
I avoid getting involved when important issues arise (5)									.45
I am absent when needed (7)									.51
I avoid making decisions (28)									
I delay responding to urgent questions (33)									.72
Eigenvalue	2.001	1.944	2.134	1.774	1.795	1.587	3.321	2.078	1.334
Factor Reliability	.66	.64	.70	.56	.59	.47	.76	.67	.33

*IIA = Idealized Influence (Attributes); IIB = Idealized Influence (Behaviors); IM = Inspirational Motivation; IS = Intellectual Stimulation; IC = Individual Consideration; CR = Contingent Reward; MBEA = Management By Exception Active; MBEP = Management By Exception Passive; LF = Laissez-faire

TABLE 13

Confirmatory Factor Analysis of Outcome Variables in the MLQ

Variables (Question No.)	Factors		
	Extra Effort	Effectiveness	Satisfaction
I get others to do more than they expected to do (39)	.81		
I heighten others' desire to succeed (42)	.84		
I increase others' willingness to try harder (44)	.86		
I am effective in meeting others' job-related needs (37)		.75	
I am effective in representing others to higher authority (40)		.74	
I am effective in meeting organizational requirements (43)		.72	
I lead a group that is effective (45)		.36	
I use methods of leadership that are satisfying (38)			.79
I work with others in a satisfactory way (41)			.79
Eigenvalue	2.097	1.982	1.256
Factor Reliability	.78	.66	.41

Carol R. Himelhoch and Mary Antonaros Raymond

TABLE 14

Statistically Significant Differences in How Leaders and Employees Perceive Leader Behaviors

		Provides me assistance in exchange for my efforts		
		Employees	Leader	Total
	N	94	26	120
	Mean	3.22	2.73	3.12
95% Confidence Interval for Mean	Std. Deviation	.929	1.116	.989
	Std. Error	.096	.219	.090
	Lower Bound	3.03	2.28	2.94
	Upper Bound	3.41	3.18	3.30
	Minimum	1	0	0
	Maximum	4	4	4
	ANOVA	Between Groups	Within Groups	Total
	Sum of Squares	4.943	111.424	116.367
	df	1	118	119
	Mean Square	4.943	.944	
	F	5.234		
	Sig.	.024		
		Concentrates his/her full attention on dealing with mistakes, complaints, and failures		
		Employees	Leader	Total
	N	93	26	119
	Mean	2.26	1.23	2.03
95% Confidence Interval for Mean	Std. Deviation	1.301	.951	1.301
	Std. Error	.135	.187	.119
	Lower Bound	1.99	.85	1.80
	Upper Bound	2.53	1.61	2.27
	Minimum	0	0	0
	Maximum	4	4	4
	ANOVA	Between Groups	Within Groups	Total
	Sum of Squares	21.444	178.422	199.866
	df	1	117	118
	Mean Square	21.444	1.525	
	F	14.062		
	Sig.	.000		

(continued)

TABLE 14 (CONTINUED)

Statistically Significant Differences in How Leaders and Employees Perceive Leader Behaviors

Provides me assistance in exchange for my efforts			
	Employees	Leader	Total
N	94	26	120
Mean	3.22	2.73	3.12
Std. Deviation	.929	1.116	.989
Std. Error	.096	.219	.090
Lower Bound	3.03	2.28	2.94
Upper Bound	3.41	3.18	3.30
Minimum	1	0	0
Maximum	4	4	4
ANOVA	Between Groups	Within Groups	Total
Sum of Squares	4.943	111.424	116.367
df	1	118	119
Mean Square	4.943	.944	
F	5.234		
Sig.	.024		

95% Confidence Interval for Mean (rows N through Maximum)

Concentrates his/her full attention on dealing with mistakes, complaints, and failures			
	Employees	Leader	Total
N	93	26	119
Mean	2.26	1.23	2.03
Std. Deviation	1.301	.951	1.301
Std. Error	.135	.187	.119
Lower Bound	1.99	.85	1.80
Upper Bound	2.53	1.61	2.27
Minimum	0	0	0
Maximum	4	4	4
ANOVA	Between Groups	Within Groups	Total
Sum of Squares	21.444	178.422	199.866
df	1	117	118
Mean Square	21.444	1.525	
F	14.062		
Sig.	.000		

95% Confidence Interval for Mean (rows N through Maximum)

(continued)

TABLE 14 (CONTINUED)

Statistically Significant Differences in How Leaders and Employees Perceive Leader Behaviors

	Leads a group that is effective		
		Employees	Leader	Total
	N	94	26	120
	Mean	3.10	3.50	3.18
95% Confidence	Std. Deviation	.974	.648	.926
Interval for	Std. Error	.100	.127	.085
Mean	Lower Bound	2.90	3.24	3.02
	Upper Bound	3.30	3.76	3.35
	Minimum	0	2	0
	Maximum	4	4	4
	ANOVA	Between Groups	Within Groups	Total
	Sum of Squares	3.328	98.638	101.967
	df	1	118	119
	Mean Square	3.328	.836	
	F	3.982		
	Sig.	.048		

TABLE 15

Post-Hoc Duncan Test for Idealized Attributes

Perceived Rate of Exertion	N	Subset for alpha = .05	
		1	2
Used to Exercise	5	2.45	
Mild Exercise	26	2.86	2.86
Do Not Exercise	6	2.96	2.96
Moderate Exercise	103		2.99
Strenuous Exercise	38		3.20

Carol R. Himelhoch and Mary Antonaros Raymond

TABLE 16

Post-Hoc Duncan Test for Inspirational Motivation

Perceived Rate of Exertion	N	Subset for alpha=.05	
		1	2
Used to Exercise	6	2.75	
Mild Exercise	26	2.76	
Do Not Exercise	6	3.17	3.17
Moderate Exercise	107	3.20	3.20
Strenuous Exercise	38		3.29

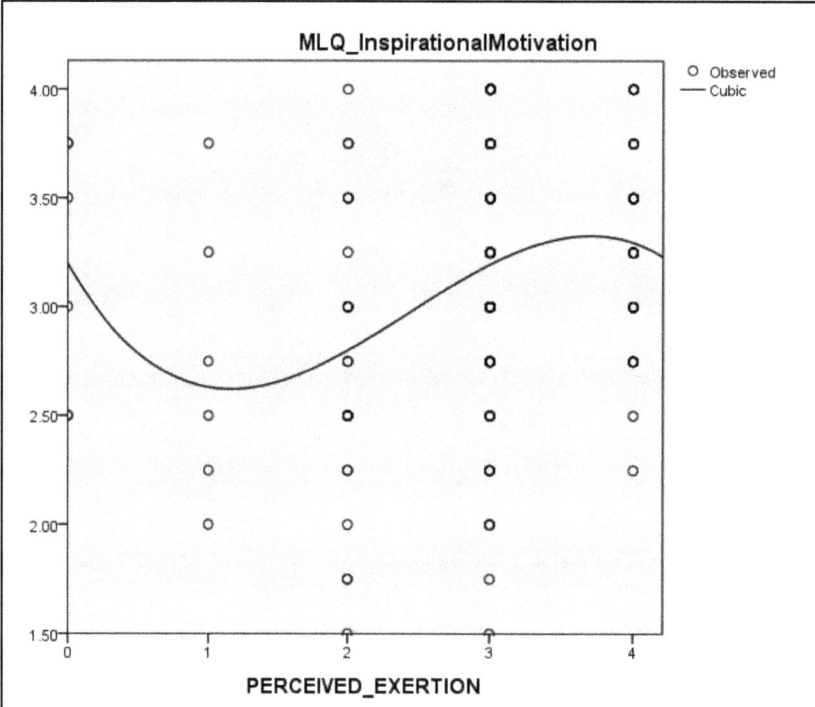

Figure 2. Curvilinear relationship between inspirational motivation and perceived rate of exertion.

TABLE 17

Post-Hoc Duncan Test for Individual Consideration

Perceived Rate of Exertion	N	Subset for alpha = .05		
		1	2	3
Used to Exercise	6	2.71		
Mild Exercise	27	2.98	2.98	
Do Not Exercise	108		3.25	3.25
Moderate Exercise	37		3.36	3.36
Strenuous Exercise	6			3.50

TABLE 18

Post-Hoc Duncan Test for Idealized Behaviors

Exercise Frequency	N	Subset for alpha=.05		
		1	2	3
One day a week	10	2.63		
Seven or more days a week	12	2.79	2.79	
None at all	8	2.87	2.86	2.86
Two days a week	37	2.90	2.90	2.90
Three days a week	14	2.93	2.93	2.93
Used to exercise	8	2.97	2.97	2.97
Six days a week	13	3.13	3.13	3.13
Four days a week	41		3.20	3.20
Five days a week	41			3.38

Carol R. Himelhoch and Mary Antonaros Raymond

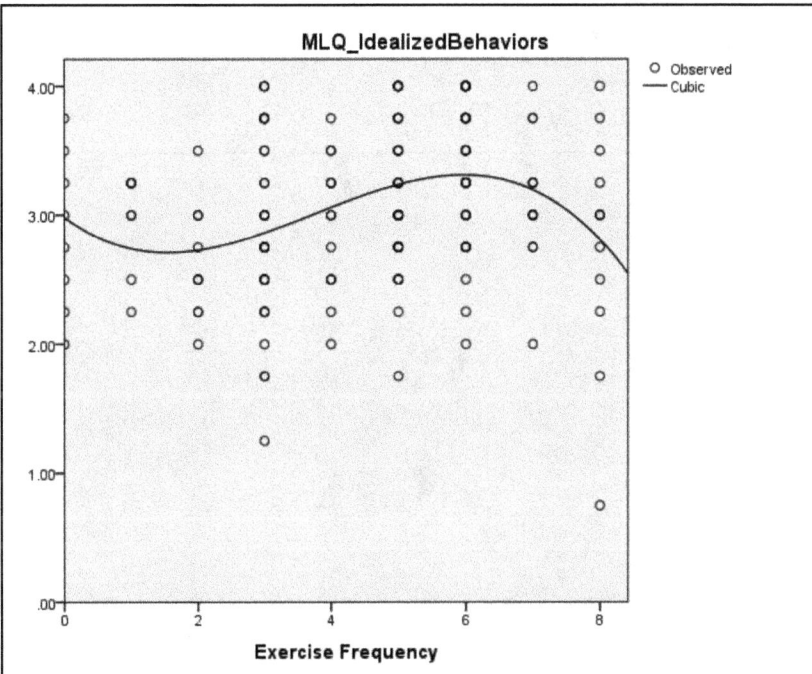

Figure 3. Curvilinear relationship between idealized behaviors and exercise frequency.

TABLE 19

Post-Hoc Duncan Test for Inspirational Motivation

Exercise Frequency	N	Subset for alpha = .05		
		1	2	3
One day a week	11	2.57		
Two days a week	36	2.96	2.96	
None at all	8	3.00	3.00	3.00
Three days a week	14	3.02	3.02	3.02
Six days a week	12		3.04	3.04
Used to exercise	8		3.09	3.09
Seven or more days a week	12		3.13	3.13
Five days a week	41		3.24	3.24
	42			3.46

Carol R. Himelhoch and Mary Antonaros Raymond

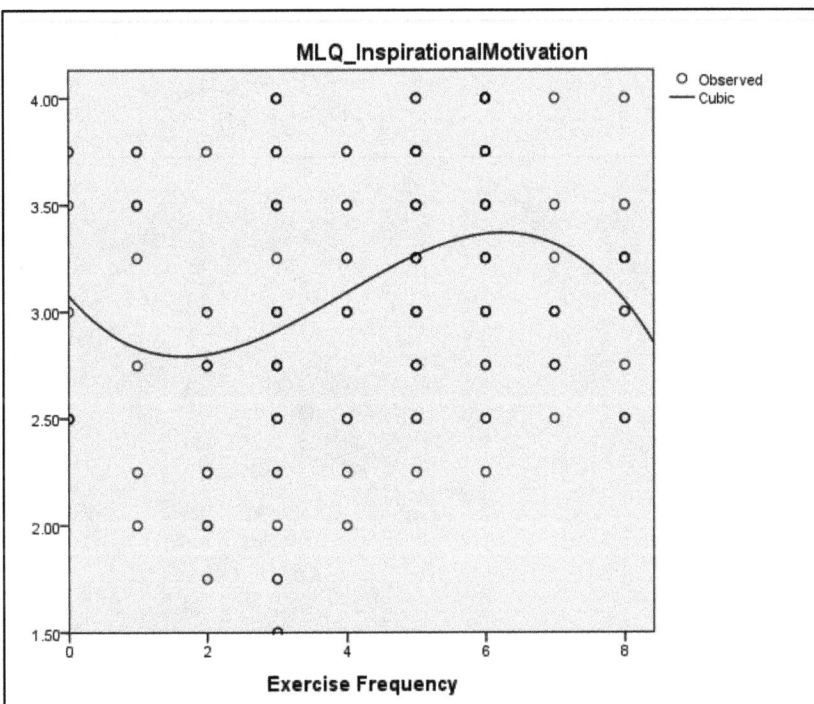

Figure 4. Curvilinear relationship between inspirational motivation and exercise frequency.

Table 20

Post-Hoc Duncan Test for Individual Consideration

Exercise Frequency	N	Subset for alpha = .05	
		1	2
Two days a week	37	2.95	
Used to exercise	8	2.97	
One day a week	11	3.11	3.11
Three days a week	14	3.16	3.16
Six days a week	13	3.01	3.01
Four days a week	42	3.32	3.32
Seven or more days a week	12	3.33	3.33
Five days a week	40	3.39	3.39
None at all	8		3.50

Carol R. Himelhoch and Mary Antonaros Raymond

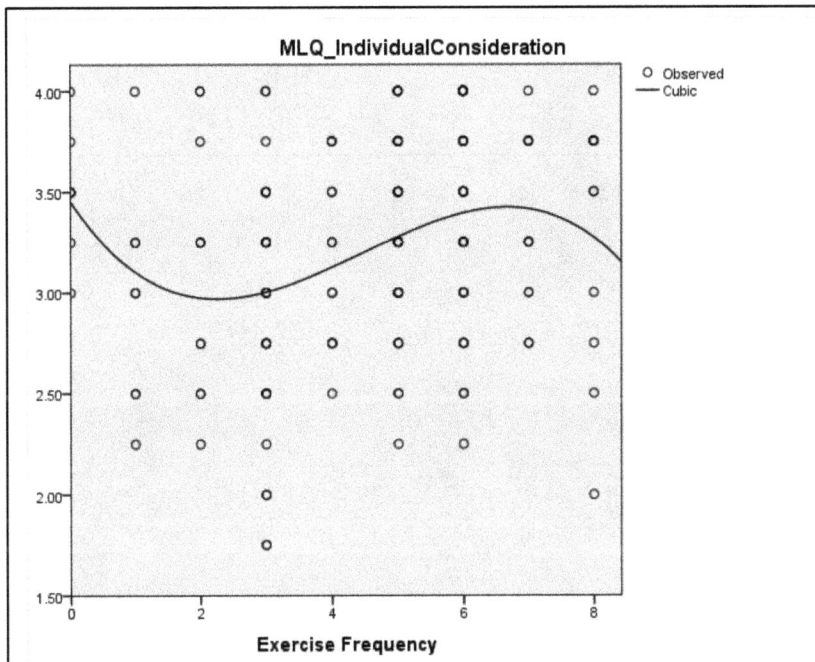

Figure 5. Curvilinear relationship between individual consideration and exercise frequency.

TABLE 21

Post-Hoc Duncan Test for Management By Exception-Active

Exercise Frequency	N	Subset for alpha = .05	
		1	2
Used to exercise	7	1.14	
One day a week	11	1.36	
Three days a week	14	1.45	
Seven or more days a week	12	1.65	
Six days a week	12	1.67	
Four days a week	42	1.79	
Two days a week	35	1.79	
Five days a week	42	1.80	
None at all	8		2.66

Carol R. Himelhoch and Mary Antonaros Raymond

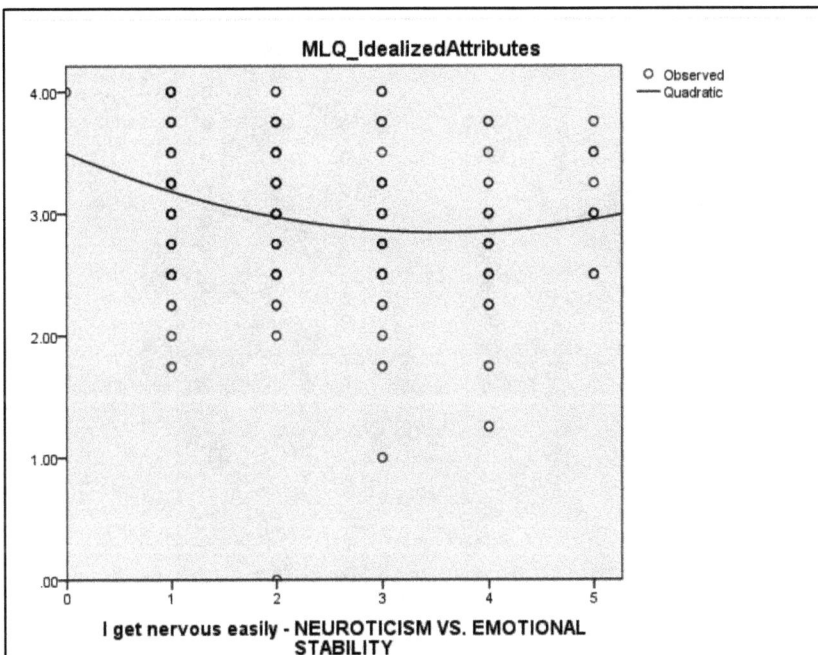

Figure 6. Quadratic relationship between idealized attributes and nervousness.

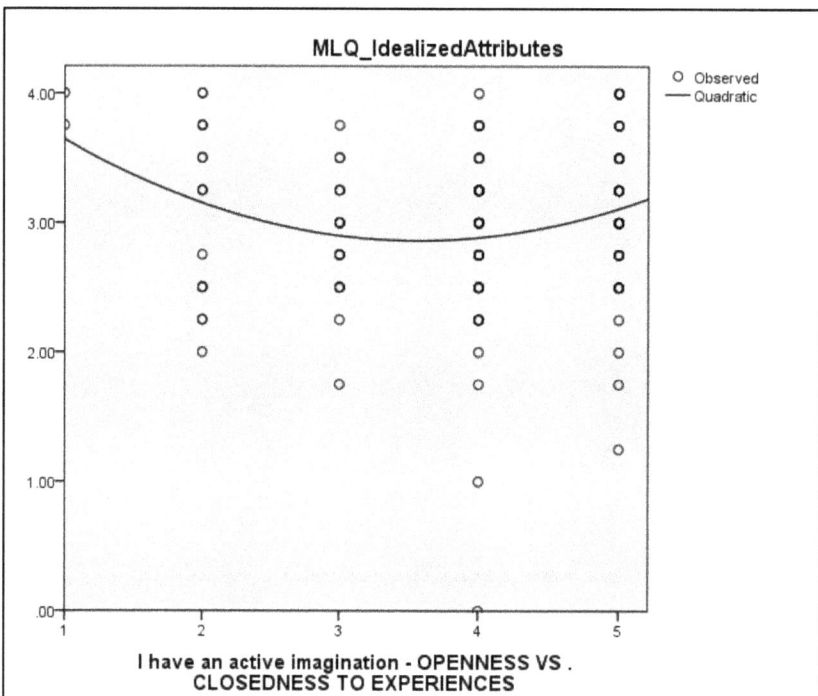

Figure 7. Quadratic relationship between idealized attributes and active imagination.

Carol R. Himelhoch and Mary Antonaros Raymond

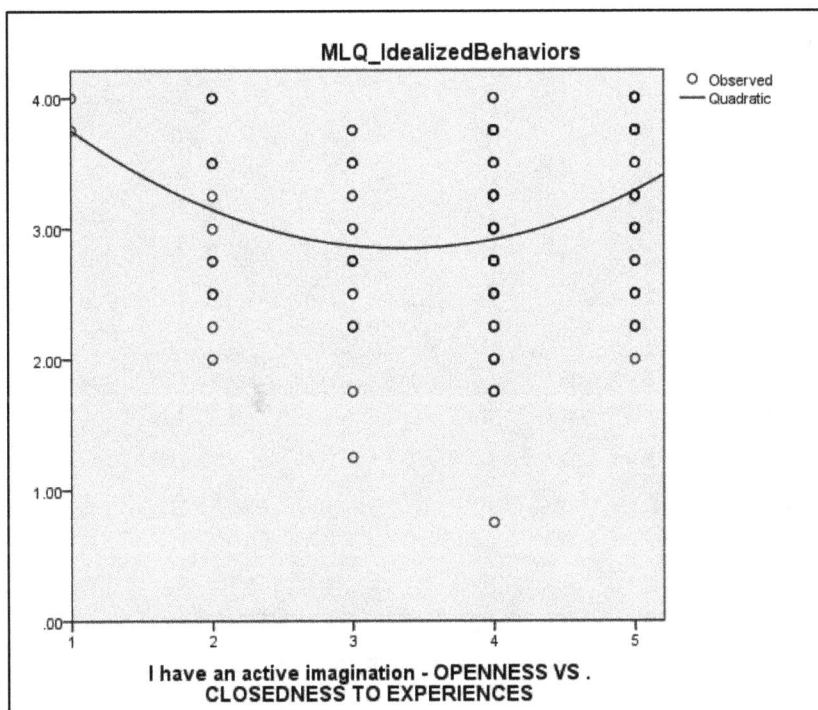

Figure 8. Quadratic relationship between idealized behaviors and active imagination.

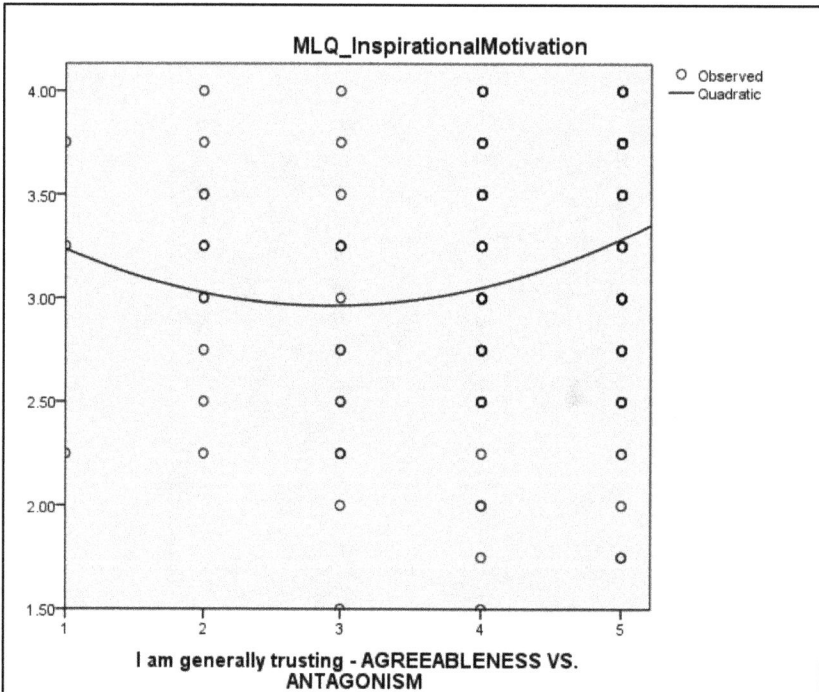

Figure 9. Quadratic relationship between inspirational motivation and trust.

Carol R. Himelhoch and Mary Antonaros Raymond

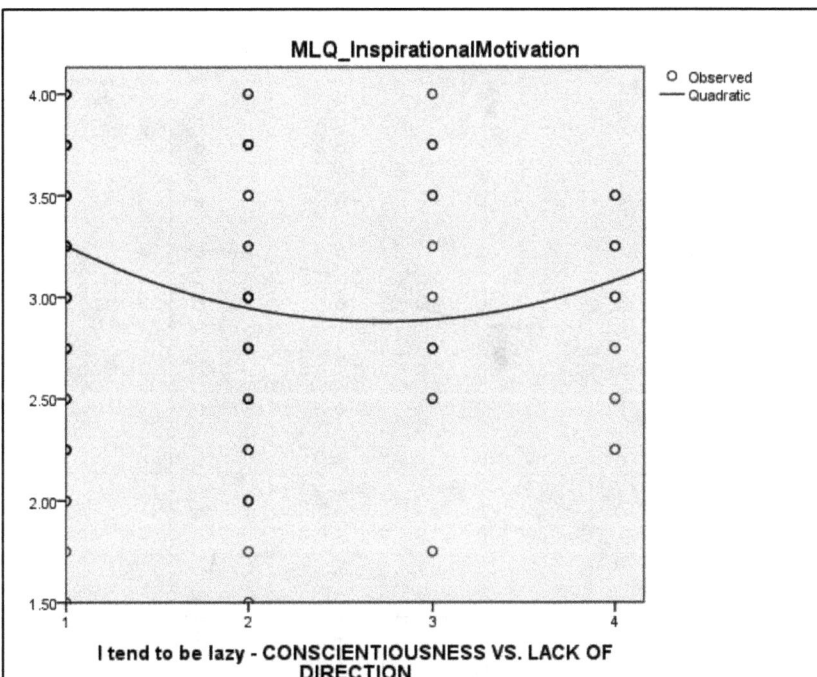

Figure 10. Quadratic relationship between inspirational motivation and tendency to be lazy.

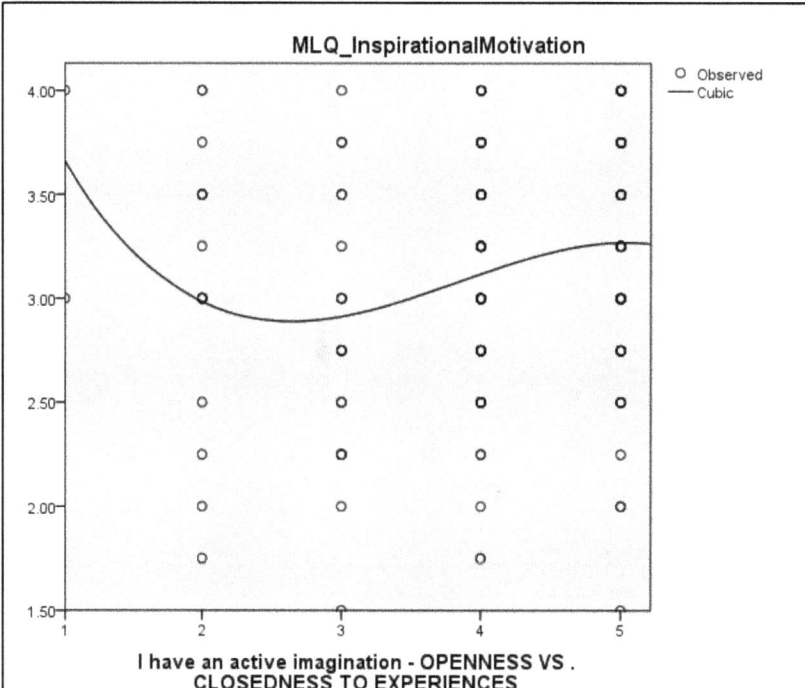

Figure 11. Cubic relationship between inspirational motivation and active imagination.

Carol R. Himelhoch and Mary Antonaros Raymond

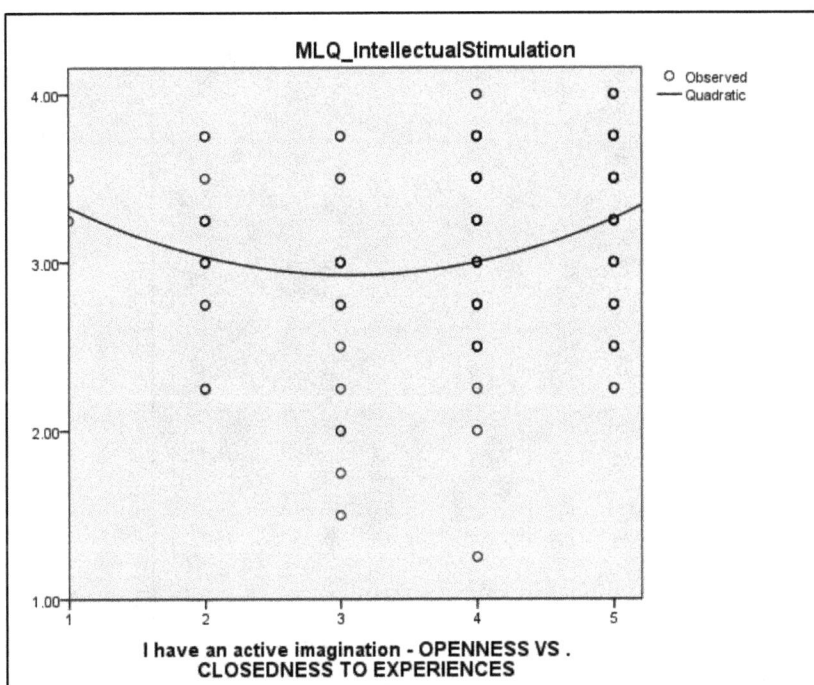

Figure 12. Quadratic relationship between intellectual stimulation and active imagination.

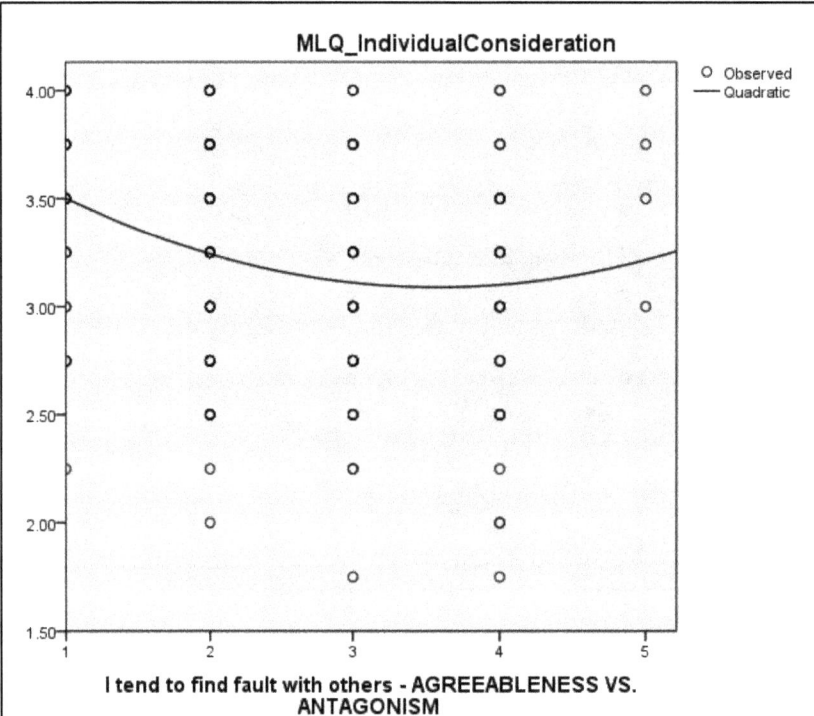

Figure 13. Quadratic relationship between individual consideration and find fault with others.

Carol R. Himelhoch and Mary Antonaros Raymond

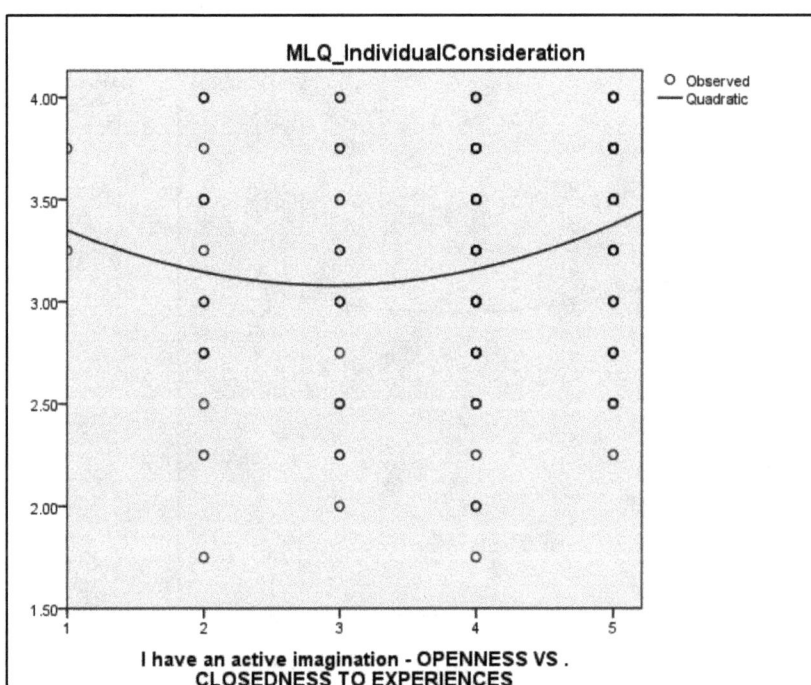

Figure 14. Quadratic relationship between individual consideration and active imagination.

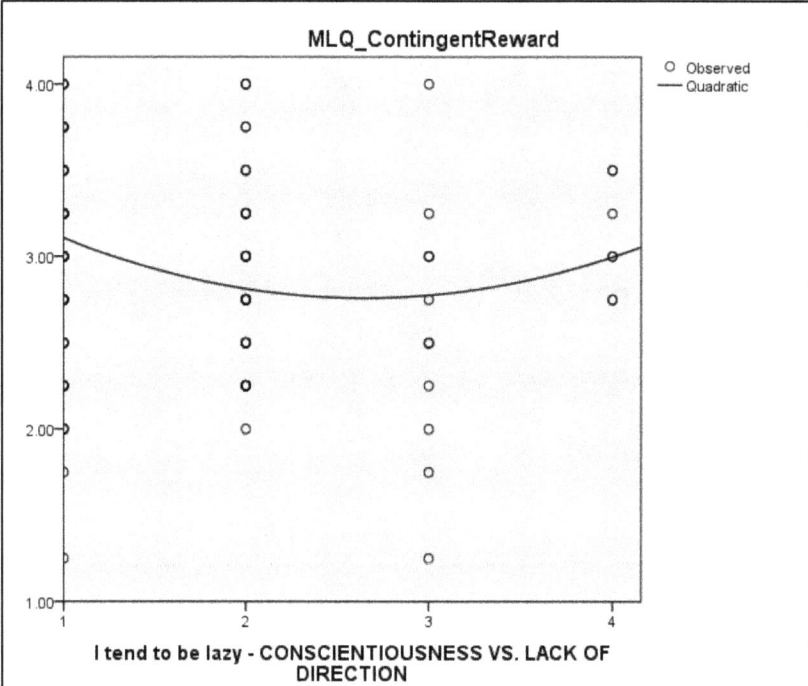

Figure 15. Quadratic relationship between contingent reward and laziness.

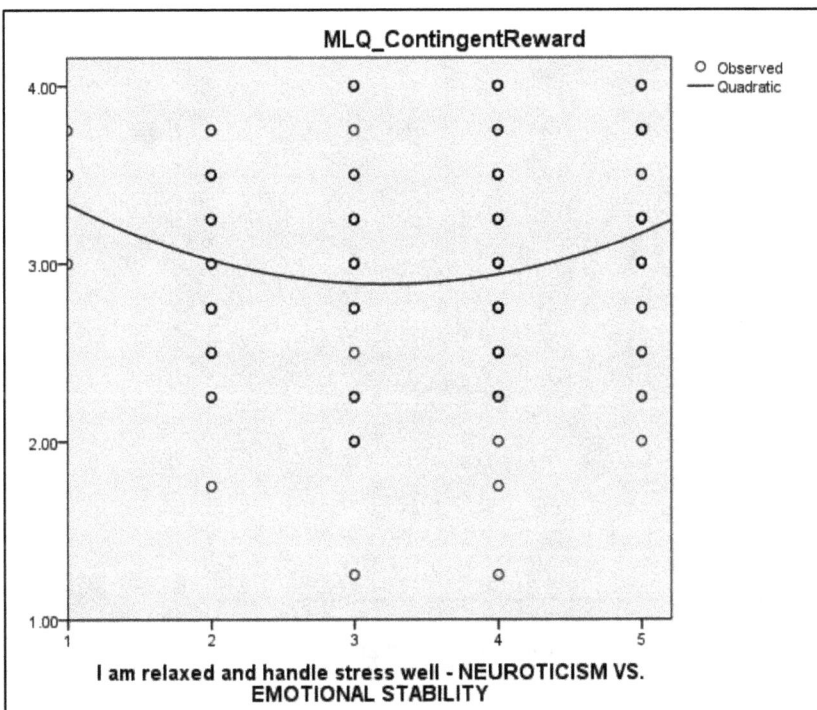

Figure 16. Quadratic relationship between contingent reward and relaxed.

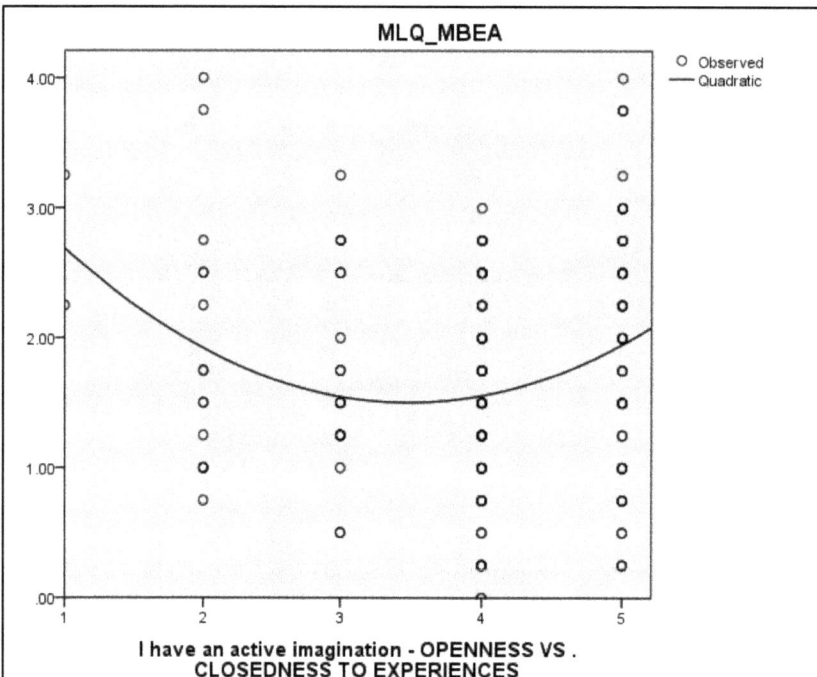

Figure 17. Quadratic relationship between management by exception active and active imagination.

Carol R. Himelhoch and Mary Antonaros Raymond

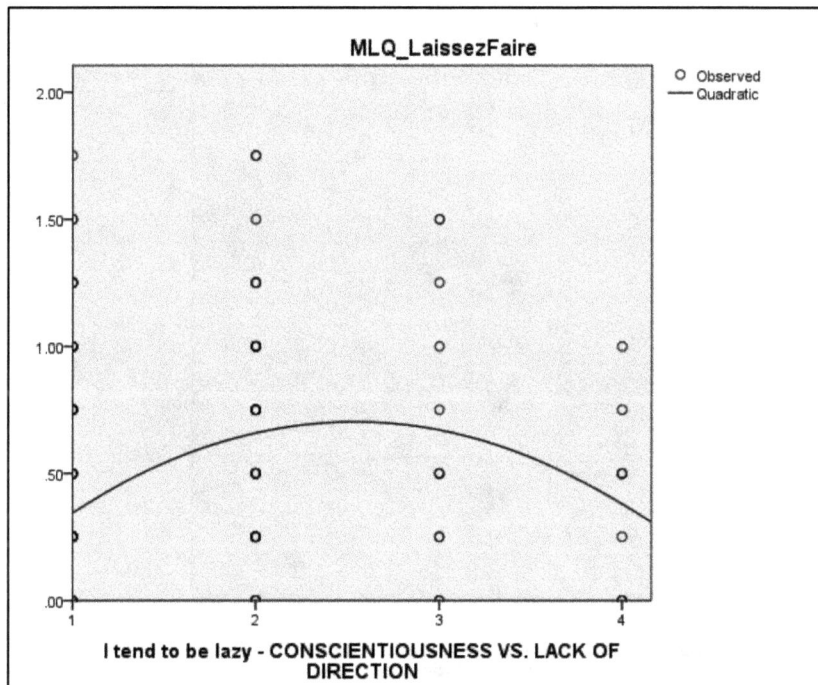

Figure 18. Quadratic relationship between laissez-faire and laziness.

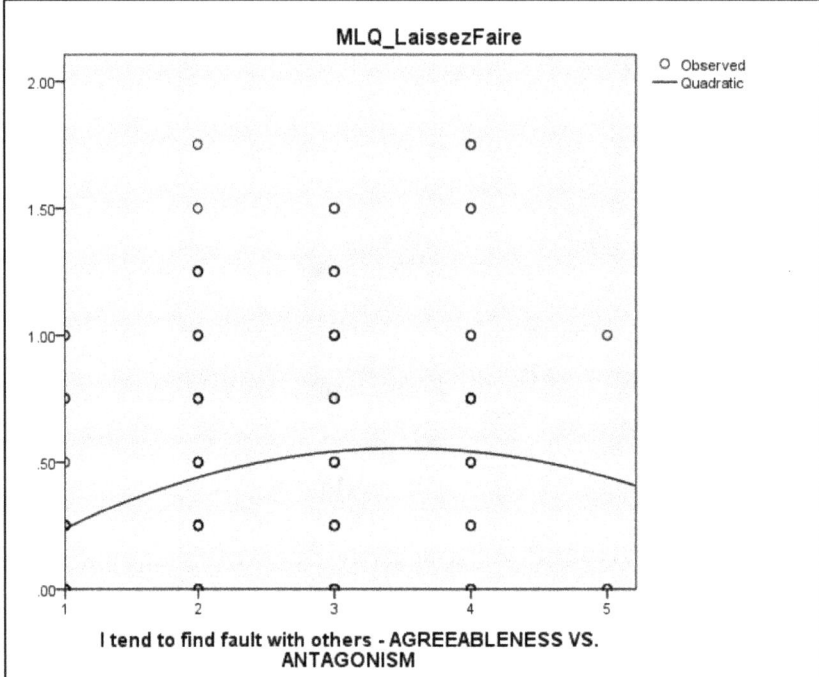

Figure 19. Quadratic relationship between laissez-faire and finding fault.

Carol R. Himelhoch and Mary Antonaros Raymond

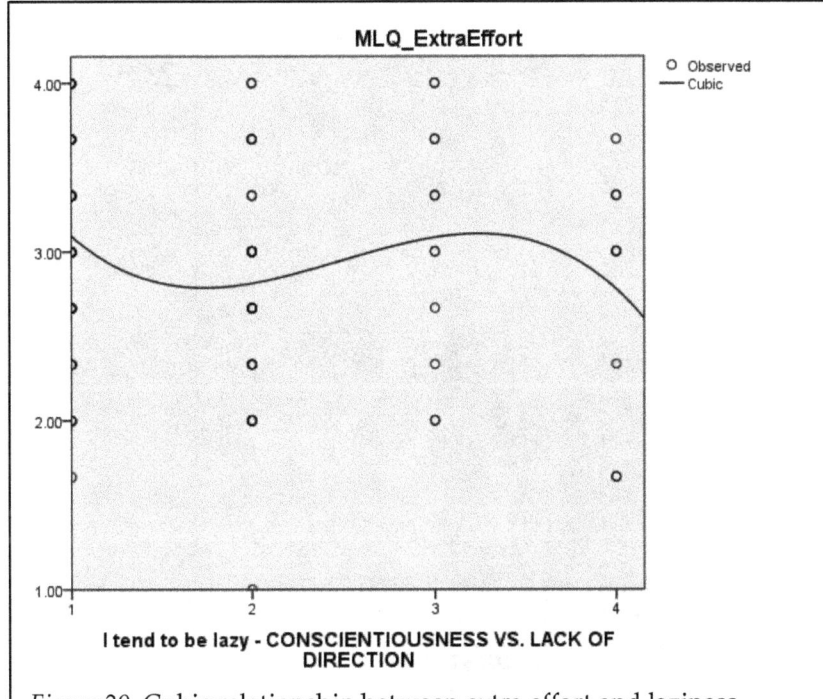

Figure 20. Cubic relationship between extra effort and laziness.

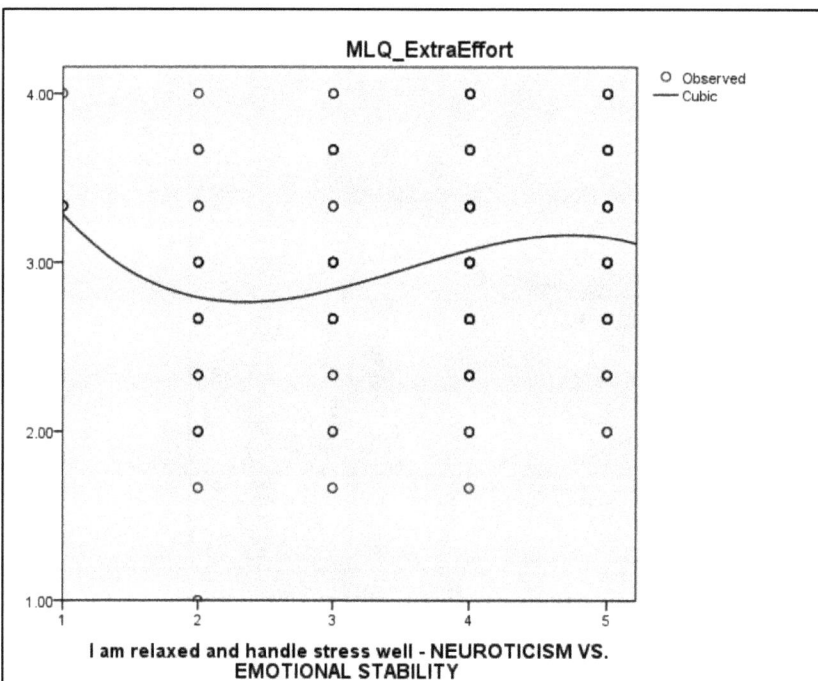

Figure 21. Cubic relationship between extra effort and relaxed.

Carol R. Himelhoch and Mary Antonaros Raymond

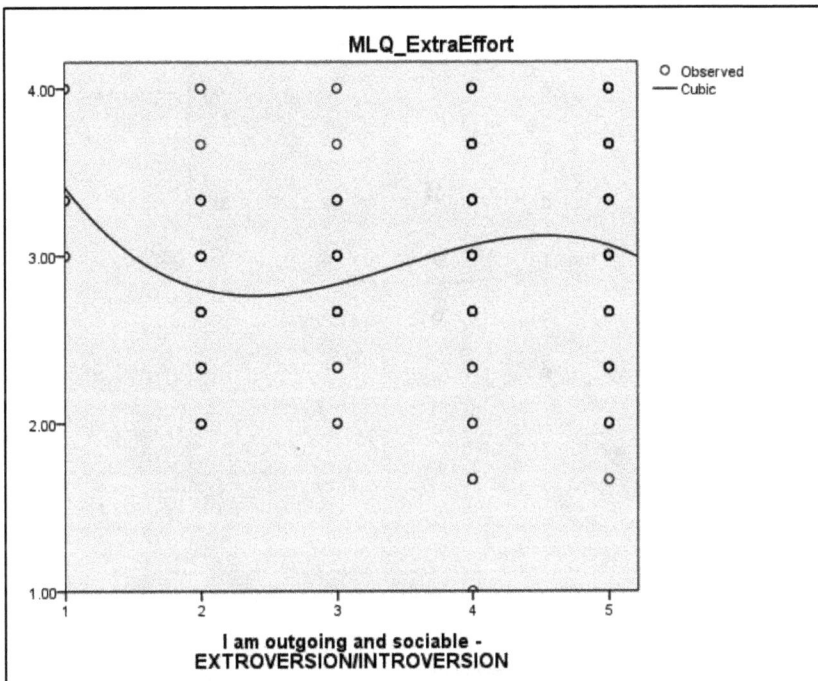

Figure 22. Cubic relationship between extra effort and outgoing.

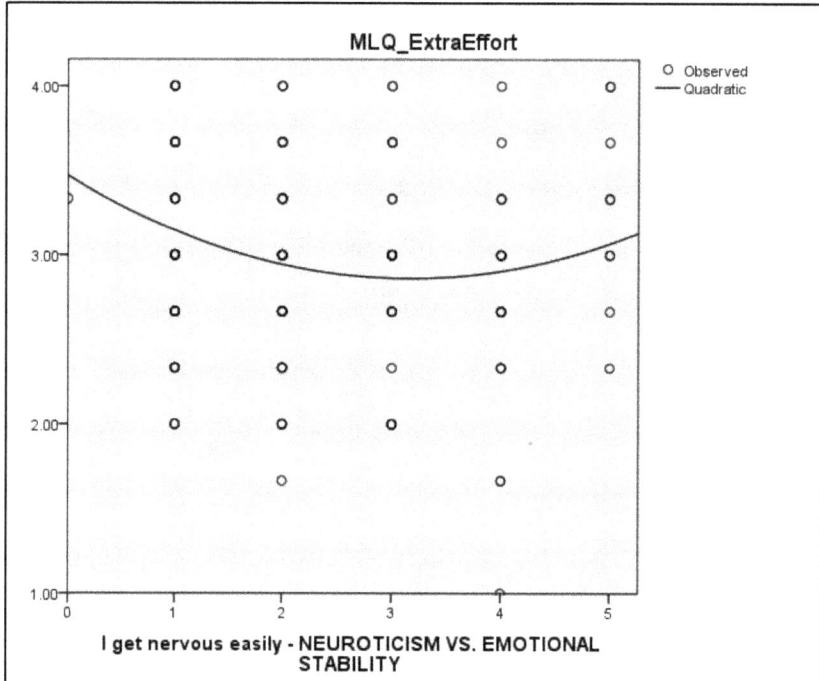

Figure 23. Quadratic relationship between extra effort and nervousness.

Carol R. Himelhoch and Mary Antonaros Raymond

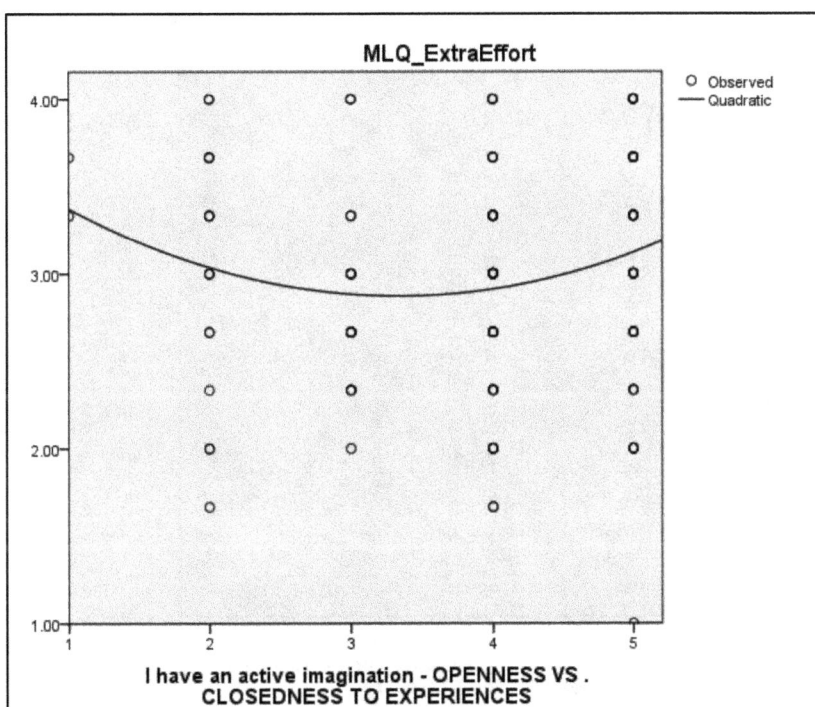

Figure 24. Quadratic relationship between extra effort and active imagination.

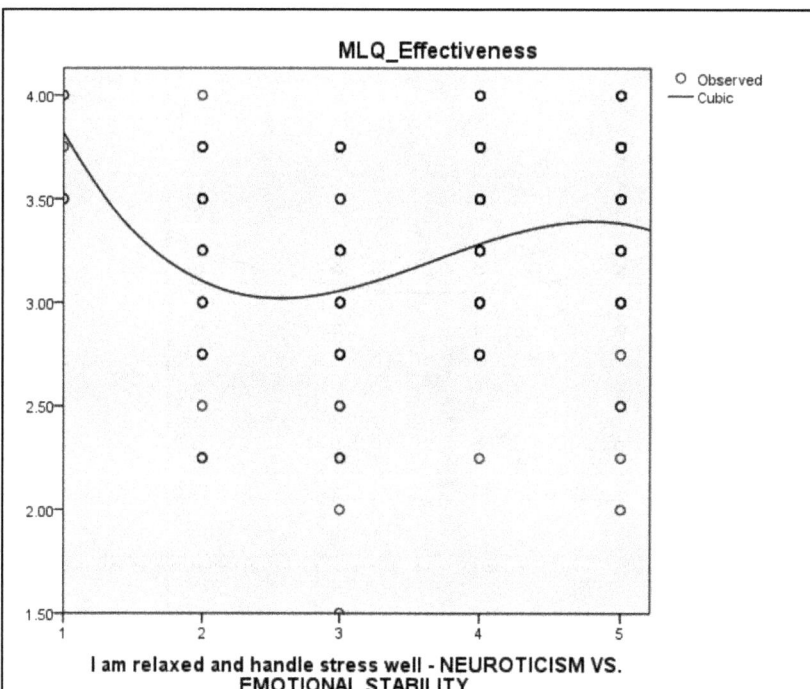

Figure 25. Cubic relationship between effectiveness and relaxed.

Carol R. Himelhoch and Mary Antonaros Raymond

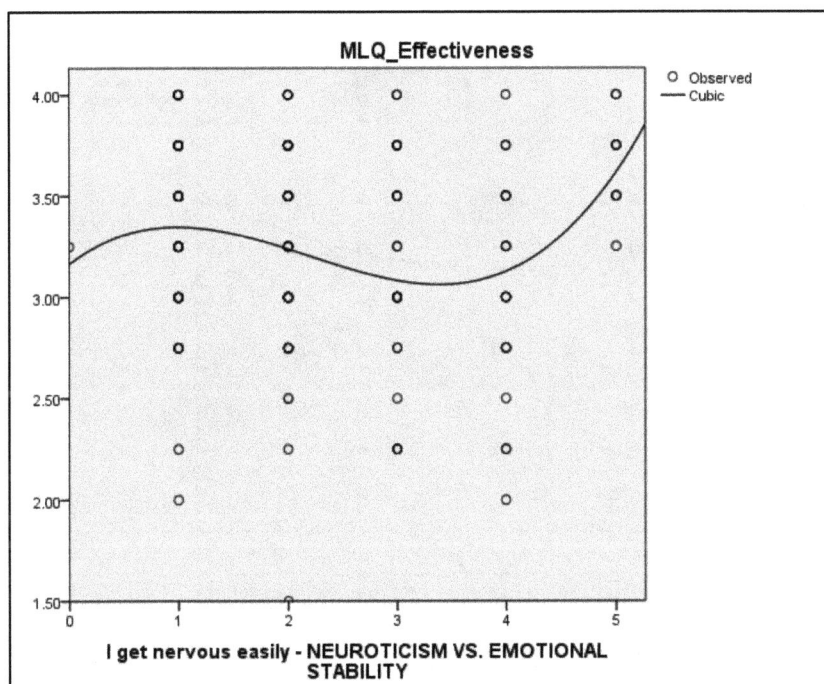

Figure 26. Cubic relationship between effectiveness and I get nervous easily.

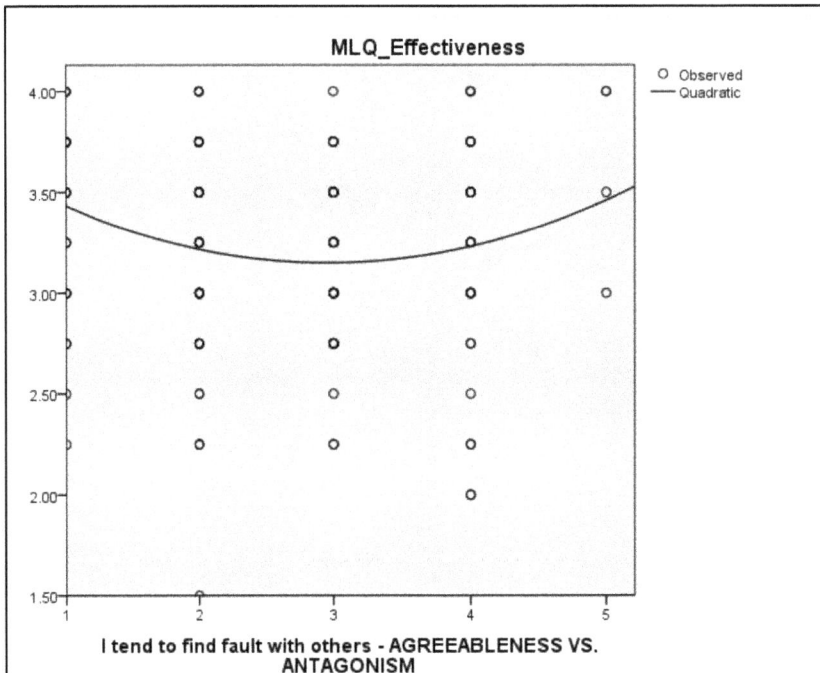

Figure 27. Quadratic relationship between effectiveness and finding fault in others.

Carol R. Himelhoch and Mary Antonaros Raymond

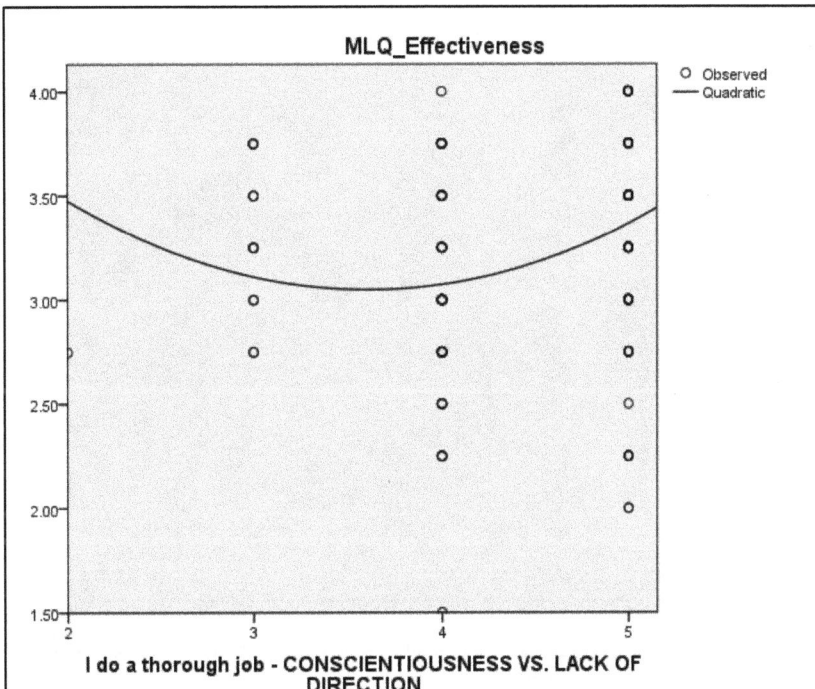

Figure 28. Quadratic relationship between effectiveness and the leader's thoroughness.

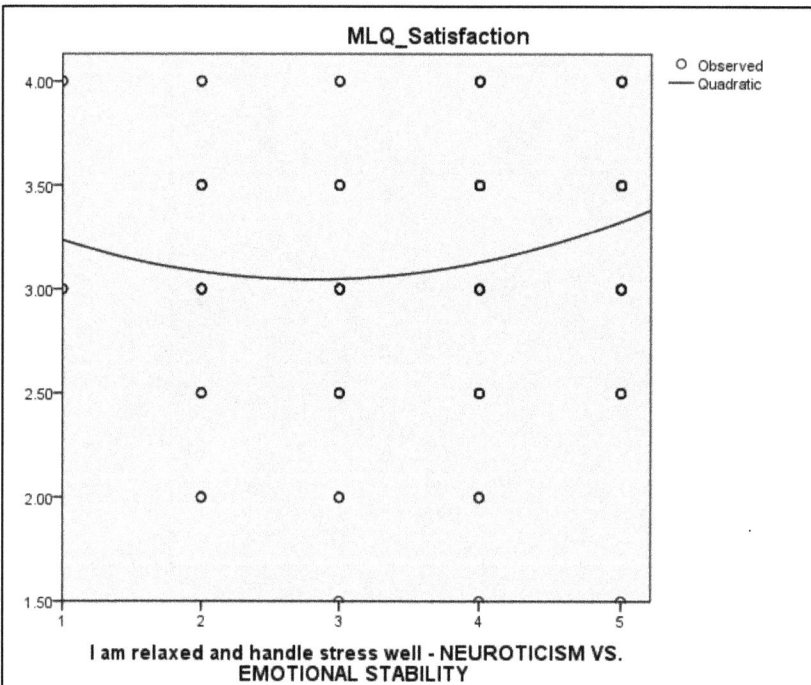

Figure 29. Quadratic relationship between satisfaction and relaxed.

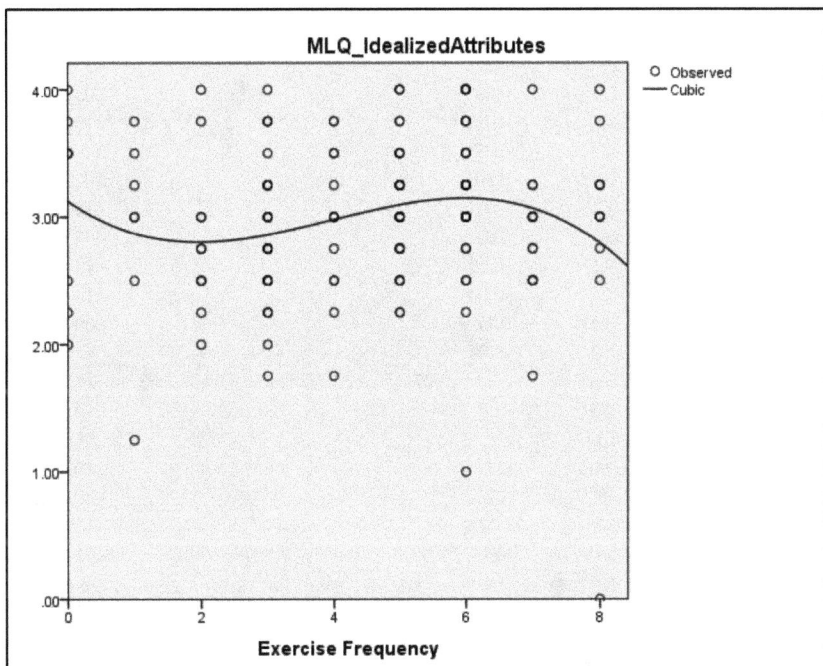

Figure 30. Curvilinear relationship between idealized attributes and exercise frequency.

TABLE 22

Curvilinear Regression of Idealized Attributes on Leader Characteristics and Exercise Habits

Predictor	Criterion							
	Idealized Attributes -Total							
	Beta	B	ΔR2	R2	ΔF	F	SE	95% CI
Step 1			.22	.22	3.151	3.151	.55	
Age	-.12	-0.07						-.16 to .02
Gender	.10	0.13						-.08 to .34
Race	.08	0.26						-.27 to .78
Position	.12	0.09						-.03 to .20
Lazy	-.05	-0.03						-.15 to .08
Relaxed	.17*	0.09						.00 to .19
Outgoing	.19**	0.10						.01 to .17
Find Fault	-.01	-0.01						-.10 to .09
Thorough	.09	0.08						-.07 to .22
Nervous	-.11	-0.05						-.13 to .03
Active Imag.	-.06	-0.04						-.13 to .06
PRE	.25**	0.17						-.09 to .02
Exercise Freq.	-.12	-0.04						
Step 2			.07	.29	.202	3.353	.53	
Age	-.10	-.06						-.14 to .03
Gender	.10	.13						-.08 to .33
Race	.09	.31						-.20 to .82
Position	.09	.07						-.50 to .18
Lazy	-.02	-.02						-.13 to .10
Relaxed	.16	.09						-.01 to .18
Outgoing	.19**	.10						.02 to .17
Find Fault	-.02	-.01						-.11 to .08
Thorough	.06	.05						-.09 to .19
Nervous	-.72*	-.35						-.69 to -.02
Nervous Squared	.62	.06						-.01 to .12
Exercise Freq.	-.06	-.19						-.30 to .18
Exercise Freq. Squared	.09	.00						-.02 to .03
PRE	.07	.04						-.43 to .52
PRE Squared	.07	.03						-.06 to .12
Active Imag.	-.12	-.76						-1.32 to -.21
Active Imag. Squared	1.17**	.10						.024to .18

(continued)

TABLE 22 (CONTINUED)

Curvilinear Regression of Idealized Attributes on Leader Characteristics and Exercise Habits

Predictor	Criterion							
	Idealized Attributes -Total							
	Beta	B	$\Delta R2$	R2	ΔF	F	SE	95% CI
Step 3			.09	.38	1.015	4.368	.50	
Age	-.11	-0.06						-.15 to .02
Gender	.11	0.14						-.05 to .34
Race	.14	0.46						-.03 to .95
Position	.08	0.06						-.05 to .17
Lazy	-.01	0.00						-.11 to .12
Relaxed	.18*	0.10						.012to .19
Outgoing	.19**	0.10						.02 to .17
Find Fault	.00	0.00						-.09 to .09
Thorough	.03	0.02						-.11 to .16
Nervous	-.73*	-0.36						-.67 to -.04
Nervous Squared	.58	0.05						-.01 to .11
Active Imag.	-1.05*	-0.65						-1.18 to -.12
Active Imag. Squared	.95*	0.08						.01 to .16
Exercise Frequency	-3.4***	-1.01						-1.53 to -.52
Exercise Freq. Sq.	7.24***	0.25						.13 to .37
Exercise Freq. Cubed	-4.22***	-0.02						-.03 to -.01
PRE	.95	0.65						-.37 to 1.67
PRE Squared	-54	-0.07						-.55 to .41
PRE Cubed	.06	0.00						-.07 to .07

*p<.05. **p<.01. ***p<.001

TABLE 23

Curvilinear Regression of Idealized Behaviors on Leader Characteristics and Exercise Habits

Predictor	Criterion							
	Idealized Behaviors -Total							
	Beta	B	ΔR2	R2	ΔF	F	SE	95% CI
Step 1			.20	.20	3.584	3.584	.56	
Age	-.08	-.05						-.13 to .04
Gender	.22**	.30						.09 to .51
Race	-.01	-.04						-.56 to .48
Position	.18*	.14						.02 to .26
Lazy	-.10	-.07						-.19 to .05
Thorough	.06	.05						-.10 to .20
Nervous	-13	-.07						-.14 to .01
Active Imag.	.05	.03						-.06 to .13
Exercise Freq.	.08	.03						-.03 to .08
PRE	.15	.12						-.03 to .24
Stren. Ex. Inten.	-.029	-4.66X10⁻⁶						.00 to .00
Step 2			.08	.28	.285	3.869	.54	
Age	-.05	-.03						-.12 to .06
Gender	.24***	.32						.12 to .53
Race	.00	.01						-.49 to .51
Position	.15	.11						-.01 to .23
Lazy	-.10	-.07						-.19 to .05
Thorough	.04	.04						-.11 to .18
Nervous	-.14	-.07						-.15 to .00
Active Imag.	-1.53***	-.98						-1.54 to -.43
Exercise freq.	.20	.06						-.17 to .30
PRE	-.13	-.09						-.57 to .38
Stren. Ex. Inten.	-.25	-3.91X10⁻⁵						.00 to .00
Active Imag. Sq.	1.62***	.14						.07 to .22
Ex. Freq. Sq.	-.08	.00						-.03 to .02
PRE Squared	.32	.05						-.04 to .13
Stren. Ex. Inten. Sq.	.20	8.3X10⁻¹⁰						.00 to .00

(continued)

Carol R. Himelhoch and Mary Antonaros Raymond

Table 23 (continued)

Curvilinear Regression of Idealized Behaviors on Leader Characteristics and Exercise Habits

Predictor	Criterion							
	Idealized Behaviors -Total							
	Beta	B	$\Delta R2$	R2	ΔF	F	SE	95% CI
Step 3			.06	.34	.279	4.148	.52	
Age	-.07	-.04						-.13 to .05
Gender	.24***	.33						.13 to .53
Race	.03	.09						.41 to .59
Position	.13	.10						-.02 to .22
Lazy	-.09	-.06						.18 to .05
Thorough	.01	.01						-.13 to .15
Nervous	-.18*	-.09						-.17 to -.02
Active Imag.	-1.38**	-.89						-1.43 to -..35
Exercise Freq.	-2.09*	-.64						-1.56 to -.13
PRE	.12	.08						-.97 to 1.14
Stren. Ex. Inten.	.18	2.86×10^{-5}						.00 to .00
Active Imag. Sq.	1.44***	.13						.05 to .20
Ex. Freq. Sq.	4.99**	.18						.06 to .30
PRE Squared	.87	.12						-.38 to .62
Stren. Ex. Inten. Sq.	-1.80	-7.4×10^{-9}						.00 to .00
Ex. Freq. Cubed	-3.01**	-.01						-.02 to -.00
PRE Cubed	-.73	-.02						-.09 to .05
Stren. Ex. Inten. Cubed	1.63	2.5×10^{-13}						.00 to .00

*p<.05. **p<.01. ***p<.001

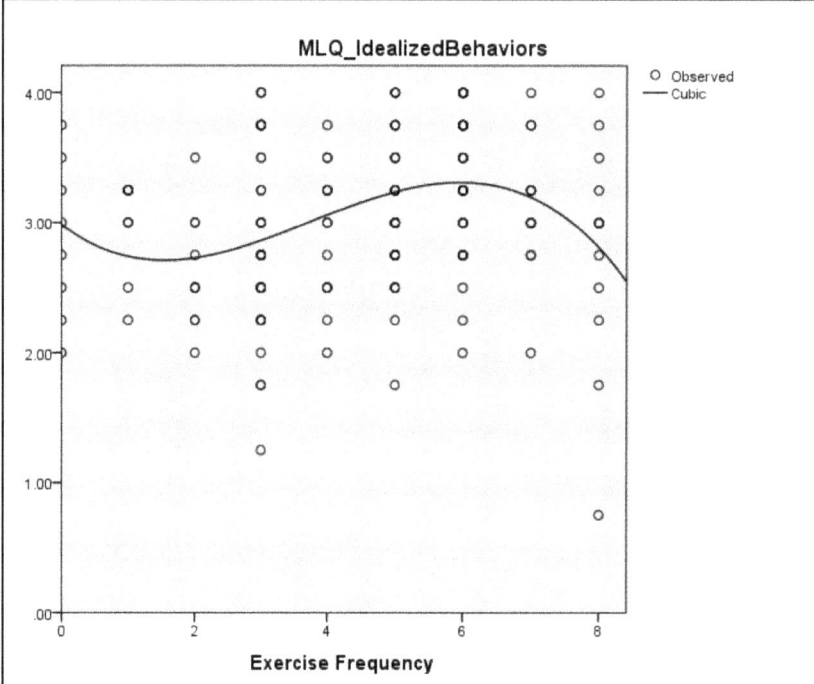

Figure 31. Curvilinear relationship between idealized behaviors and exercise frequency.

Carol R. Himelhoch and Mary Antonaros Raymond

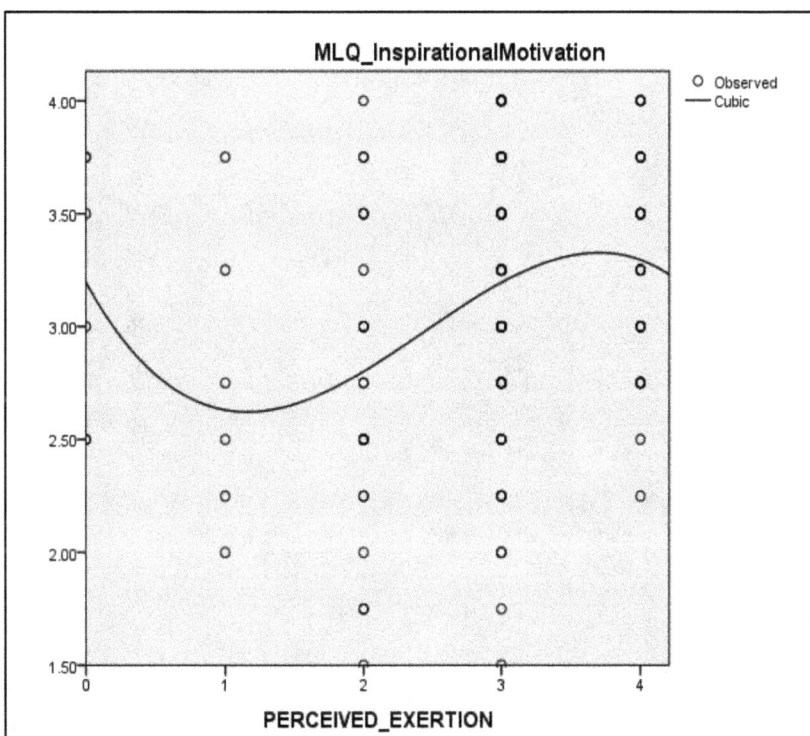

Figure 32. Curvilinear relationship between inspirational motivation and perceived rate of exertion.

TABLE 24

Curvilinear Regression of Inspirational Motivation on Leader Characteristics and Exercise Habits

Predictor	Criterion									
	Inspirational Motivation -Total									
	Beta	B	$\Delta R2$	R2	ΔF	F	SE	95% CI		
Step 1			.29	.29	3.707	3.707	.51			
Age	-.14	-.08						-.16	to	.01
Gender	.07	.09						-.11	to	.28
Race	.07	.21						-.24	to	.65
Position	.18*	.13						.02	to	.24
Reserved	.04	.02						-.06	to	.10
Trusting	.15	.09						-.00	to	.18
Lazy	-.14	-.10						-.21	to	.02
Outgoing	.18*	.09						-.00	to	.18
Find Fault	-.01	-.01						-.09	to	.08
Thorough	.05	.40						-.10	to	.18
Nervous	-.18*	-.01						-.16	to	-.02
Active Imag.	.08	.05						-.04	to	.14
Exercise Freq.	.13	-.04						-.02	to	.10
PRE	.10	.07						-.06	to	.19
Stren. Ex. Inten.	.18	5.45×10^{-5}						.00	to	.00
Total Ex. Inten.	-.21	-5.37×10^{5}						.00	to	.00
Step 2			.04	.33	-.855	2.852	.51			
Age	-.11	-.06								
Gender	.08	.11						-.15	to	.02
Race	.08	.24						-.10	to	.31
Position	.15	.11						-.21	to	.69
Reserved	-01	-.01						-.01	to	.22
Trusting	-.00**	-.00						-.10	to	.08
Lazy	-.56	-.41						-.59	to	.58
Outgoing	.16	.08						-.96	to	.13
Find Fault	-.00*	-.00						-01	to	.17
Thorough	.02	.02						-.09	to	.09
Nervous	-.15	-.07						-.12	to	.15
Active Imag.	-.52	-.31						-.15	to	.00

(continued)

Carol R. Himelhoch and Mary Antonaros Raymond

TABLE 24 (CONTINUED)

Curvilinear Regression of Inspirational Motivation on Leader Characteristics and Exercise Habits

Predictor	Criterion									
	Inspirational Motivation –Total									
	Beta	B	ΔR2	R2	ΔF	F	SE	95% CI		
Exercise Freq.	.48	.14						-.87	to	.24
PRE	-.40	-.26						-.09	to	.37
Stren. Ex. Inten.	.16	4.89 X10⁻⁵						-.73	to	.20
Tot. Ex. Inten.	-.082	-2.07 X10⁻⁵						.00	to	.00
Trusting Sq.	.16	.01						.00	to	.00
Lazy Sq.	.44	.07						-.07	to	.09
Active Imag. Sq.	.62	.05						-.05	to	.13
Ex. Freq. Sq.	-.33	-.01						-.04	to	.01
PRE Squared	.46	.06						-.02	to	.05
Stre. Ex. Inten. Sq.	.00**	8.82 X10⁻¹²						.00	to	.00
Total Ex. Inten. Sq.	-.14	-3.56 X10⁻⁹						.00	to	.00
Step 3			.09	.42	.508	3.360	.49			.
Age	-15*	-.08						-.17	to	.00
Gender	.11	.15						-.05	to	.34
Race	.08	.25						-.19	to	.69
Position	.11	.08						-.03	to	.19
Reserved	-.06	-.03						-.11	to	.06
Trusting	-.16	-.10						-.66	to	.47
Lazy	-.58	-.43						-.96	to	.10
Outgoing	.11	.06						-.03	to	.15
Find Fault	.01	.01						-.08	to	.09
Thorough	-.02	-.01						-.15	to	.12
Nervous	-.16*	-.08						-.15	to	-.00
Active Imag.	-.78	-.47						-2.73	to	1.79
Exercise Freq.	-.82	-.24						-.74	to	.26
PRE	-1.71*	-1.14						-2.14	to	-.13

(continued)

TABLE 24 (CONTINUED)

Curvilinear Regression of Inspirational Motivation on Leader Characteristics and Exercise Habits

Predictor	Criterion										
	Inspirational Motivation –Total										
	Beta	B	$\Delta R2$	R2	ΔF	F	SE		95% CI		
Stren. Ex. Inten.	.71	.00						.00	to	.00
Total Ex. Inten.	-.35	8.86 X10⁻⁸						.00		.00
Trusting Sq.	.29	.02						-.05	to	.10
Lazy Sq.	.46	.08						-.04	to	.20
Active Imag. Sq.	1.46	.12						-.58	to	.82
Ex. Freq. Sq.	2.49	.08						-.03	to	.20
PRE Squared	4.91**	.65						.18	to	1.13
Stre. Ex. Inten. Sq.	-1.80	-6.28 X10⁻⁸						.00	to	.00
Total Ex. Inten. Sq.	.91	2.47 X10⁻⁸						.00	to	.00
Active Imag. Cubed	-.58	.01						-.08	to	.06
Ex. Freq. Cubed	-1.64	-.01						-.02	to	.00
PRE Cubed	- 3.21**	-.09						-16	to	-.03
Stren. Ex. Inten. Cubed	1.47	4.83 X10⁻¹²						.00	to	.00

*p<.05. **p<.01. ***p<.001

Carol R. Himelhoch and Mary Antonaros Raymond

TABLE 25

Curvilinear Regression of Intellectual Stimulation on Leader Characteristics and Exercise Habits

Predictor	Criterion									
	Intellectual Stimulation –Total									
	Beta	B	ΔR2	R2	ΔF	F	SE	95% CI		
Step 1			.10	.10	3.113	3.113	.47			
Age	.04	.02						-.06	to	.09
Gender	.03	.04						-.13	to	.21
Race	-.13	-.33						-.74	to	.08
Position	.15*	.10						-.00	to	.19
Exercise Freq.	.23**	.06						.02	to	.10
Mod. Ex. Inten.	-.06	-4.68X10^{-5}						.00	to	.00
Trusting	-.10	-.05						-.13	to	.03
Active Imag.	.14	.07						-.01	to	.15

(continued)

TABLE 25 (CONTINUED)

Curvilinear Regression of Intellectual Stimulation on Leader Characteristics and Exercise Habits

Predictor	Criterion									
	Intellectual Stimulation –Total									
	Beta	B	ΔR2	R2	ΔF	F	SE	95% CI		
Step 2			.04	.14	.401	3.514	.46			
Age	.06	.03						-.05	to	.10
Gender	.03	.03						-.14	to	.20
Race	-.13	-.34						-.74	to	.06
Position	.14	.09						-.01	to	.19
Exercise Freq.	.20*	.05						.01	to	.09
Mod. Ex. Inten.	.34	.00						.00	to	.00
Trusting	-.10	-.05						-.13	to	.03
Active Imag.	-.90	-.45						-.92	to	.02
Mod Ex. In. Sq.	-.41*	-1.13×10^{-7}						.00	to	.00
Active Imag. Sq	1.05*	.07						.01	to	.14
Step 3			.01	.15	.048	3.562	.46			
Age	.06	.03						-.05	to	.10
Gender	.04	.04						-.13	to	.21
Race	-.15	-.38						-.78	to	.02
Position	.14	.09						-.01	to	.18
Exercise Freq.	.19*	.05						.01	to	.09
Mod. Ex. Inten.	.87*	.00						.00	to	.00
Trusting	-.08	-.04						-.12	to	.04
Active Imag.	-.95*	-.48						-.95	to	-.01
Mod Ex. In. Sq.	-1.94*	-5.39×10^{-7}						.00	to	.00
Active Imag. Sq.	1.09*	.08						.01	to	.14
Mod. Ex. In. Cubed	1.08	9.99×10^{-11}						.00	to	.00

*p<.05. **p<.01. ***p<.001

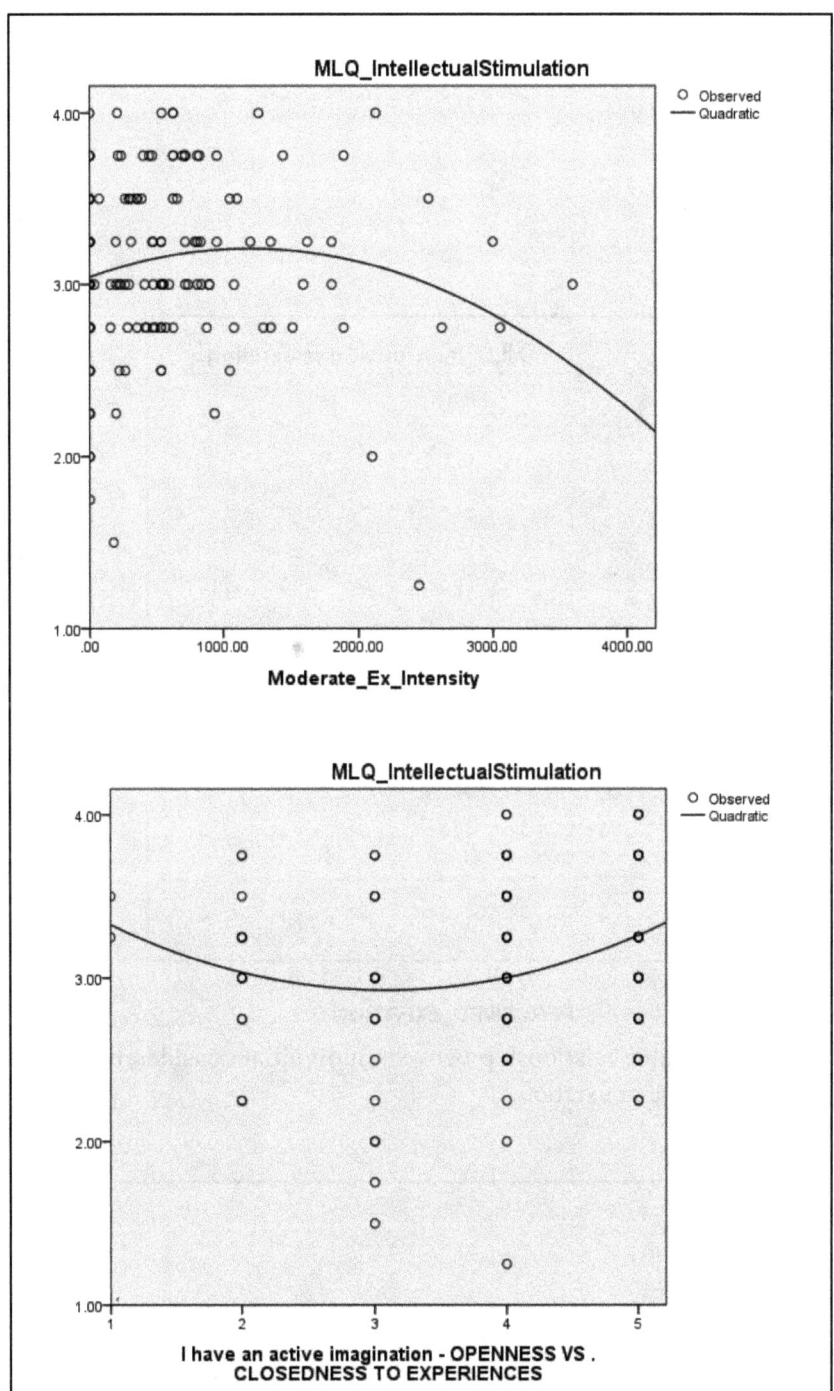

Figure 33. Quadratic relationships between intellectual stimulation and moderate exercise intensity and active imagination.

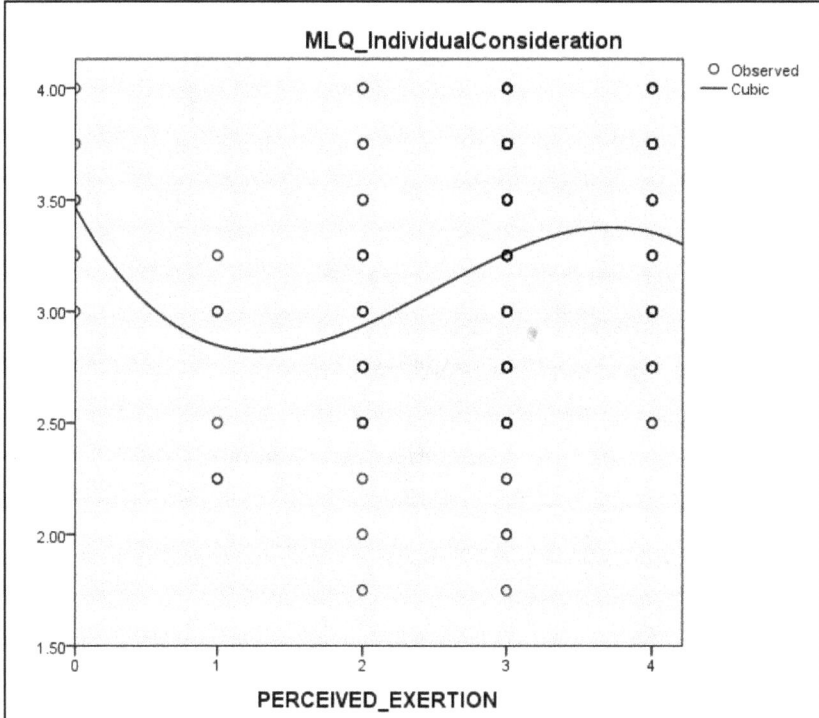

Figure 34. Cubic relationship between individual consideration and perceived rate of exertion.

TABLE 26

Curvilinear Regression of Individual Consideration on Leader Characteristics and Exercise Habits

Predictor	Criterion									
	Individual Consideration -Total									
	Beta	B	ΔR2	R2	ΔF	F	SE	95% CI		
Step 1			.22	.22	4.341	4.341	.48			
Age	.02	.01						-.07	to	.08
Gender	.21**	.25						.07	to	.43
Race	-.14	-.43						-.88	to	.02
Position	.08	.05						-.05	to	.15
PRE	.12	.07						-.02	to	.17
Lazy	.02	.02						-.09	to	.12
Relaxed	.14	.07						-.01	to	.14
Thorough	.21*	.16						.04	to	.29
Find Fault	-.10	-.05						-.13	to	.02
Active Imag.	.15*	.08						.00	to	.16
Step 2			.04	.26	-.39	3.948	.47			
Age	.04	.02						-.06	to	.10
Gender	.23**	.26						.09	to	.44
Race	-.14	-.42						-.86	to	.03
Position	.08	.05						-.05	to	.15
PRE	-.36	-.22						-.53	to	.08
Lazy	.04	.03						-.08	to	.13
Relaxed	.11	.06						-.02	to	.13
Thorough	.21*	.17						.04	to	.30
Find Fault	-.19	-.10						-.47	to	.28
Active Imag.	-.47	-.26						-.75	to	.23
PRE Squared	.51*	.06						.00	to	.12
Find Fault Sq.	.11	.01						-.06	to	.08
Active Imag. Sq.	.64	.05						-.02	to	.12

(continued)

TABLE 26 (CONTINUED)

Curvilinear Regression of Individual Consideration on Leader Characteristics and Exercise Habits

Predictor	Criterion									
	Individual Consideration -Total									
	Beta	B	ΔR2	R2	ΔF	F	SE	95% CI		
Step 3			.04	.30	.702	4.650	.46			
Age	-.02	-.01						-.08	to	.07
Gender	.24**	.28						.10	to	.45
Race	-.16*	-.49						-.92	to	-.06
Position	.07	.04						-.06	to	.14
PRE	-2.24***	-1.38						-2.15	to	-.62
Lazy	.02	.01						-.09	to	.11
Relaxed	.02	.05						-.02	to	.12
Thorough	.20*	.16						.04	to	.29
Find Fault	-.17	-.09						-.45	to	.28
Active Imag.	-.38	-.21						-.69	to	.26
PRE Squared	5.80**	.72						.31	to	1.12
Find Fault Sq.	.10	.01						-.06	to	.07
Active Imag. Sq.	.57	.04						-.02	to	.11
PRE Cubed	-3.55**	-.10						-.16	to	-.04

*p<.05. **p<.01. ***p<.001

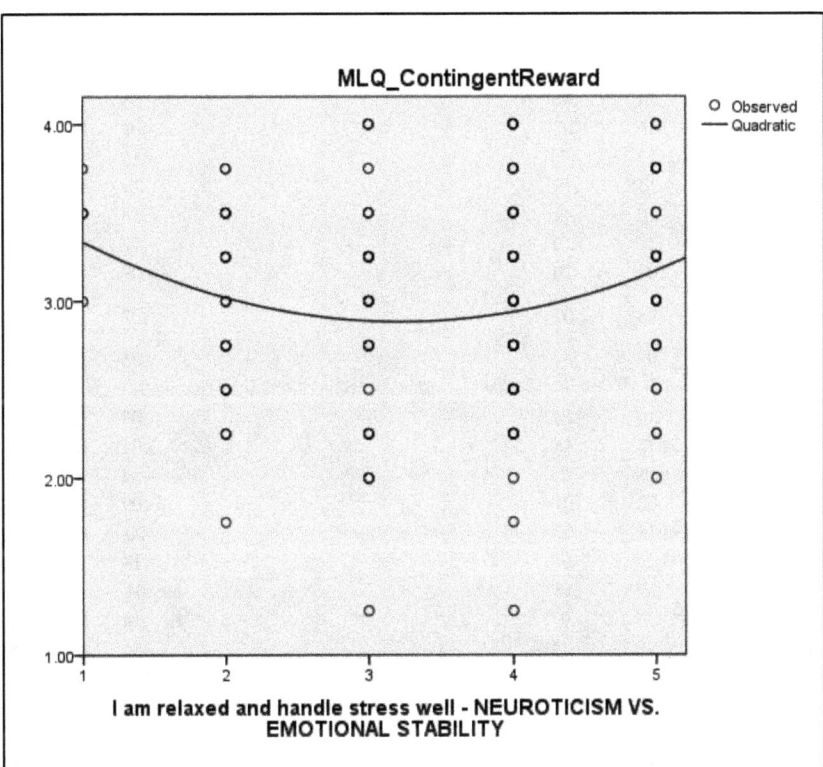

Figure 35. Quadratic relationship between contingent reward and being relaxed.

TABLE 27

Curvilinear Regression of Contingent Reward on Leader Characteristics and Exercise Habits

Predictor	Criterion									
	Contingent Reward –Total									
	Beta	B	ΔR2	R2	ΔF	F	SE	95% CI		
Step 1			.22	.22	3.497	3.497	.51			
Age	-.03	-.01						-.09	to	.06
Gender	.18*	.22						.03	to	.41
Race	-.07	-.19						-.59	to	.22
Position	.04	.03						-.08	to	.13
Outgoing	-.09	.07						-.01	to	.14
Find Fault	.23	-.05						-.13	to	.03
Thorough	-.13*	.19						.05	to	.33
Nervous	-.01	-.06						-.13	to	.01
Lazy	-.02	-.01						-.12	to	.10
Relaxed	.08	-.01						-.09	to	.07
Exercise Freq.	.08	.02						-.02	to	.06
Trusting	.07	.04						-.05	to	.13
Step 2			.05	.27	-.163	3.334	.50			
Age	-.02	-.01						-.09	to	.07
Gender	.13	.16						-.04	to	.36
Race	-.09	-.23						-.64	to	.17
Position	.02	.02						-.09	to	.12
Outgoing	.14	.07						.00	to	.14
Find Fault	-.10	-.06						-.14	to	.03
Thorough	.22*	.18						.04	to	.32
Nervous	-.14	-.07						-.14	to	.01
Lazy	-.19	-.14						-.65	to	.38
Relaxed	-1.27**	-.64						-1.10	to	-.18
Exercise Freq.	-.06	-.02						-.17	to	.14
Trusting	.22	.13						-.42	to	.68
Lazy Squared	.20	.03						-.08	to	.15
Relaxed Squared	1.26**	.09						.03	to	.16
Ex. Freq. Sq.	.16	.01						-.01	to	.02
Trusting Squared	-.11	.01						-.08	to	.07

(continued)

Carol R. Himelhoch and Mary Antonaros Raymond

TABLE 27 (CONTINUED)

Curvilinear Regression of Contingent Reward on Leader Characteristics and Exercise Habits

Predictor	Criterion									
	Contingent Reward –Total									
	Beta	B	$\Delta R2$	R2	ΔF	F	SE	95% CI		
Step 3			.03	.30	.014	3.348	.49			
Age	-.02	-.01						-.09	to	.07
Gender	.13	.16						-.04	to	.36
Race	-.06	-.17						-.57	to	.24
Position	.02	.02						-.09	to	.12
Outgoing	.16*	.08						.00	to	.15
Find Fault	-.10	-.05						-.14	to	.03
Thorough	.20*	.17						.03	to	.31
Nervous	-.15	-.07						-.14	to	.01
Lazy	-.15	-.11						-.62	to	.40
Relaxed	-1.18*	-.60						-1.05	to	-.14
Exercise Freq.	-1.17*	-.32						-.65	to	.00
Trusting	1.82	1.06						-1.22	to	3.34
Lazy Squared	.17	.03						-.09	to	.14
Relaxed Squared	1.15*	.09						.02	to	.15
Ex. Freq. Sq.	3.03*	.10						.01	to	.19
Trusting Squared	-4.07	-.33						-1.04	to	.39
Ex. Freq. Cubed	-1.83*	-.01						-.01	to	.00
Trusting Cubed	2.38	.03						-.04	to	.10

*p<.05. **p<.01. ***p<.001

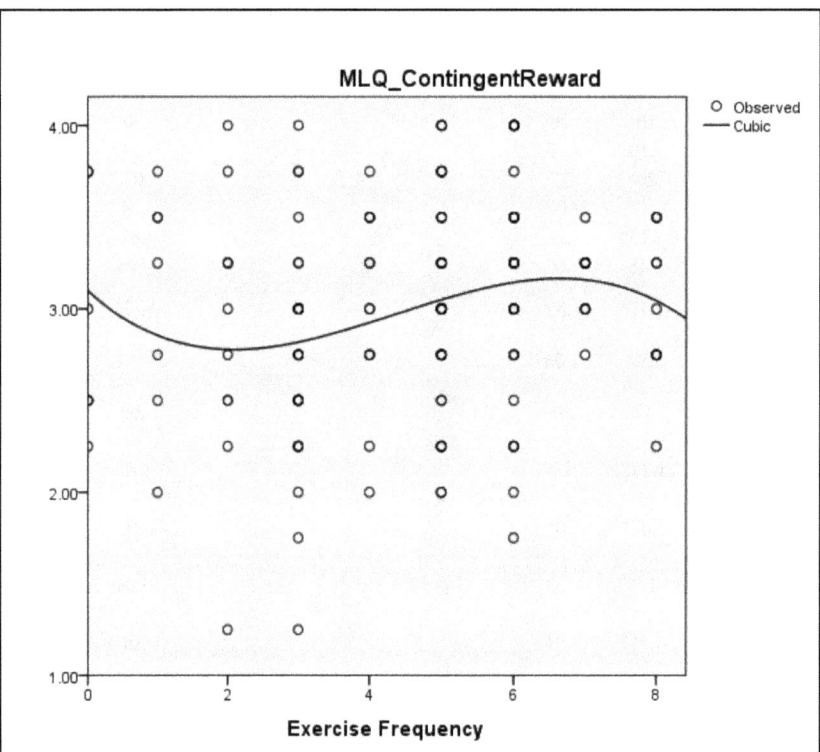

Figure 36. Cubic relationship between contingent reward and exercise frequency.

Carol R. Himelhoch and Mary Antonaros Raymond

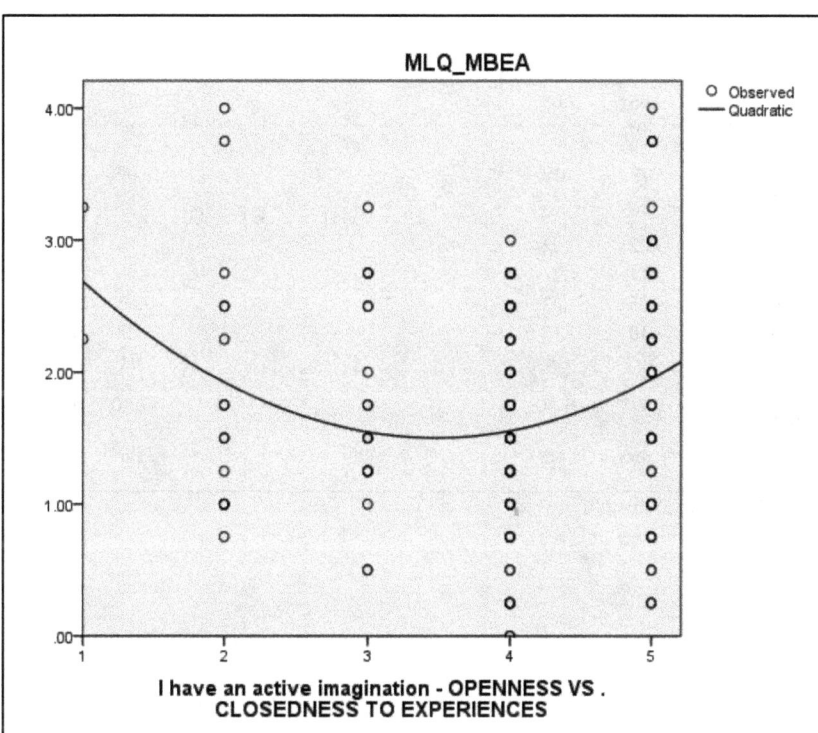

Figure 37. Relationship between active imagination and management by exception active.

TABLE 28

Curvilinear Regression of Management By Exception-Active on Leader Characteristics and Exercise Habits

Predictor	Criterion									
	MBEA -Total									
	Beta	B	$\Delta R2$	R2	ΔF	F	SE	95% CI		
Step 1			.07	.07	1.930	1.930	.83			
Age	-.04	-.03						-.17	to	.10
Gender	-.13	-.25						-.54	to	.04
Race	-.06	-.26						-.91	to	.38
Position	-.06	-.06						-.23	to	.10
Find Fault	.20*	.17						.04	to	.29
Active Imag.	.05	.05						-.09	to	.18
Step 2			.06	.13	1.441	3.371	.80			
Age	-.02	-.02						-.14	to	.11
Gender	-.14	-.27						-.55	to	.02
Race	-.05	-.22						-.85	to	.40
Position	-.10	-.11						-.27	to	.06
Find Fault	.20*	.16						.04	to	.29
Active Imag.	-1.49**	-1.30						-2.10	to	-.50
Active Imag. Sq.	1.57**	.19						.08	to	.30

*p<.05. **p<.01. ***p<.001

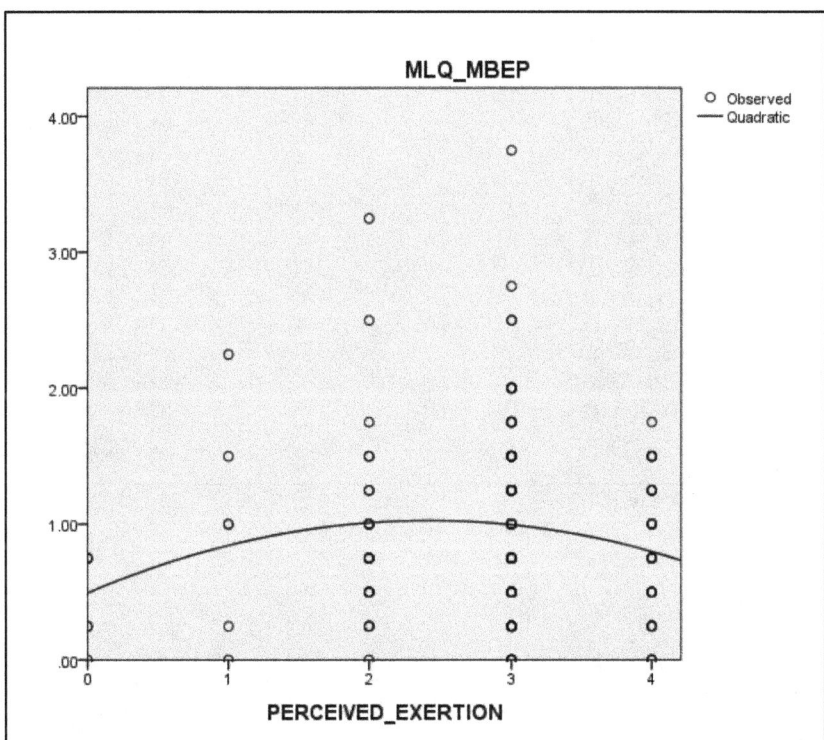

Figure 38. Quadratic relationship between management by exception passive and perceived rate of exertion.

TABLE 29

Curvilinear Regression of Management By Exception-Passive On Leader Characteristics and Exercise Habits

Predictor	Criterion									
	MBEP -Total									
	Beta	B	ΔR2	R2	ΔF	F	SE		95% CI	
Step 1			.12	.12	3.011	3.011	.59			
Age	-.09	-.05						-.14	to	.04
Gender	.06	.08						-.13	to	.29
Race	.02	.05						-.44	to	.54
Position	.03	.02						-.10	to	.14
Lazy	.19*	.15						.03	to	.27
Thorough	-.21*	-.19						-.34	to	-.04
PRE	.04	.03						-.09		.14
Step 2			.02	.14	.297	3.308	.58			
Age	-.11	-.06						-.15	to	.03
Gender	.04	.05						-.16	to	.26
Race	.01	.03						-.46	to	.51
Position	.01	.01						-.11	to	.13
Lazy	.18*	.14						.01	to	.26
Thorough	-.21**	-.20						-.34	to	-.05
PRE	.58*	.42						.05		.78
PRE Squared	-.56**	-.08						-.15	to	-.01

*p<.05. **p<.01. ***p<.001

Carol R. Himelhoch and Mary Antonaros Raymond

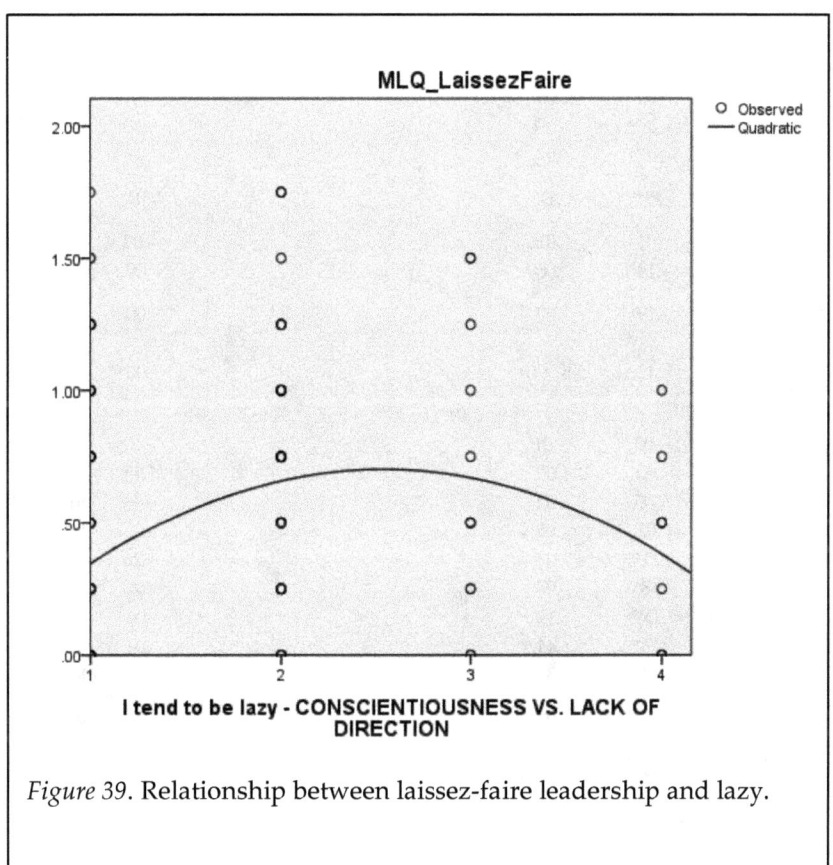

Figure 39. Relationship between laissez-faire leadership and lazy.

TABLE 30

Curvilinear Regression of Laissez-faire Leadership on Leader Characteristics and Exercise Habits

Predictor	Criterion									
	Laissez-faire -Total									
	Beta	B	$\Delta R2$	R2	ΔF	F	SE	95% CI		
Step 1			.26	.26	4.700	4.700	.42			
Age	-.03	-.01						-.08	to	.05
Gender	.00	.00						-.15	to	.15
Race	-.04	-.10						-.45	to	.25
Position	.00	.00						-.09	to	.08
Thorough	-.26**	-.19						-.30	to	-.08
Nervous	.18*	.07						.01	to	.13
Active Imag.	.23**	.11						.04	to	.18
Lazy	.01	.01						-.08	to	.09
Find Fault	.14	.06						.00	to	.13
Mod. Ex. Inten.	-.19*	.00						.00	to	.00
Mild Ex. Inten.	.12	5.51X10-5						.00	to	.00
Step 2			.04	.30	-.267	4.433	.41			
Age	-.03	-.01						-.08	to	.05
Gender	.00	.00						-.15	to	.15
Race	-.05	-.11						-.46	to	.23
Position	.02	.01						-.07	to	.10
Thorough	-.21**	-.15						-.26	to	-.04
Nervous	.18*	.07						.01	to	.13
Active Imag	.23**	.11						.04	to	.18
Lazy	.76*	.44						.04	to	.84
Find Fault	.74*	.34						.01	to	.66
Mod. Ex. Inten.	-.16*	.00						.00	to	.00
Mild Ex. Inten.	.09	4.46X10-5						.00	to	.00
Lazy Squared	-.77*	-.10						-.19	to	-.01
Find Fault Sq.	-.62	-.05						-.11	to	.01
Mild Ex. Int. Sq.	.04	2.57X10-9						.00	to	.00

(continued)

Carol R. Himelhoch and Mary Antonaros Raymond

TABLE 30 (CONTINUED)

Curvilinear Regression of Laissez-faire Leadership on Leader Characteristics and Exercise Habits

Predictor	Criterion									
	Laissez-faire -Total									
	Beta	B	$\Delta R2$	R2	ΔF	F	SE	95% CI		
Step 3			.01	.31	-.113	4.320	.40			
Age	-.01	.00						-.07	to	.06
Gender	-.01	-.01						-.16	to	.14
Race	-.05	-.12						-.47	to	.23
Position	.03	.02						-.07	to	.10
Thorough	-.21**	-.15						-.26	to	-.04
Nervous	.18*	.07						.01	to	.12
Active Imag	.23**	.11						.04	to	.18
Lazy	.66	.38						-.03	to	.79
Find Fault	.79*	.36						.03	to	.68
Mod. Ex. Inten.	-.16*	.00						.00	to	.00
Mild Ex. Inten.	-.30	.00						.00	to	.00
Lazy Squared	-.66	-.09						-.18	to	.00
Find Fault Sq.	-.67	-.05						-.11	to	.00
Mild Ex. Int. Sq.	1.60	9.52×10^{-8}						.00	to	.00
Mild Ex. Int. Cubed	-1.22	-7.72×10^{-12}						.00	to	.00

*p<.05. **p<.01. ***p<.001

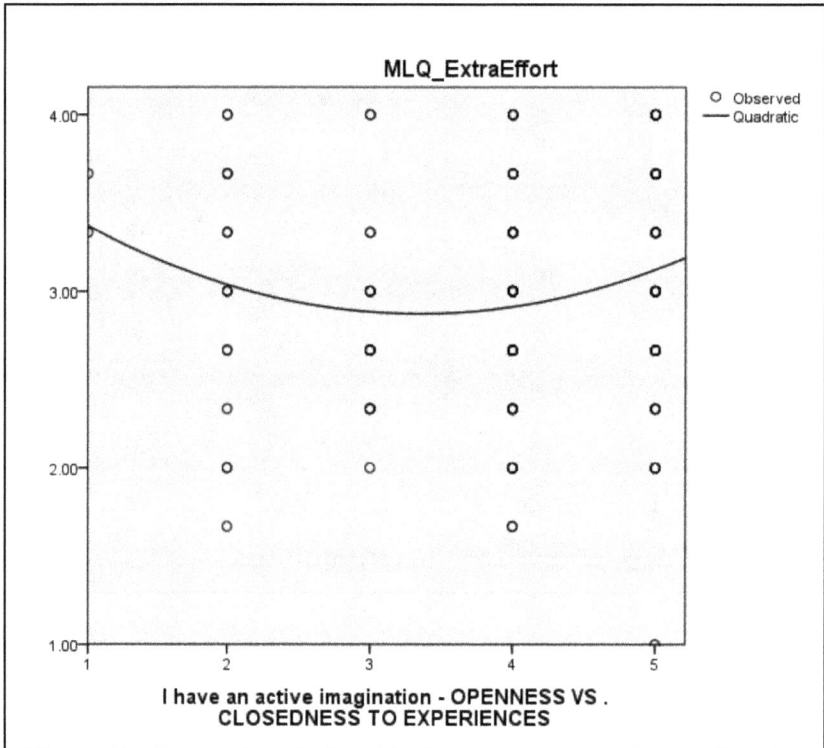

Figure 40. Quadratic relationship between extra effort and active imagination.

Carol R. Himelhoch and Mary Antonaros Raymond

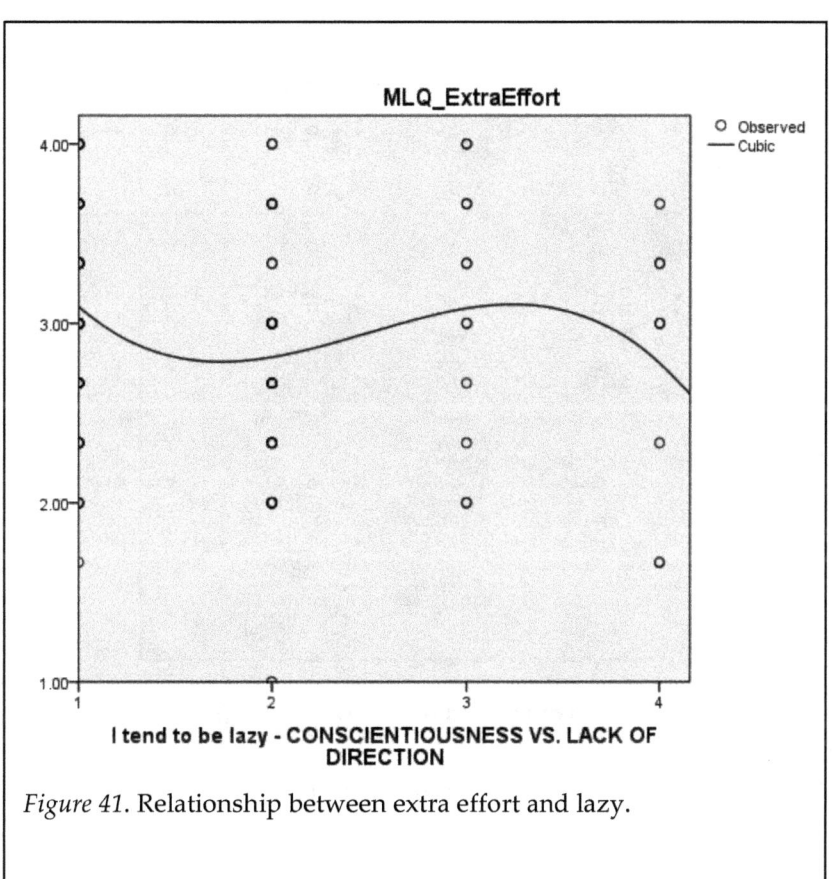

Figure 41. Relationship between extra effort and lazy.

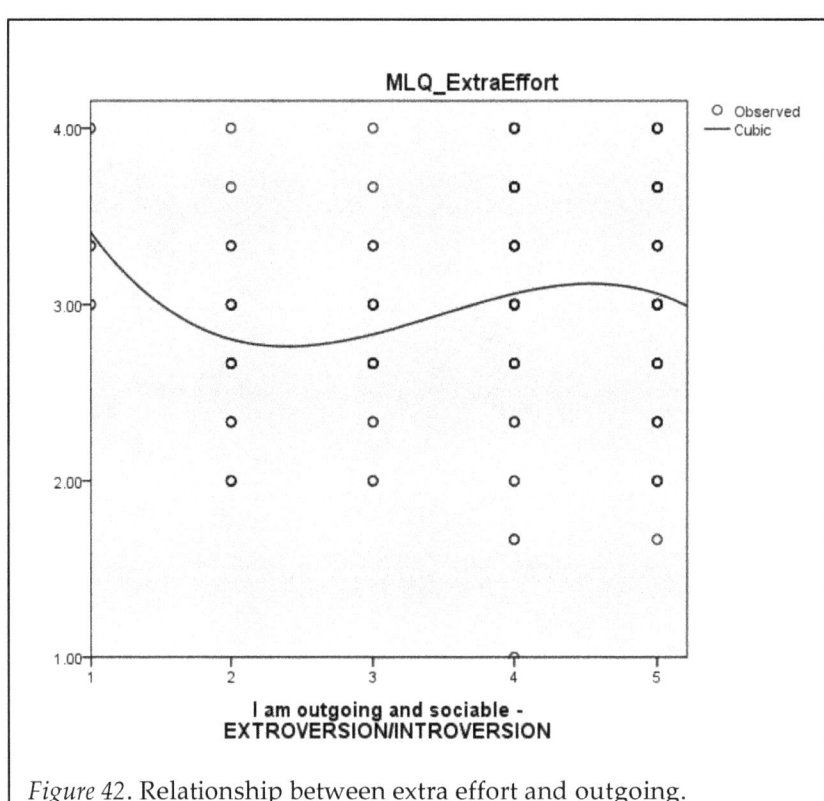

Figure 42. Relationship between extra effort and outgoing.

Carol R. Himelhoch and Mary Antonaros Raymond

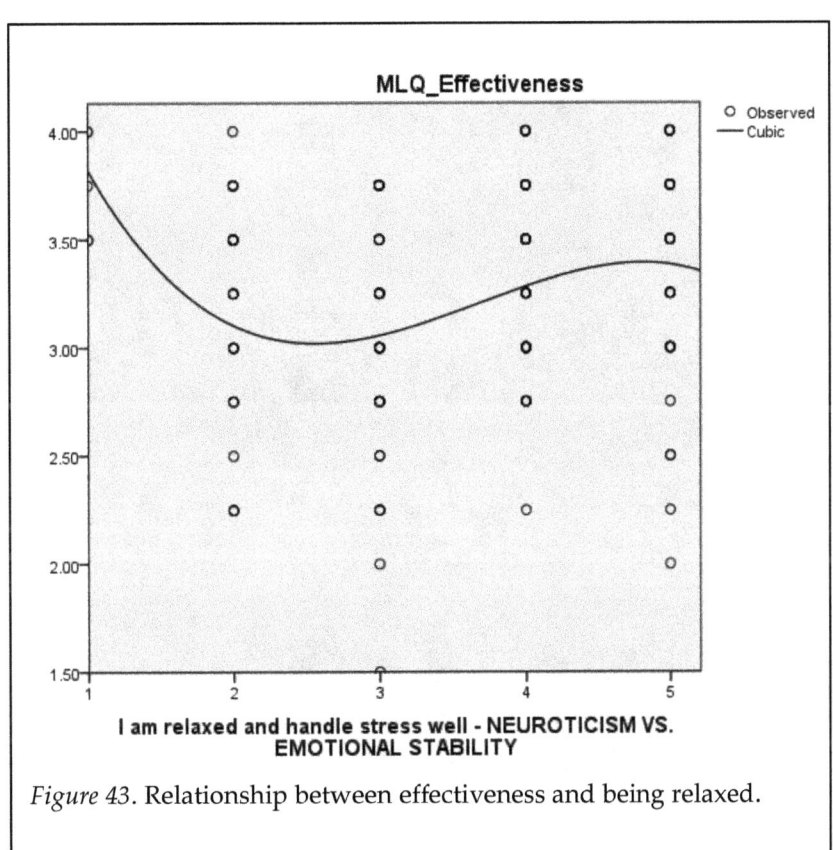

Figure 43. Relationship between effectiveness and being relaxed.

AUTHOR'S BIOGRAPHY

Dr. Carol R. Himelhoch received her PhD from the University of Michigan. She is a Professor of Management and Organizational Behavior at Siena Heights University in Adrian, Michigan. Her management experience spans Tier 1 automotive manufacturing operations, marketing, advertising, and retail management. Carol contributes to the field of management by publishing in peer-reviewed journals and speaking at management and leadership conferences. Carol has been active in consulting since the mid-1980s. She has been an avid HIIT athlete since 2005.

Dr. Carol's first book *"Transformational Leadership and High-Intensity Interval Training"* was an exploratory study of how leaders who participate in high-intensity interval training perceive the influence of HIIT on their leadership styles. She is back at it again, this time in a quantitative follow-up study of 189 leaders at all managerial levels, and at all levels of exercise from none at all to very high intensity. Her follow-up study also includes subordinate perceptions of their leaders to minimize leader self-report biases. Her recent research culminates in the discovery of nuanced factors in the relationship between exercise and leadership.

AUTHOR'S BIOGRAPHY

Dr. Mary Antonaros Raymond earned her PhD at the University of Michigan in 2010. She is an Associate Professor of Professional Communication and Coordinator of the Professional Communication Major at Siena Heights University. She has conducted research as well as published and presented papers on topics related to leadership for over 14 years, with special emphases on gender differences in leadership style and the influence on leader effectiveness as well as the influence of exercise on leadership styles and leader effectiveness.

COPY EDITOR'S BIOGRAPHY

Michele Spilberg Hart, MA, RYT, is an editor and restorative yoga teacher. She has a vast array of experience copy editing books, journals, newspapers, marketing materials, and website copy. She studied at the University of Rochester and received a master's degree in Writing & Publishing from Emerson College, where she was the head proofreader of the Beacon Street Review. She has been the staff copy editor for medical publishers and corporate communications departments in addition to working on freelance editing projects for the past seventeen years. Michele is currently the Director of Marketing and Communications for a leading autism education and research institute in New England.

She is also interested in health and wellness and is a certified Relax and Renew trainer under Judith Hanson Lasater, PhD, and received her 200-hour yoga teacher training from Natasha Rizopoulos through Yoga Works.

ABOUT MINDBODYMED PRESS

Thank you for your interest in publishing with MindBodyMed Press.

WE ARE: MindBodyMed Press, an indie publishing company seeking to publish manuscripts dealing with nutrition, mind- body and integrative medicine.

YOU ARE: A newly emerging or established author, clinician, practitioner, research scientist, or academic with a finished manuscript between 7,500 and 80,000 words looking to publish a high-quality nonfiction book or mini-monograph in trade paperback and on popular e-book platforms.

Why Publish with MindBodyMed Press?

- Easy publication process
- Retain copyright
- Collect royalties
- Augment your authority

Ready for the next step in the publication process?

Visit us on the web at http://mindbodymedpress.com/ to find out how easy it is to publish your nonfiction book or mini-monograph.

THANK YOU FOR READING!

WE INVITE YOU TO SHARE YOUR THOUGHTS

AND REACTIONS

Please write a custom review for this title on:

WWW.MINDBODYMEDPRESS.COM

Spring Lake | Michigan | United States

Alternatively, directly share the title with your friends via:

CPSIA information can be obtained
at www.ICGtesting.com
Printed in the USA
FSHW022018020319
55973FS

9 780990 329749